WHY IT'S OK TO TALK ABOUT TRAUMA

HOW TO MAKE SENSE OF OUR PAST AND GROW THROUGH THE PAIN

CHARLIE WEBSTER

WELBECK
BALANCE

First published in 2024 by Welbeck
An Imprint of HEADLINE PUBLISHING GROUP

1

Cataloguing in Publication Data is available from the British Library

Trade Paperback 978-1-80129-302-0

Typeset in Avenir by Lapiz Digital Services
Printed and bound in the United Kingdom by Clays Ltd

Headline's policy is to use papers that are natural, renewable and recyclable products and
made from wood grown in well-managed forests and other controlled sources. The logging
and manufacturing processes are expected to conform to the environmental regulations of
the country of origin.

HEADLINE PUBLISHING GROUP
An Hachette UK Company
Carmelite House
50 Victoria Embankment
London EC4Y 0DZ

www.headline.co.uk
www.hachette.co.uk

"This is a powerful and empowering book about a difficult subject, and it's long overdue. Charlie writes not as a victim, nor a survivor, but as a pioneer for how to process and deal with trauma."
Dr Ranj Singh, NHS doctor, TV presenter and author

"Charlie's book is a compassionate guide for those seeking to unravel the threads of trauma in their lives. *Why It's OK to Talk About Trauma* is not just a narrative; it's a toolbox filled with empathy, courage and practical strategies. An invaluable resource for anyone on the path to healing."
Andy Serkis, actor and director

"When Charlie Webster developed PTSD and was looking for help, all she could find were 'intimidating textbooks full of academic jargon, which didn't feel like real life'. Books by people like me. I am pleased to say that this book is free from academic jargon, and is definitely based on real life – her own. If something similar were to happen to me as happened to Charlie, this is the kind of book I would want to read."
Professor Sir Simon Wessely, Regius Chair of Psychiatry, King's College London

"This is an incredibly important, extremely brave and unwaveringly honest book. Charlie's openness about the effects of trauma on her life, and how she's come to understand, process and survive the pain in her past, is empowering for us all, whether trauma has affected us or not."
Sean Fletcher, TV broadcaster, journalist and mental health advocate

"Charlie has taken a deeply complex topic and created a practical and empowering book – one that shows the reader that there is light at the end of the tunnel. Essential reading for anyone who has experienced trauma or is supporting someone who has."
Dame Professor Clare Gerada, President of the Royal College of General Practitioners

"Charlie Webster's book on trauma is a compelling and transformative exploration of the subject, weaving together her very personal anecdotes that draw readers into a nuanced and brave exploration of what trauma truly entails. Through her own experiences, Webster skillfully navigates the intricate web of emotions that accompany the processing of trauma, allowing readers to identify with her struggles and triumphs. The book also serves as a powerful guidebook, gently encouraging readers to embark on their own journey of understanding, empowering them to confront and process their own traumatic experiences.

For people suffering with trauma this book should stand as a beacon of hope, offering explanation, solace and actionable insights. This is truly an essential read for anyone who is eager to foster a more empathetic and supportive understanding of the human experience."
Professor Paul Gringras, President of the International Paediatric Sleep Association

"Charlie's book highlights the long-lasting impact that childhood abuse can have on people's lives, and through sharing her own experiences, she shows how the right support can help people start to recover from the trauma they've experienced."
Sir Peter Wanless, CEO of the NSPCC

"As a national domestic abuse charity, we are so proud of Charlie (a long-term and valued ambassador for Women's Aid) for writing so powerfully about her own experiences. This book articulates why being trauma-informed is vital when working with those who have survived horrific experiences and abuse, and will raise important awareness and understanding."
Farah Nazeer, CEO of Women's Aid

"Charlie has created a book that is truly inspiring. She shows that you can be in the darkest place and come out of the other side – it delivers hope. She is an amazing human with the courage to speak her truth, which in fact reflects many of ours. The impact this book will have is incredible."
Justin (JC) Coghlan, co-founder of the Movember Foundation

"As the CEO of Malaria No More UK, it fills me with immense pride to see Charlie, our dedicated ambassador, share her deeply personal journey and insights into the aftermath of malaria as part of her story.
In this powerful narrative, Charlie bravely delves into the trauma associated with the disease, shedding light on its long-term impact on mental health. Drawing from her own experiences, she courageously explores the emotional toll of malaria, showcasing the importance of discussing and understanding the trauma that often accompanies such life-altering events.

Charlie continues to be a powerful advocate for those grappling with trauma, fostering a sense of connection and understanding. I encourage everyone to read this impactful book, as it not only shares Charlie's malaria journey but also provides a source of encouragement and empathy for others navigating their own paths of recovery."
Dr Astrid Bonfield CBE, CEO of Malaria No More UK

"Charlie deserves huge respect and heartfelt thanks for writing this brave and brilliant book. With extraordinary candor, she gives us a unique window into many of the horrific things she's been through and into how these experiences shaped her thinking, feelings and behaviour. But that's not the half of it.

What sets this book apart is the way Charlie interweaves her story with expert voices and the practical techniques she learnt on her therapeutic journey. Her commitment to equip her readers with the knowledge and confidence to acknowledge, process and grow through whatever life has thrown at them is the driving force of this book and is a testament to the exceptional woman Charlie is."

Alison Baum OBE, founder and President of Best Beginnings

About the Author

Charlie Webster is an award-winning broadcaster, journalist, writer, campaigner, documentarian and international speaker. She is the host and creator of *Scamanda*, the number 1 Apple podcast of 2023.

Charlie is an ambassador for Women's Aid, Malaria No More and an NSPCC Campaigner for Childhood. She does extensive advocacy work and sits on the Ministry of Justice's victims advisory panel. She has covered global events for major networks including the BBC and Sky, and her powerful documentary, 'Nowhere to Run: Abused by Our Coach', broadcast on the BBC, led to a change in UK law and international policy.

Prologue

'Do you want to place a flower or a stone to represent your birth?', my clinical psychologist asked. 'Remember, a stone represents something bad that happened and a flower a good thing.'

'I don't know.'

I paused, but not for long.

'Both. It's a flower and a stone.'

There is no way I would ever have ended up like this. I was a survivor. Tough, resilient and could withstand anything. Shut up, put up and get on with it – that was me. I went into everything with a confidence that stemmed from the fact that I knew I had no choice but to push on and keep fighting. I only had myself to rely on, and I wanted to prove that I was enough. I didn't trust the branch I was sitting on – or, for that matter, the tree that it grew off. But I *did* trust my own wings to keep flying every time it broke, which it did. A lot.

I was raised in Sheffield in the north of England, where a cup of tea is the answer to any problem (I still buy into that philosophy), and steel is the heart of our city and its people.

My mum became pregnant with me at the age of 16. She hid her bump through her safety-pinned jeans and baggy jumpers for six months while going to school. When the school found out about this 'horrific sin', she was kicked out.

My mum and dad – who was only a year older than her – were miserable. They were forced to marry so that they could keep me.

They got divorced when I was three.

We were homeless for six months, living on the kindness and charity of my mum's friends.

After a stop at the dole office (as the benefits or welfare office was referred to back then), we were turned away. After all, we were only another number in the system. My mum and I eventually moved into a narrow, terraced two-up two-down. It had a coal fire that doubled as our heating, and had a little cubby hole where we cooked potatoes for dinner. We didn't eat meat because we had no way of cooking it, and couldn't afford it anyway. The house was always musty with the aroma of smoke from the coal.

I was seven when my mum met my step-dad. I was also seven when this grown man thought I was plotting against him. I just wanted this new dad to love me. He didn't. He just wanted me out of the way so he could have my mum all to himself.

He told me he would ultimately win and get rid of me. He called me 'thick', 'ugly' and, when I cried, 'pathetic'. This verbal abuse then progressed to physical abuse and isolation – I'd be too scared to come out of my room, even to go to the toilet. He would monitor our food to make sure I hadn't eaten any, and when it came to 'treat' foods, like yoghurts, he'd declare I wasn't deserving of them. Anything that would remind him that I existed under 'his roof' would cause an outburst of violence. Ironically, it wasn't his roof – he had moved in with us. I buried my feelings deep inside. It was the only way I could get through each day.

By the time I was a teenager, I was being sexually abused by my running coach. I walked around in an all-consuming fog that had taken up permanent residency in my head.

I kept fighting through the fog, one distressing experience after the other, living with trauma all the way into adulthood.

Until, one day in my mid-30s, it got to the point where I just couldn't fly anymore. The branch was broken, the tree was broken, I was broken.

PROLOGUE

At that time, I wrote the below:

An overwhelming feeling of pain from the inside out.
It's mental but I can physically feel it inside,
deeply tucked away but also at the surface.
Feelings, thoughts, flashbacks,
I could be right back there,
struggling to breathe, unable to swallow, powerless to see.

My sense of touch is electric.
My hearing is acute.
My mind is wired.
I feel everything and nothing at all.
Trapped in my own head.

This is what trauma feels like.

Contents

Introduction

This book is the book that I needed when I was desperately searching for help and for something that I could actually relate to; all I could find were intimidating textbooks full of academic jargon, which didn't feel like real life.

I want to begin by acknowledging that, yes, I've had quite a lot of awful experiences in my life, as you'll come to read. But to live with trauma isn't about how 'bad' it was, or a comparison of whose was worse.

Trauma comes in many forms. From repeated bullying, emotional abuse in a relationship, being raised in a dysfunctional home, or critical illness, to a mother going through childbirth. All these are traumatic, and all have been normalized by society. Often, we *ourselves* downplay it, to fit in with that 'normal' narrative; this is a very common reaction, and a coping mechanism for trauma.

For a long time, I didn't even consider that I was struggling with trauma. It was just my life – I'd been dealt a shitty card. I felt it was just who I am – and I deserved it, otherwise why would these bad things keep happening to me? That's the story I told myself for the longest of times. I just wasn't enough.

Whatever has happened to you, whatever your distressing experience, we will face it together in this book. If you're reading this to support someone else, this book is also for you. Each chapter will take us on a journey through the stages of coming to terms with and processing your trauma. We will learn exactly what trauma is, why our painful experiences have such a profound after-effect on our lives, and how trauma impacts us mentally, emotionally and physically. We'll look at how trauma influences our

1

day-to-day behaviours and affects how we connect in relationships. I'll be drawing on my own experience, research and experts along the way.

I believe having a full understanding of what trauma is is the first step to starting to recover from it and living a healthier life mentally, emotionally and physically. Our hurtful past experiences don't stand alone from our present daily lives.

ABOUT THIS BOOK

I've divided the book into three parts. I'd strongly recommend reading it chronologically and revisiting points that really resonate with you.

- **Part I – What is trauma?** This is all about understanding what trauma actually is and identifying its impact on ourselves or how to recognize it in others.
- **Part II – Trauma in our lives.** This looks at how trauma shows up in our lives and what to do with it.
- **Part III – Growth through and after trauma.** Here, we examine what happens as we grow through trauma, and what recovery really means.

By the time you turn the final page, my intention is that you will feel different. Although what has happened to you won't disappear, it will hopefully feel more manageable; you will have the knowledge and some of the tools you'll need to deal with trauma and life moving forward.

BEGINNING YOUR JOURNEY

It takes so much courage to look inside of ourselves. It can be incredibly exposing and make us feel so vulnerable. It did for me. Making sense of our past and how it impacts us is not an easy road to take. I wish I could tell you it was, but staying where you are in your trauma is much harder. I know that first hand. For far too long I avoided the road of dealing with what I'd been through, and suffered repeatedly because of it.

Our past isn't just a story – our past has feelings and emotions that stay with us. They live in our present and influence our behaviours. We can't change what has happened to us or the way people have treated us in the past, but we *can* change the present and the way we treat ourselves.

I spent far too long living and reliving my trauma. Everything that follows is what has helped me. I truly believe what I outline in this book will have the same impact on you.

I hope that you give it a try, but take your time with it. Be gentle on yourself as you go through the journey of this book. I say this because I wasn't, and I wish somebody had said that to me.

I have laid out everything that I've learnt about trauma over my life, and I've combined my own experience with integrative emotional and behavioural psychology specific to trauma.

PROFESSIONAL ADVICE

Alongside my own story, I'll share invaluable insights from Dr Rachel O'Beney throughout the book. Dr Rachel is a consultant clinical psychologist for the National Health Service, and the lead for Psychology services in South Westminster in London, England. She works for the South Westminster mental health hub, a part of the Central and North West London Mental Health Foundation NHS Trust. Back in 2017, I became one of Dr Rachel's patients in her Psychology department. I saw her for two years; three times a week to start with, until we were able to reduce the frequency to twice and then once weekly. In the second year of my treatment, Dr Rachel started a small weekly psychotherapy group which she asked me to be part of – we called it our trauma group. I received a mixture of narrative exposure therapy and schema therapy specific to trauma, the latter I went on to study in depth. I truly believe Dr Rachel saved my life.

The book contains descriptions of my own inner work that I did while seeing Dr Rachel. When I told Dr Rachel I would be writing about my own experience, she did bring up questions around my own disclosure – about whether I wanted to put it all out there. Up to this point everything I'd discussed with her when I was her patient was only ever between us: doctor–patient confidentiality. When I considered if I wanted to share everything with the world, I realized I wouldn't know how *else* I could write a book on trauma that would be truly useful if it weren't to include my own journey, and show that in the darkest depths of trauma there is a way through.

'The whole reason for our contact in the psychology department was about you finding your voice,' Dr Rachel said in her support of my decision to write these words. Ironic given I've spent my adult life being a voice on TV and campaigning for social change.

This is real-life, humanized therapy.

There are also contributions from Dr Niki Snook, a highly experienced lead consultant in the Intensive Care Unit (ICU) who pioneered the idea of follow-up clinics for ICU patients to help them process the trauma of their experience.

EXERCISES, TECHNIQUES AND CONNECTION CARDS

Scattered throughout the book are exercises and techniques that I have used and learnt throughout my own journey.

Exercises

The exercises are designed to help you work through a concept, to identify how you are feeling and apply the information to your life in a practical way. The exercises will increase your awareness of how you behave because of what you've experienced in your past, help you grow through it and give you the ability to change your thinking and behaviour. Please give these all a try, but don't worry if an exercise doesn't work for you. It might be that you need to return to it at a future time, once you've read a bit more of the book.

Techniques

The techniques are ones that I have used – and still use – myself. These are specific actions that we can take to provide immediate comfort or relief, or help us get out of a difficult spot with really challenging feelings and thoughts. Many are of particular help when things feel overwhelming and everything is just too much to cope with. Again, don't worry if something doesn't work for you – different techniques work for different people. Once you find one that does help you, you can use these tools forever and in many life situations.

Connection cards

An important part of my recovery is to go back over what I've learnt. To be able to revisit key learnings easily, I use what I like to call 'connection cards'. These are blank or lined index cards that contain important strategies or techniques that we repeat to help change our thought patterns that we get stuck in because of trauma. I use index cards, as they can fit in most bags and even some purses and wallets. Alternatively, you could treat yourself to a notebook that you use purely for this journey; or you could use a mixture of cards and a paper or electronic notebook – whatever works for you.

Throughout the book, I will reference these connection cards and suggest you create one when there's something to practise and repeat or that you might need to refer to quickly. Your notes don't need to be anything fancy or for anyone else to be able to read but they will be really helpful on your recovery journey.

An example of a well-used connection card. This is my dog-eared Emotionally Healthy Messages connection card that I carry with me in my wallet.

You'll find a key to all exercises, techniques and connection cards straight after this introduction.

WHEN I FIRST REALIZED I WASN'T OKAY

It wasn't the time I self-harmed by cutting myself with screwdrivers. It wasn't the time I had suicidal thoughts and drank myself into a numbness. It wasn't the many failed relationships and unemotional sex, or the times I would starve myself or be unable to lift my head off the pillow from crippling depression.

No. It was when I was catching a train.

* * *

I look around, there are people everywhere, moving unpredictably. I'm in a video game, my character bouncing lightly back and forth, idle, while everything else spins around me. The other characters are already deep into the game. It's so echoey and booming. Why are my controls not working?

Get a grip! You've caught a train a million times.

I know this station well. It's Leeds.

I focus my gaze on the barriers ahead to insert my ticket. My head is down, my chin is almost touching my chest. I'm watching myself from a distance, urging myself to keep going, and at the same time ashamed of how pathetic I feel.

I'm through the barriers and walking down the train platform.

I try to walk toward the door, but everybody else just keeps walking in front of me leaving me behind. I'm back in the video game, somebody else has the controls, and is playing my character. I try to catch the others, but instead just spin round and round on the spot, going nowhere.

I can't do this. I can't get on the train. I need to go back. I just want to be in bed and pull the covers tight over my head.

'What are you doing? I need to get on.' A throaty voice comes from behind me followed by an accompanying nudge in the middle of my back.

I scramble up the train steps as the voice pushes me forward and onto the train. The doors beep behind me and swipe firmly shut. I look left and all I can see is a rough sea of heads bobbing up and down trying to find a seat. I look right and the sea spills into every carriage. Where am I supposed to go? The train starts moving. The tannoy roars overhead, announcing the destination as London. What am I doing here? I look down. My phone is clenched in my hand, my knuckles poke through, milky white against my tanned skin. I'm sweating, I can feel it trickling down my back. An immense pain hits my chest – it feels like my heart is exploding through my coat. I slump down onto the floor, gripping my head.

My neck's prickly and spasming. My mouth is dry. I cough to try and release a breath. My throat won't clear. My breathing is sharp and comes out as a high-pitched gasp. Thoughts are flying through my mind, but I can't catch hold of even one of them to help me figure this out.

I'm in the hospital. Tubes everywhere.

I'm staring at the ceiling.

My coach is leaning over me. Stale blue-cheese breath.

The slipperiness of baby oil.

My step-dad is screaming in my face.

'Pathetic.'

The bitter stench of alcohol.

I'm in the hospital.

'You're dying.'

The doctor is leaning over me.

Tears are pouring down my face, dripping onto my hands and down my arms into the crease of my elbows.

'Hello. Are you okay? Do you need help?'

A man is towering over me, his face pixelated. He has a white paper bag in his hand.

'Madam, you need to take a deep breath.'

I'm holding my breath watertight. I grip at my neck fighting for air. The ventilator is being jammed down my throat. I can see characters in the video game running the gauntlet, collecting the energy stars, defeating the obstacles – but not mine. My character has no power, no stars and no weapons to stop me from being swallowed into the void of darkness.

I can see the red train door.

The man passes me the paper bag as he crouches down next to me. I try to pull myself up, embarrassed.

'Breathe into this madam. I think you're having a panic attack.'

What is he talking about? I take the paper bag off him as he ushers it gently toward my face like an oxygen mask, and I start to breathe in short sharp squeals. His hand is still holding onto one edge.

'Are you going to London?'

London?

I remember now. I'm going to London. I look down to see my whole body trembling. I nod.

'That's better. Do you want to get off at the next stop?'

'No, no.' My nose is pouring with snot. A wave of humiliation brings me back to reality.

'I'm sorry.'

'Can I look at your ticket?' I had it gripped in my hand protectively alongside my phone.

He twists his head to look.

'Come with me. Let's go and sit you in first class. It's quieter. Is there anyone I can phone for you?'

I shake my head. I pull myself up and follow him through the carriages keeping my head low, embarrassed and ashamed. The red and grey floor offers some comfort. The man puts me in a sunken spacious seat. The sea is calmer here.

'I'll come and check on you in a bit.'

'Thank you,' I whimper.

I'm still holding the paper bag with my ticket and my phone. I dial my best friend, Adele.

'Hey babe, you okay?'

'No. I'm a fucked-up mess.' My words come out as an aggressive spit.

'I can't understand what is going on. I don't know what I'm doing. I'm going crazy. I can't even get a train. I can't do this anymore.'

I put my head on the window, the cold from the outside adding to the feeling of loneliness.

I need help.

* * *

I was 33. A year later, I walked into a mental health facility and sat face to face with Dr Rachel. She said that I'd been living with the impact of trauma for the majority of my life, and that, if I didn't get help, she feared for my life.

The only reason I was sat in that stereotypically white therapy room was because I had very nearly lost my life eight months earlier.

MY TIPPING POINT

I was in intensive care on life support, paralysed and in a coma. I had a rare strain of malaria, and three other hard-to-pronounce deadly tropical diseases that were eating me alive. I'd contracted them while completing a 3,000-mile charity cycling challenge from London to Rio de Janeiro, Brazil.

I had arrived in Rio feeling on top of the world, yet 24 hours later my lungs were collapsing, my kidneys had failed and I was told by the doctor I was dying. Still to this day, it's hard to get my head around what happened. It was like every bad moment in my life came flooding to the very forefront of my mind. Not quite 'my life flashed before my eyes', more my life hit me in the face.

I was once again trapped inside my own body. I was a 15-year-old being sexually abused by my running coach; I was a frightened 9-year-old, pinned to my bedroom door by my step-dad, and holding my breath for fear of making a noise. I was locked in a coma with emotions that I'd spent my life running away from. I couldn't escape. An all-too-familiar feeling in my life. I didn't know it at the time, but distressing experiences trigger past distressing experiences – trauma triggers trauma. While I was in a physical coma, my brain replayed everything that had happened to me, forcing me to confront my painful past within what was a very frightening present.

After coming out of hospital, I was diagnosed with Post Traumatic Stress Disorder (PTSD). It was causing crippling anxiety and depression, and opened a whole can of worms. Sometimes trying to get help would make me feel even worse, because it was dragging up painful feelings and thoughts that I'd convinced myself I had moved on from. This was one of the ways I'd always coped, by simply refusing to accept that what had happened to me was now having an impact. It was the biggest lie I told myself for years. Of course, it affects me. How can we go through trauma and not be shaped by it?

I absolutely hate the phrase 'the past is the past' – who spun that bullshit? I now say to myself, 'Of course you feel like this, how can you not? It's understandable. Look at what you've been through.' 'Leaving it in the past' doesn't mean it's not there; our past just seeps out in other ways. Emotionally unhealthy and self-destructive behaviours, angry outbursts, deep, dark lows, pushing people away (I was an expert at this); and impulsive behaviours such as substance misuse, consuming large amounts of food (comfort eating) or alcohol, and intrusive, sometimes suicidal thoughts. The symptoms of trauma can make you feel constantly fearful, helpless and isolated, with no hope of escape. I wonder if this is something you can relate to?

BEGINNING TO PROCESS

The symptoms of trauma listed in the *Diagnostic and Statistical Manual of Mental Disorders*, the bible for the diagnosis of mental health disorders, are:

- Flashbacks
- Anxiety
- Intense emotional reactions
- Hypervigilance (always being on guard)
- Depression
- Nightmares
- Detachment from emotion (suppressing our feelings, denial, avoidance)
- Agitation
- Irritation
- Numbness
- Confusion
- Sadness
- Exhaustion
- Guilt and shame
- Self-defeating and destructive patterns of behaviour
- Physical sensations, including hyperventilation, severe headaches, tense muscles, irritable bowel syndrome (IBS), nausea and vomiting
- Memory lapses around a specific traumatic experience
- Intrusive and suicidal thoughts

If you are feeling any or all of the above, it's likely you've been through some sort of disturbing or distressing experience or multiple experiences. Maybe you've been through something similar to me, or maybe what you've been through is different. The fact is, these times in our lives do have an emotional, mental and physical impact, whether we like it or not; and, unfortunately, there is no getting away from that. It doesn't matter how or what you endured, it's that this experience left you with trauma, and trauma is trauma. There's no dancing around it.

But know this: *recovery is possible and can lead to a more fulfilled life.*

'Unprocessed trauma' means we feel emotionally and physically unsafe, like we are back in those moments of distress. This leads to unhealthy (i.e. more harmful than helpful) ways of coping with our vulnerability.

I wonder if you're like me – I hate feeling vulnerable.

I would ignore my feelings. Shut them out. Push them deep down. Run away from them. Do anything other than face them and feel them.

I ran away from the things that had happened to me – 'put the past behind me' – but they chased me, and they chased hard. The more I disengaged from my feelings and avoided the emotional pain, the more overwhelming things became for me; the louder my past shouted and the more heightened my mind grew. It's as if the more I tried to fight the sadness, the harder it fought back to attack me.

It was only when I started to understand what was going on and why, that I could start to make different choices. You can't change things that you don't realize you do.

Many of us don't talk about what we've experienced until later in our lives, if at all. It's okay to talk about trauma, but it's not easy … because it's not *just* about talking about it. You have to emotionally connect to your trauma – and that hurts.

'Processing' is to feel, to emotionally connect, not just think. So, when I use the word 'processing' trauma, it doesn't just mean to mentally connect to your distressing experiences and work through them but to emotionally feel them too. We'll talk about it further on, but one of the most common ways of coping with trauma (coping mechanisms) is to emotionally detach – but that coping mechanism is what actually prevents us from healing.

Once I took the step to work through my trauma, I found myself starting to open up more, let my guard down (well a little bit anyway, but that was a start) and allow people in. I was less reactive, less defensive, and I could see logic in situations where before I would have only seen self-loathing, personal rejection and my own failure.

I will only be honest and open with you throughout this book. I will give you the understanding and knowledge of an ongoing recovery, which includes awareness, learning and adapting from trauma. The book will help you develop a more compassionate approach to what you've been through and toward yourself. I will help you work toward an acceptance of your trauma and how it's impacted you, so you can see it as part of your story rather than something to hide or run away from. But there is no quick fix that makes it all better; recovery takes work, and it takes you being honest with yourself.

'It's totally understandable. We all want a quick fix, don't we? To make all our uncomfortable feelings go away. This can be a problem for people who constantly think they need more therapy because they aren't the finished product yet. I'm afraid to say we are never the finished product. It's always work, and it's our work of internalizing and practising what we've learnt.'

Dr Rachel O'Beney

I am with you on this journey.

EXERCISES, TECHNIQUES AND CONNECTION CARDS

I know that even starting this book may have brought up intense emotions. So, before we go any further, I wanted to flag that throughout the book I've included different techniques for emotional regulation. Think of them a little bit like building a scaffold around yourself, to support your journey.

The tools will be introduced as we work through this book together, but you can also turn to them whenever you need. For instance, the grounding techniques can be used to gently pull you away from any overpowering emotions and thoughts from the past; and the box breathing technique can be used when everything feels overwhelming – it's even used by top athletes, due to its profound impact.

Exercises

Techniques

PART I

What is trauma?

Trauma can have a serious impact on us – emotionally, mentally and physically.

When I refer to 'trauma' throughout this book, it is that exact impact on us that I am addressing, and the heaviness we continue to suffer because of it. It's not *what* happened to us, but what it's left us with.

How can we know what trauma is when we so often normalize our fear, pain and suffering?

Because of the way we, as humans, innately deal with threat, it can be hard to see how much our past pain influences our present behaviour and the decisions we now make. It's those behaviours and decisions that can keep us in our trauma, keep us stuck and keep us repeating past trauma cycles.

Identifying what we've been through as trauma means we have to acknowledge it – and acknowledging it and then seeing how much it affects us is painful, scary and may not be what we want to see. Acknowledging trauma can shine a light on things that are hard for us to face and admit to ourselves; it can be overwhelming, especially when we are trying to cope and manage with what we have going on right now in our day-to-day life. Dealing with our past is the last thing most of us want to do. Ignoring, denying and avoiding it are all ways that comfort us; we tell ourselves,

'It wasn't really that bad,' and, 'Well, that person over there has been through much worse.' Hiding and convincing ourselves otherwise are all strategies to try and cope with the very thing we are denying and hiding from.

I was so busy protecting myself from my own feelings that I didn't acknowledge what I'd been through. While that can seem like great self-protection, it actually kept a deep but empty reservoir inside me that was still suffering; even though I was no longer living in the moment of the traumatic experience, I was reliving the consequences of it.

Part I of this book will help you understand what trauma is and how that relates to your own life. This is the foundation of working through trauma. We can do everything else on the surface, but if we don't understand what trauma is and how it shows up for us, we can't recognize what we need to heal.

1

The impact of what you've been through

No wonder you feel like you do – look at what you've been through.

We've all been through something adverse in our lives. I've never met anybody that hasn't. It's far more common than we realize. Most of us will live through at least one distressing experience in our lifetime, and some more than others. Over 70% of the world's population have experienced at least one traumatic event, and the average adult experiences one major life event every four years. The world's population is over 8 billion. I've never been great at maths, but even I know that's a hell of a lot of people.

I suppose we could say, 'Well, that's life.' And we can't avoid life! Even if we tried to, and locked ourselves away in a fortress, that would be traumatic in itself! What we *can* do is make sense of how our hurtful experiences – trauma – affect us and find a version of healing and recovery.

The awful experience(s) causes initial emotional distress, but what causes the long-term damage? It's the fact that the majority of us don't deal with the emotional pain of it, or give ourselves the time and space to mend. If we broke our leg, we'd need time for it to heal, potentially have surgery and specialist help, like working with a physio. If none of those things happened after the initial break, you wouldn't be able to walk, and even if it healed you would have problems walking normally. Our mind is no different.

Trauma is what stays with us *after* the painful experience itself is over. Our life physically moves on from that time, as if the 'traumatic' experience is not *actively* happening anymore, but our brains, emotions and nervous system don't move on. This is because, nine times out of ten, when something awful happens to us, we push it away or bury it deep down inside. And that's exactly what I did, so you're definitely not alone.

Trauma takes from us, it degrades us, it cuts into the very essence of who we are. Trauma makes us close down and internalize our feelings and the emotional pain we are in. So, imagine what happens inside when we lock that away and keep it all to ourselves.

UNDERSTANDING OUR PAIN

When I first started working with clinical psychologist Dr Rachel O'Beney and she asked me what I was feeling from my trauma, I couldn't think of how to describe it. Dr Rachel asked me again and all I could think of was the word 'pain'. 'I'm just in pain,' I said to her. 'Emotional, heart-wrenching pain, and it's always there, no matter what I do.'

Pain that I'd buried for so long had become my normal state of being. I was always in emotional pain, no matter how many good things were happening in my life on the outside.

Pain is most commonly attributed to a physical sensation, but it's also mental and emotional, and this sort of pain can feel far worse than physical pain. In fact, I've used physical pain in the past – self-harming and obsessive exercising – to help me cope with my emotional pain. Experts call this 'pain offset relief' – the feeling of relief that comes when (self-inflicted) physical pain starts to subside tricks the brain into thinking it's in lesser emotional pain. Self-harming can also be sneaky, as it can manifest in subtle ways: I'd over-exercise, push myself to breaking point, overwork, deprive myself of sleep and food. All of those things constitute self-harm, yet are completely normalized, often seen as admirable and even encouraged. Understanding what we do to cope with the way we feel, and how this comes from your past experiences, is fundamental in recovering from trauma. We'll revisit and work through this as we go.

So, what *is* trauma then?

TRAUMA DEFINED

The UK Trauma Council defines trauma as:

'A distressing event or events that are so extreme or intense that they overwhelm a person's ability to cope, resulting in lasting negative impact.'

UK Trauma Council

Definitions of trauma from organizations throughout the world are very similar; while I think the UK Trauma Council sums it up well, I struggle a little with certain words.

Firstly, with the use of the word 'event'. An emotionally distressing or neglectful childhood is a continuous experience over time, not a singular event – as is repeatedly being bullied at school or work, or being ridiculed and degraded in a relationship; they are not even a *series* of events.

Secondly, the experiences mentioned above are often not seen as 'extreme'; in fact, they are repeatedly normalized in society – but all can cause long-lasting trauma.

So, my own definition of trauma is:

'The disturbing and painful experiences we've been through, that stay with us and influence our behaviour and our actions in a way that keeps us in this same emotional pain.'

Charlie Webster

Memories and feelings of past hurts live in present daily life, and we close ourselves down in protection to try and avoid feeling this pain and anymore coming in.

Dr Rachel said she's not particularly a fan of the word 'trauma'. She explains it's 'because people say "I'm traumatized" because their bus doesn't come ...' The use of the word trauma in such a scenario clearly minimizes what trauma actually is and what causes it. Your bus not coming might upset you, make you angry, or stress you out, but it doesn't leave you with trauma.

Dr Rachel defines trauma as:

'The awful things that one has experienced. The moments where you were really worried about your survival – mental or physical, or both. Some people have had general neglect, not specific moments of intense worry about survival but general failure to thrive. It's important for them to tell their story, the story of their sadness. Trauma is moments when you really doubt you're going to get through, mentally or physically, and you are terrified.'

Dr Rachel O'Beney

But Dr Rachel wants to take it further than a basic definition. She believes an understanding of trauma centres on people's stories. She says, 'I'm much more interested in understanding the story of each person. If you can bear to tell your own story and for it to be heard by another, you can work through how it is affecting you.' This approach can be known as narrative exposure therapy, and focuses on telling and validating your own story. This is very much the opposite of what trauma makes you do: downplay and often hide your story.

HOW OUR UNDERSTANDING OF 'TRAUMA' DEVELOPED

The study of trauma started well over a century ago (although it wasn't called that then). The word 'trauma', when describing a psychological concept, only started to be used after the 1960s. For the first half of the 20th century the only reference to trauma in psychiatry is 'traumatic brain injury', which is a physical state – for example, a literal bullet through the brain. A hundred years later, it still means this now in Accident and Emergency. But back in Paris in 1887, Jean-Martin Charcot first proposed that 'hysterical' patients were suffering because of their past. After conducting a study, it was his student Pierre Janet that described how these memories returned not as stories of what had happened, but as intense emotional reactions, aggressive behaviour, physical pain and bodily states, which were all part of the experience the patient had previously suffered.

Then Sigmund Freud came to the party, and in 1920 described how patients suffering from trauma couldn't always recall these memories, concluding that 'perhaps they are more concerned with *not* thinking of it'. Freud saw how horrible life experiences destroyed people's ability to function long after their painful experience.

Meanwhile, the two World Wars prompted conversations about trauma in line with Freud and Janet, and the term 'shell shock' was coined by British physician Charles Myers in 1915. Although the phrase was banned in 1917 by the British Army, it has become part of our culture and language ever since. In World War I, the army had to create five large tented hospitals solely to deal with the psychological problems of the servicemen. British psychiatrist Sir Simon Wessely told me that the site of ShellShock Hospital Number 5 is, if you've ever caught the Eurostar, at the Calais terminus car parks and where the huge supermarket is, where everybody stocks up on wine when crossing the UK–France border.

Trauma was again brought to the forefront of conversation in the 1970s after the Vietnam War, but the history and understanding of psychological trauma is much more complex than simply 'war to enlightenment'. It's a constant merry-go-round, still 'two steps forward, two steps back,' as Sir Wessely explained to me.

As more progression was made within mental health, correlations were found that people using mental health services had higher rates of trauma in childhood or adulthood than the general population, and were more likely to have experienced violence. It also became clear that trauma is widespread throughout society, a significant problem and a costly public health issue.

When I first started campaigning against domestic and sexual abuse over 15 years ago, I spoke about the long-term mental health impact and how government policy doesn't work if it is not understood from an approach of what the individual is going through. My point was: how can we have domestic abuse policy or law when there is a lack of understanding about the trauma the victim is in, which will influence how they behave? For example, a victim of domestic or sexual abuse might not engage with the police – not because they don't need help, but because they are in trauma (scared and in survival mode) rather than in a place of healing and empowerment.

I was invited to sit on the Ministry of Justice Victims' Panel, and now (nine years later), although a lot still needs to change, the phrase 'trauma-informed approach' is at least in the conversation. Although, it's not just about professionals being informed, but people being *supported* to recover. Right now, the latter piece is missing. There's no point in being informed if there's no action to help people and to change a system that isn't working.

In 2019, I gave a TED Talk where I described a flashback I'd experienced. I then said, 'But I don't want to talk to you about what happened and how it happened. I want to talk to you about the bit that we never hear about – that no one ever talks about. What happens after. The aftermath of a traumatic experience.'

A trauma-informed and healing-centred approach would ask, 'What happened to you?', rather than, 'What is wrong with you?' As Dr Rachel says, it's about your story, and how you truly feel about it.

WHERE WE ARE NOW

Now, we are finally talking about trauma. Recently in the press, there have been multiple articles published about 'trauma' being an overused buzzword of the zeitgeist, and concern about the 'wrong type' of trauma conversation. It goes back to Dr Rachel's dislike of the word 'trauma' because people use it in a flippant context: 'That meeting traumatized me' or 'I went on an awful date – it was traumatizing'. I've had a few of those meetings and dates in my time, but they didn't cause me trauma – just disappointment and often a good story to tell my friends. An annoying or awkward experience is *not* trauma.

We've also seen this flippancy with the word 'depressed'. People use 'depressed' when they have a normal reaction of sadness after a life event that *was* sad, but it doesn't mean the person has depression. Being sad is a normal human emotion that we all have.

It's important to understand what trauma is and what it's not so that it's not diminished (equally with depression), and talking about trauma should be encouraged. But saying that 'trauma' is a buzzword can make those of us that are living with trauma hide even more.

We are finally starting to understand the impact of trauma on us as individuals and collectively as a society. Even more so now, given the heightened political and economic environment and following the Covid-19 pandemic. Let's not undo that by now saying 'trauma' is just something of the moment. There's already been many lifetimes of discouragement, mocking and shame when it comes to people's experiences. For a long time, people have gone unheard and unseen. Labelling 'trauma' as a buzzword is just another trap to keep people from thriving. It doesn't help anybody.

For far too long now trauma has been dealt with in isolation – by an individual with medical professionals – if dealt with at all. But the power of an open conversation is clear. Once one person's trauma is openly validated, it leads to another person opening up and sharing their experience.

Talking about trauma, getting it out into the open, validating experiences, is how we recover. It *is* okay to talk about trauma. We shouldn't normalize what has happened to us, but we *should* normalize the impact of it – it is normal that something distressing will have an effect on our emotional and mental state of being.

THE COMMON EXPERIENCE OF EMOTIONAL PAIN

Emotional pain is something we all have in common. There are collective ways we all react and feel from trauma, but they may appear in different ways in your life. We often hear the phrase 'everyone's experience is different' and the idea that emotional pain is subjective. Yes, it is, and that's important to acknowledge, and we also have different ways of coping; but I want to introduce another concept that we hear far less about: the concept of commonality in how our painful experiences make us feel.

When frightening and upsetting things happen to us, we have common experiences of emotional pain, loss, rejection, worthlessness, loneliness, abandonment, anxiety, depression, fear and often shame.

We all have the same basic needs of safety, secure attachment to others and freedom to express our needs and feelings in a safe environment. A distressing experience shakes all of those things at its core.

For much of my life I believed that my trauma made me different, which just isolated me further and strengthened the idea that there was something wrong with me. If I had known about the concept of commonalities in painful experiences earlier on, I believe that would have made all the difference to me.

After having individual treatment with Dr Rachel, I joined the psychotherapy 'trauma group'. Many of the attendees had experienced multiple emotionally painful things and/or neglect. I have to admit, I didn't want to be part of the group. I felt like I had too much going on, I was in survival mode, and I didn't feel like I could take the time out to sit in a room with a bunch of strangers for two hours a week. Even the thought of it brought about panic. When I first started going, I was very defensive; I came across as closed off, and I didn't contribute much. But when members of the group opened up, it dawned on me that we all felt the same, despite our widely differing backgrounds, cultures and ages. The more I listened and let my guard down, the more I heard myself in each person every time they spoke. I saw my own emotional pain in theirs. It was an epiphany moment that, for the first time, genuinely made me feel less alone.

When I came out of hospital toward the end of 2016, I was referred by my renal consultant to an Intensive Care Unit (ICU) follow-up mental and emotional support service at St James's University Hospital in Leeds. I'd gone from an ICU and semi-intensive care in Rio, to being repatriated on a medical plane (which took 20 hours, five stops and two doctors), to the tropical diseases unit and then the renal unit in St James's. The focus shifted from the diseases I had, to the consequences: saving my kidneys. The follow-up service was run by Dr Niki Snook, the highly experienced lead consultant in the ICU, who was one of the first people to set something like this up. Dr Niki told me that trauma was never talked about when she first became a consultant, and she set up the clinic because she wanted to know what happened to her patients after the ICU. At the time (1999), there were only two other ICU follow-up services in the UK, in Reading and Liverpool:

'It took a little while to convince people. It was just not talked about back then. Naively, I thought we ought to check up to see how patients were doing with their physical healing. I looked at it as a bit of an MOT. It didn't take long from me talking to patients to suddenly realize it wasn't just about physical health. Patients were struggling emotionally and mentally after what had happened to them physically. Nobody was looking at the patient as a whole. I now get letters from all over the country to see people. ... If you can imagine an ICU as a place for the sickest patients – consultants send their patients into an ICU when they are really sick; it's a case of getting them better and just bringing them out again. Actually, the experience of an ICU is a huge burden both to the patient and the families. An ICU is noisy, uncomfortable, disorientating, and some of the drugs we use cause patients to hallucinate or to dream. It's also bed rest, and, no matter how fit you are, you will lose muscle mass; but in your head, you don't actually understand that. This is why young people struggle for longer than older people. We call it "the burden" – it's a whole package of psychological emotional stress as well as physical.'

Dr Niki Snook

Dr Niki talks about 'the burden'. I like this way of describing the aftermath of a difficult experience. The word burden is defined as 'a load, typically a heavy one'. That's exactly what some of my past experiences feel like – a heavy load I have to carry everywhere I go.

During my treatment, I saw Dr Niki one-on-one; now they operate a patient support group.

'It's an individual journey, but knowing lots of people have done that journey, and you're not alone, is important. People come from all over the country for the patient support group, just to sit in a room and chat with fellow patients who have been through what they have.'

Dr Niki Snook

After my ICU experience, I felt very alone. It's hard to describe what being critically ill felt like or what it feels like, not just in the immediacy but after. Nobody in my circle or my daily life could relate to what it was like or what it had left me feeling, which is why a support group is so important. It brings you together with people who do have that common experience. The focus of my doctors, my family and me was on my physical health, understandably, but our body, mind and emotions don't work separately – everything is interconnected.

Being part of Dr Rachel's group convinced me that sharing with other people who truly understand what you've been through and what you're feeling is how we start to heal.

The narrative of 'our experience is our own and we've all experienced it differently' does not promote recovery; all it does is isolate us in our own trauma – in our own head. The truth is, there are many, many of us struggling in isolation with the same thing.

WEATHERING AND REVISITING THE PAIN

There has been significant research on group therapy and peer-to-peer support that shows they are highly effective in aiding trauma recovery. Dr Rachel even wrote a research paper on it: 'An exploration of members' experiences of group therapy'. The research found that everyone who persisted with group therapy – even in the difficult moments – found the therapy was effective.

'Powerful feelings emerged in the group, linked to painful experiences evoked from earlier groups such as family or school. Experiencing and bearing to share these feelings with other group members was found to be challenging, but also extremely helpful and reparative, giving rise to new learning and understanding. We called this process of 'staying to understand when we feel like leaving and avoiding' "weathering". Weathering was a word used by one of the group members I interviewed in my research, who described being able to "make up" with another member, who she realized had reminded her of her mother and their difficult relationship. She said, "So yeah, we weathered it".'

Dr Rachel O'Beney

Weathering refers to the capacity of individuals to sit with their uncomfortable emotions, which then gives them an opportunity for observing and understanding them, rather than shutting them down. In the research, group members reported this process felt very difficult at times, but that it was helpful in reducing their sense of feeling overwhelmed and feeling like the 'only one' who struggled. The research paper's findings suggested that those who were able to remain engaged with this process of sharing their experiences learnt how to process and manage their distressing thoughts and feelings more effectively, and went on to experience long-term personal growth and change.

If I had only one sentence to explain how to recover from trauma, it would be this: I don't believe there is any other way but to go back into the hurt, weather the strong emotions that come up, and learn to understand 'why'. You can only make sense of something if you go back to it. It's called processing and digestion.

There are therapies like hypnosis and EMDR (Eye Movement Desensitization and Reprocessing) where people hope that they can move forward without going back to the pain, and, of course, pills and medication. But even EMDR still needs a degree of processing and working through.

EMDR was devised by psychologist Francine Shapiro in 1987. My mum has recently had EMDR work for her trauma. While she had to go back over her past painful memories and work through processing them, the EMDR – which involved crossing her arms across her chest and tapping her hands on each arm – helped her do so in a calmer and controlled manner. Shapiro came up with EMDR when, while walking in the park one day, she was struggling with an upsetting memory so distracted herself by moving her head back and forth to look at the surrounding nature, and she realized the sting from the memory started to ease.

It's totally understandable that one of the main reasons people don't recover and grow from trauma is because it *is* emotionally painful to go back over old wounds. It's the vicious cycle of trauma.

Dr Niki first started her patient group because of Covid-19, which brought what she described as 'wellness' into the light. She said, 'I didn't want it to be just a Covid legacy. We wanted it to be all patients that have gone through an ICU.' Commonality is far more important in trauma than our individual experiences. As with so many things, we have more in common than we have different.

Dr Niki said that she had a group of patients that had been on ICU during the Covid-19 pandemic and had had a horrible experience. In the support group, these patients met a man who had been in an ICU for about six weeks before the pandemic. She told me, 'He was very supportive. He said, "I was in an ICU for six weeks and had to learn how to walk again and I couldn't speak or move." Everyone's jaw just dropped. He's rebuilding his life, a bit like you really. It just puts everything into context for the other patients. Everyone has to go at their own pace but it also helps other people to see somebody who has gone through what you have and who's living a "normal" life.'

TOGETHER WE RISE

I do wonder if it is a protective mechanism to say, 'Everybody's experience is different'. I am convinced that with trauma it is isolation that does the most damage – the loneliness in our own thoughts and feelings inhibits our recovery and growth, and keeps us in the same place of trauma.

In January 2023, a friend from my running group, who was also abused by my coach and testified in the court case, died by suicide. She was 38 years old. I know that she tried so hard to leave what happened to us, and to her, behind. She changed her name, from Katie to Katia, and she worked hard to achieve incredible physical feats – from competing in Muay Thai to winning CrossFit competitions – pushing her body to the limits. I can relate to a lot of what Katie did to try and cope. Sue, Katie's mum, said Katie couldn't rest or be still because that's when the loneliness and intrusive thoughts of her abuse came in. She was surviving on adrenaline all the time, and struggled to find normality. I can't say what exactly was going on in Katie's mind, but I do know that she didn't want her life to end – she wanted the isolation in her own thoughts and the torment in her head to stop.

I also want to mention Georgina, who also died by suicide. She was another friend from my running group. She died at the age of 19, a year after the court case. I strongly believe that if we'd connected after all this happened, been supported together, talked with each other as a group about what happened to us and what it made us feel, and not been separated and sent on our own 'merry' way to deal with things on our own, isolated in our extremely young minds, things would have been very different. We were all suffering: even those that hadn't been physically abused were dealing with the trauma of the emotional abuse we suffered, of the violation of our trust and of knowing what had happened to their closest friends. There was far more commonality in the trauma we were left to deal with than there was different, but we all had to deal with it in isolation. For more than 15 years, before we reconnected, I had believed that it was my fault, that it had started with me (it didn't, I found a long line of victims before me/us), and that the way I was feeling was because there was something wrong with me. There was nothing wrong with me, and it wasn't my fault.

'In a group, you are not alone. People come to it thinking they are a little bit mad (with a small "m"), because they think it's only them that feels like this. The real joy of a group is actually in realizing you're not alone, realizing you're the same as others. What you are feeling is a very understandable response to something unpleasant and horrible that may have happened to you, and that other people are in exactly the same boat.

'Of course, you can be much more objective when you see other people's struggles. A group is like a mirror. Understanding our trauma can be an intellectual exercise until we see other people behaving and struggling like us. The real "ah ha" moment is when you recognize someone else in the group doing what you do. For example, "shutting down" when others reach out. You have evidence right in front of you of how unhelpful (unintentionally) this behaviour can be. It's much more powerful if a peer or a friend points something out; you really take note. It's expert by experience.'

Dr Rachel O'Beney

I want this book to be that mirror for you. We are more similar than we know. We cope in similar ways, we also heal in similar ways – and very rarely is that on our own.

2

Cause and effect

I'm going to focus this book on how trauma influences us, how to recognize it and how to grow through the impact – rather than on the actual experience of trauma itself.

We've all had different painful experiences – there may be some of mine you can relate to and some you may not. What's happened to us may be different, but we have commonality in how we all feel and cope after.

At this stage, I want to name some of the causes of trauma to help you recognize them in your own life. Be aware that denial after a distressing experience is a common reaction, but denial stops you from recovering. If you deny what's happened to you, how can you recover from something that your brain is telling you didn't happen?

NAMING YOUR TRAUMA

Naming your experience and acknowledging it as 'a trauma' is the first step to being able to work through the impact it's having on you and your life. Before I started to get help, I would never have said my painful experiences were 'trauma'.

The most common causes of trauma

- Sexual abuse
- Physical assault
- Domestic abuse
- Natural disasters
- War
- Displacement
- Accidents (car, bike, etc.)
- Long-term illness
- Acute and critical illness
- Childhood abuse

Other causes of trauma

- Childbirth
- Bereavement
- Childhood adversities: neglect, divorced parents, having a parent in prison or with mental illness or addiction, poverty, school bullying, death of a parent(s) or sibling, living in a violent community
- Bullying in the workplace or in adult friendships
- Witnessing something distressing or violent
- Divorce, infidelity, broken relationships
- Family conflict
- Financial/legal problems
- Homelessness
- Long stays in hospital and intensive care
- Injustice and discrimination based on race, religion, gender, class, disability, sexual identity, etc.
- Collective 'mass' trauma, such as ongoing war; the pandemic has been named a collective trauma, however we didn't all have

a collective traumatic experience of Covid-19 – some had it far worse than others

- Moral injury: witnessing or doing something that goes against your values and moral beliefs; this is common among doctors, nurses, therapists, first responders, human rights workers, soldiers and veterans, and survivors of abuse and political violence

You might be surprised by some causes on that list. There may be things you would never think of pinpointing as trauma. We do a very good job of dismissing both other people's experiences and our own by normalizing, shaming or comparing – all of which keep us stuck.

Types of trauma

It's also helpful to know the three types of trauma:

1. Acute trauma. A single incident – such as a car accident.
2. Chronic trauma. Repeated and over time – such as domestic abuse, childhood abuse, bullying, war and community violence.
3. Complex trauma. Exposure to multiple different traumatic experiences, often caused by or involving another person. This is often seen in people who have been imprisoned, sexually abused, sex trafficked, are refugees, and those exposed to long-term conflict.

While these categories are useful, it is really important to understand that the impact of your trauma is valid no matter the type or cause. The emotional response we have after, and the symptoms we get from this, is completely understandable and normal, and something we can work through together, irrespective of the different things we've all been through.

With complex trauma, there tends to be less of a clear beginning and end; often the experience occurs in secrecy and has stigmatized connotations that can create a fear of shame and prevent openness and acceptance. Also, in trauma that started in childhood or adolescence, a developmental factor needs to be considered because the brain is still growing. If this is you, don't worry, this is also me; and although it can leave us with repeated difficulties with emotions, stability and safe relationships, it is something we can change and grow through.

CAUSES OF TRAUMA

Trauma can be considered to have four different root causes:

1. Random
2. Neglect
3. Negligence
4. Hate and animosity

Understanding the cause of our trauma can help us separate ourselves from why this 'ordeal' happened to us. As well as recognizing that your experience is trauma, it's important to connect to why it happened. Our mind is very good at blaming ourselves for our experiences. The number of times I've said to myself, 'Why me? Why does all this shit keep happening to me? What's wrong with me? It's my fault.' But it's not that you have shit luck or there's something wrong with you. As much as we don't like to accept it, some horrible experiences are purely random. It's hard to accept because it means we are not in control of life and something awful might randomly happen to us or a loved one, and we can't do anything about it. That's why society likes to victim blame: 'Well, they shouldn't have walked home at night,' or, 'Why did they go there? It's a dangerous place; I'd never go there,' or that age-old 'Look at what they were wearing – they were asking for it.' Such victim-blaming remarks give the false perception that we're safe and the only reason something bad happened to the person was because of their own actions. And that's not true! Victim blaming is an individual and societal protective coping mechanism.

Random trauma

Random trauma is something that is beyond anyone's control, for example a natural disaster, an accidental fire, a car accident. You could say that my critical illness in 2016 when I ended up in intensive care fighting for my life was random. I had malaria, a disease from a mosquito bite. I'm pretty sure the mosquito didn't set out to find me to give me malaria and nearly kill me because it had it in for me or because it thought I wasn't good enough. I also had life-threatening Shigella and HUS (Haemolytic Uraemic Syndrome), which caused my kidneys to fail and all my red blood cells to self-destruct. I'm not sure what I could have done to prevent this apart from wrapping myself in cotton wool and not leaving the house. I was just in the wrong place at the wrong time. Random trauma is something that happened that shouldn't have – it is unintentional.

Trauma from neglect

Trauma from neglect is also unintentional, but avoidable – something didn't happen that should have, it's a trauma caused by inaction. My mum was in an abusive relationship throughout all of my upbringing and young adulthood. Her partner also abused me. My mum didn't do anything about that, but it wasn't because she didn't care, it was because she was also in trauma; her inaction was her way to keep us as safe as possible and prevent further danger.

Trauma from negligence

Trauma from negligence is also a result of inaction, but intentional inaction. That is, someone knew there was a problem and failed to do anything about it. This makes me think back to my school being aware that something wasn't right at home, but opted to ignore it because they felt they 'couldn't be seen to be interfering'.

Trauma from hate and animosity

Finally, trauma from hate and animosity involves intentional, deliberate hurtful or violent action. The coach that was grooming and sexually abusing me and others in my running group caused harm to all of us with intent – he knew what he was doing.

All of these root causes of trauma, you and I aren't responsible for. It happened, but it wasn't your fault; it wasn't because of you as an individual. Trauma from animosity may make you feel like it was you, as you were targeted; but the abuser's actions and accountability is always on them, it's their own repeated pattern of behaviour. Abusers will always find someone to make their victim – it wasn't because of you and who you are.

A WORD ABOUT PTSD

Before we move forward, I want to talk about PTSD, Post Traumatic Stress Disorder. PTSD occurs from trauma, but experiencing trauma doesn't necessarily mean you will get PTSD. The likelihood of developing PTSD can differ based on the type of trauma experienced. The highest rate of PTSD is in rape victims: estimates vary but between 33%–45% will get PTSD. The likelihood of developing PTSD after being directly involved in a serious terrorist incident (such as the 2005 London bombings) is around 20%.

In 2019 the first comprehensive epidemiological study of trauma and PTSD in young British people found that one in three young people experienced trauma, and one in four of those exposed to trauma developed PTSD by the time they were 18 years old. Repeated exposure to traumatic experiences can lead to a higher chance of PTSD, which is why people who work on the frontline or military personnel may be more susceptible, as are those who have complex trauma. However, anyone can get PTSD and from any type of trauma.

PTSD is a mental health illness with a specific set of symptoms that make you relive the traumatic experience – flashbacks and nightmares – persistently over an extended period of time. It's where a trauma response keeps going and going, like a broken record, over and over again, and impacts your ability to function day to day. PTSD can appear seemingly out of nowhere years after a distressing experience, particularly when the trauma has not been worked through, which is why it's so important to deal with our past.

'People with PTSD have flashbacks and nightmares. This is different from having intrusive memories. Flashbacks and nightmares are when the experience comes back again and again, as if the here-and-now isn't there anymore; you are back reliving what happened, as if it was today. So, the dreadful experience feels like it's really happening to you again and again.

'Intrusive memories, which people with trauma also tend to have, are really sad and painful memories of something awful happening to them in the past, but you do know that it happened in the past and so in this way have a bit more control over them.'

Dr Rachel O'Beney

I remember having flashbacks a lot after I fell critically ill in Rio. The one that always sticks prominently in my mind was when I was brushing my teeth one evening before getting into bed, a routine activity that I had obviously done all my life.

* * *

I feel like the toothbrush is jammed down my throat, I take it out and let go of the handle, the toothbrush drops into the sink. I can't breathe. My whole throat tightens, it grips me from the inside and I'm desperately gasping for air. Tears pour down my cheeks as I start to cry in panic. I try to scream, but only sharp coughs come out as I try to clear my airways.

I'm in the hospital room grabbing hold of my bed but I can't move. The ventilator tubing is being pushed aggressively down my throat, through my body and into my lungs, but I don't know what it is. I'm gagging so hard it's ripping my throat. It feels like the most intense pressure on my chest as if I'm trapped underneath the largest rock. I can feel the damp as my tears pour down the sides of my eyes and into my hair. I'm so scared. I'm alone. I can no longer breathe.

Suddenly I'm back in my bathroom. I'm sitting on the floor. I don't remember sitting down. My head feels like it's swimming in the roughest ocean. I'm scared, alone and confused. I crawl out of the bathroom, unable to stand, and into my bedroom. I curl up on my bed, sobbing. I feel so exposed and so vulnerable. I cry myself to sleep trying to escape, but there is no escape as I climb into the same feeling, the same place of helplessness in my sleep, in my nightmares.

* * *

There was physically nothing wrong with me. If you had been able to watch me you would have just seen a woman brushing her teeth, in her own bathroom, getting very upset for no apparent reason. Yet for me, at that moment, all I could feel was the ventilator that I was on when critically ill in Rio, making me feel like my airways were blocked (even though the ventilator was breathing for me). My mind was telling me that I couldn't breathe. It was so very real to me that I was actually physically choking and struggling to breathe in my bathroom, even though nothing was choking me. I was just brushing my teeth.

I also used to have a lot of flashbacks about the sexual abuse I suffered at the hands of my coach. Those were moments of real, intense fear for me, so they came back into my present as if they were happening again and again.

Memories don't just disappear (they form who we are), so why would emotions? There is an analogy used to help understand and explain what is actually going on in the brains of people with dementia, which I find useful for explaining trauma and the power of emotions and our memories. The analogy goes like this: There are two bookshelves in our brain. One is solid oak and sturdy, and contains our emotions. The other is made from flimsy plywood and is easily rocked, and holds our memories. Dementia affects the flimsy bookshelf and knocks the books off. The solid oak bookshelf holding all the emotions attached to each particular memory isn't moved in the slightest, it remains intact and outlives the memory.

My 'nanan' (grandmother) had dementia. She kept forgetting that my grandad had already passed away but she felt immense sadness, pain and loss, and would leave him notes on his pillow asking him to please come home. She had no memory of his death (the flimsy plywood bookshelf), but she felt the emotion (the solid oak bookshelf) of it every second of every day. Trauma memories may be in the past, you may have pushed them so deep down that you can't fully recall the trauma, but the emotion of the memory is as powerful today, if not more so, than when it happened. The feelings attached to our memories are stronger than the memory itself.

What our brain does with memories

To understand PTSD, it helps me to imagine the brain has a filing cabinet where all our memories are stored. Normal memories get filed neatly and in chronological order – they are processed. Traumatic frightening memories are a little different, they don't get filed and are left unprocessed. During distress, the survival part of the brain takes over and the memory filing cabinet in our brain locks itself – it goes into self-protection mode and shuts down.

When I was being sexually abused, my brain shut off to try and protect me as best it could. The awful memories were left disordered and floating around the brain, because at the time of the distress the memories couldn't be neatly filed away (processed). Traumatic memories remain in the brain as fragments of images, sounds and physical sensations until they are processed. That's why sometimes disturbing moments from your past – flashbacks – will appear out of nowhere and make you feel the same emotion or physical reaction as if you were right there experiencing the same thing again. Most likely, the memories will come in bits and pieces because they aren't filed.

To start to recover from trauma, we need to file those memories so they can be accessed if and when we want to remember under our own control and in safety. The memories will always be there – we can't undo the memory unfortunately, but we can be more in control of it and, as a consequence, of how it makes us feel. If we process and file the memory, we deal with the emotion of it.

HOW OUR EXPERIENCE OF TRAUMA CAN SHIFT

I still feel the hurt, but in a reflective way rather than as an overwhelming sensation. I used to push the feelings away or try to fight them. I'd notice the pain appearing, which then created a self-loathing cycle of, 'Why do I still feel like this, what's wrong with me?' or, 'I hate these feelings'. Instead, I now experience my pain by accepting that I'll always have those feelings, in some way, about the things that have happened to me – how could I not? When we start to see our pain as a normal response to something bad that's happened, and accept there will always be a feeling toward it, the intensity of the pain actually lessens, which is surprisingly freeing and empowering.

'It's a work in progress until the day we die. I know my trigger points and I talk to myself when I notice what's happened. Instead of taking two days to come out of that feeling from my past, it can now take as little as five minutes; but it's still there, and we still have to work on our trauma and recognize where our feelings are coming from.'

Dr Rachel O'Beney

I had a friend who once said to me when he was dealing with depression, 'Well if I have to live with feeling like this then I don't want to live.' It made me wonder what he thought about my life (he knows a lot about my past and trauma) – does he think my life is not worth living? I don't believe so. However, he made me realize how, despite my trauma and despite sometimes having painful feelings, it doesn't mean my life isn't worthy. Dr Rachel helped me process what I struggled with after I fell critically ill in Rio.

'Everyone wishes for a magic wand or a magic pill. There isn't one. But what does change is how you deal with it. … Rio was very much a hotspot for you. When we first met you couldn't even use the word "Rio". You said, "We'll talk about it next time". And when we did start talking about Rio, it was really fragile and tricky. But now you can say "Rio" and speak about what happened; it still hurts, but you worked through and acknowledged the pain. Before, you were constantly in avoidance and refused to speak about what happened to you in Rio and what you suffered.

'The way you manage it now is much more effective and healthier. You acknowledge your feelings. Once you acknowledge the feeling, it's still very sad but the sadness doesn't stay with you for every moment of

every day, it does not paralyse you, you are not constantly "on the run" from it, which was exhausting.'

Dr Rachel O'Beney

I struggled a lot connecting with the underlying emotion because of how painful it was and how scared I was of feeling it. I was scared that if I allowed myself to feel sad it would cripple me, and I wouldn't be able to come out of the sadness. I also feared that other people couldn't handle my sadness and pain, and would run a mile from me, both from a professional and personal perspective.

These emotionally painful experiences that we've had do affect how we behave outwardly to the world and inwardly toward ourselves.

MOVING TOWARD 'ACCEPTING' OUR TRAUMA

If you're anything like me, I refused to accept my trauma because I believed that if I accepted it then that would mean I had to accept all those horrible things that have happened to me. I ran away from them for good reason. What I'd been through made me feel like 'damaged goods' and unlovable.

In reality, I was just suffering the aftermath of some horrible things that had happened to me. It took me a while to see it like that. It's understandable if you are reading this and hearing my words from the page but not quite taking them on board – that's completely normal. If you think how long you've felt like this and lived with your trauma, it's not going to change in the opening chapter of a book.

But I do want you to start recognizing that refusing to accept and ignoring your painful past experience(s) mean the feelings from the past are still going to be there. Your body and your inside self (rather than the 'outside you' that you show everyone) still feels it, and that does impact how you behave toward yourself and others without us even realizing it most of the time. This is normal. How could it not be? Look at what you've been through.

In my psychology sessions, I'd often be in the middle of telling Dr Rachel about something difficult when I would just blank, my eyes would glaze over. She could see it happening and would say, 'You aren't here anymore, are you?' My emotions would just switch off and I'd have no idea what I was talking about. I could be in floods of tears – feeling so vulnerable – one minute, and then the next I'd be dry-eyed and numb. My brain's sneaky little way of repressing my feelings, and protecting me from any further emotional pain; which actually sounds sensible – why would I want to keep bringing it up?

Repressing our trauma may help prevent the pain in the short term, but it also prevents us from easing the pain in the long term. I am grateful for our brain's ability to shut off, because this is actually our survival mechanism. If our brain didn't do this during distress we would malfunction, it'd all be too much. We need it when we are going through something horrific – but when this survival mechanism remains and is ongoing, that's when it can become a problem. It's like your brain is a guard dog that's alerting you of danger irrespective of whether there is any.

I imagine a guard dog outside a gated building. The dog knows when danger is approaching, it might hear or see somebody suspicious creeping about unexpectedly at night, and the dog gives off a warning signal – it barks loudly and repeatedly to alert its owners of the danger.

Now imagine if the dog did this all the time at anything and everything, even the slightest breeze in the air caused the dog to bark non-stop. This is what our brains do when trauma isn't worked through (processed). We become hypersensitive and overly alert, even when we don't need to be, and we react accordingly. Our brain in trauma is always alerting us of danger even when there isn't any.

Dr Rachel once said to me, 'It must be exhausting living in your head.' It was. It still is sometimes. But seeing and understanding why helped me; because if that's what's going on in my head all the time, then no wonder I felt like I did. Imagine that poor guard dog if it was constantly barking, how exactly would it be able to carry on functioning? It would eventually collapse on the floor in a heap! This is what trauma does to us.

RAW EMOTIONS

My aim is to give you as much understanding of this thing called trauma as I possibly can. In doing so, it will very likely bring up lots of different emotions – which is what we want to do, as this is a good thing. It may feel a bit wobbly though. We need to let the emotions come to the surface. Trauma recovery is about the relationship between understanding and also feeling it. I'm the type of person who would be quite happy just learning about trauma and not having to feel any of my emotions. I wish I could tell you (and myself) otherwise, but we do have to allow ourselves to feel what's going on in order to recover.

To help when things are feeling a little overwhelming, try the following technique.

SAFETY BUBBLE TECHNIQUE

- Imagine a big bubble that fits round you. Create your own bubble; make it any colour(s) you like, make it the perfect escape full of beauty. The bubble is strong and safe; nothing harmful or unsafe is allowed in the bubble.
- Place yourself inside the bubble. You can stay in your bubble as long as you want – until you feel it's safe to come out.
- When you come out, make sure you take a few deep breaths and take a minute or so before doing anything else.

This exercise tends to work for people who use escapism to cope. This exercise doesn't always work for me because, according to Dr Rachel, I'm always 'vigilant' and alert. My bubble felt a little claustrophobic, so I made it transparent so I could see out of it from every angle, because at that point I needed to always be aware of my surroundings to feel in any way safe.

Don't worry if it doesn't work for you.

'If you've got a big imagination, and can be a little bit in your own world, the bubble will suit you', explains Dr Rachel. 'If it doesn't work, don't feel dreadful about yourself, because it just means that you've just used a different way of coping with the trauma.'

3

How to recognize trauma in ourselves

Fear, anxiety and depression are the main staples of trauma, no matter the cause of your trauma. Our brains and bodies are set up to learn how to respond emotionally to things.

Trauma and fear go hand in hand. When something 'traumatic' happens to us, we have a reaction of fear. This reaction is a normal and natural response to something threatening (whether emotional, mental or physical) and distressing, which helps us survive. When the fear stays for a prolonged time and stops us from functioning, that is unprocessed trauma, and potentially PTSD.

Anxiety is a response to feelings of fear; it's a vicious cycle: anxiety can create a fear of re-experiencing what happened, which then creates more anxiety.

The subsequent emotional impact – increased stress hormones and feelings of worthlessness and shame (which we will explore further in the book) – can lead to depression. Trauma in childhood is associated with an increased risk of depression in adulthood.

TRAUMA VERSUS TRAUMATIC EXPERIENCE

Many of us find it hard to recognize an experience as traumatic, never mind being able to recognize what it's left us feeling. One of the impacts of trauma is low emotional awareness (the ability to recognize and understand your emotions because of your experience). If we have difficulty naming and seeing an experience as causing trauma, then it's very hard to tend to the feelings around what's happened. This can lead people who are dealing with trauma to avoid emotional situations as much as possible, to stay clear of those uncomfortable feelings, which can be really life-limiting.

In identifying trauma, it's important to differentiate between the traumatic experience and the trauma. The distressing experience itself is different from the trauma after-effect of it.

The **experience** is what happened to you in the outside world. My parents got divorced; I was abused in my childhood; I was groomed and sexually abused; I spent months critically ill in intensive care; and so on.

The **trauma** is our internal emotional and physical response to the emotionally painful experience; the trauma is how your brain and body are responding afterward.

I found it hard to see that the things that happened to me were connected to what I was feeling, and how all this influenced how I behaved to myself and others. This is very common.

I was first diagnosed with depression when I was 17 years old, but I had had the symptoms of depression for as long as I could remember. The doctor prescribed me anti-depressant pills and sent me on my way. Nobody looked into why I was having the symptoms of depression. The doctor didn't ask and I didn't say a word. I was silent because I didn't understand trauma – the word wasn't even in my vocabulary – or what I was feeling; add to that the fact I didn't know life could be any different and my very low self-esteem. I was sad and empty, I felt everything and nothing, but I was also irritable and easily frustrated. Nobody asked any questions. If they had, they would've found out that I was living in a domestic abuse household; my childhood had been chaotic and unstable since birth; I was being abused physically and emotionally by my step-dad – I was scared to death of him and what he was capable of; and for the last three years had been groomed and sexually abused by my running coach – and, to make it worse, running was about the only thing that helped me deal with my home life. No wonder I was feeling the way I was. But I didn't connect the dots for a long time. I thought there was just something wrong with me.

Depression is common after trauma – it is one of the symptoms of trauma.

HOW TRAUMA PRESENTS (AND HIDES) ITSELF

Our brain in trauma does everything it can to cope with our emotional pain and anything potentially harmful to us. We try to avoid our hurt and keep overwhelming emotions away by whatever means. In doing so, we keep ourselves in pain, because we don't allow any healing in. In trauma, we create ways of coping based on our fear of feeling the hurt, and avoid any situation that could lead to feeling those same things again. This drives us to behave in certain ways that can be harmful to us and sometimes others. In psychology, these ways of coping with our trauma that actually keep us in trauma and increase the symptoms of it are known as 'maladaptive coping behaviours'; they are things like avoidance, overcompensating and disconnecting from emotions.

People dealing with unprocessed trauma (unprocessed distressing memories) are very good at masking it. They are so convincing that they can even mask their trauma from themselves (I'm putting my hand up here).

I use the word 'unprocessed' because initial feelings of sadness, anxiety, dissociation, numbness and exhaustion to something awful happening are completely normal responses. We can't go through something distressing without having some kind of reaction after.

'Unprocessed' trauma is when those feelings stay with you after the initial reaction and start causing you problems in your daily life – problems that you may not realize are connected to what you've been through. But think about all those feelings you're left with – they inevitably sneak out into your behaviour.

COPING BEHAVIOURS
(MALADAPTIVE/UNHEALTHY)

There was a woman in my trauma group, let's call her Anna, who always cried. The two of us couldn't have been more opposite in how we coped with our trauma. Anna would cry when she spoke about anything. She would also cry whenever the psychologists addressed her. In her day-to-day life, if she was challenged on anything she would cry. Compare that to me. When I spoke about anything in the group, it was with very little emotion – it came across as nonchalance and as if I had better places to be. If somebody challenged me, I'd look impassive, normally through gritted teeth.

The way Anna and I coped was very different but came from the exact same place of hurt and that neither of us felt like we were good enough. I coped by shutting off, exhibiting an outward confidence and stoic nature to make it clear to anyone to keep their distance – this was my protective mechanism. Anna coped by crying at everything to avoid conflict or challenge, which was her way of protecting herself.

It came to a head one day when Anna told the group how she wasn't coping in a relationship and at work. She then made a dig at me from across the circle. I hadn't yet said a word in the group that day – it was completely unprovoked and out of the blue. It really hurt me. She said, 'I know, Charlie, you won't approve and wouldn't do that. You'd do better than me.' She was saying that she felt judged by me, and that she saw me as someone that would not let themselves be treated that way. I didn't say anything, I just looked at her. She started to cry. In my head, I was thinking, 'Unbelievable! She has a dig at me. I don't say a word or do anything to her, yet she cries like she's the one that's been hurt.'

Dr Rachel and Dr Rebekah Honey, a clinical psychologist who was also part of our group, turned to me and asked me if I was okay. I was so taken aback – I was so used to not getting my feelings tended to, to not being comforted when I was hurt, to not being seen because I didn't show my emotion and didn't cry, that I didn't know what to say. Normally, the person crying is who everyone feels sorry for. I was asked again, even though Anna was now sobbing even louder. I said, 'Well, not really. I already feel totally shit; I haven't said a word, and then I get comments made at me as if I'm a horrible person.' Both psychologists comforted me and said that what Anna did wasn't acceptable.

Dr Rachel then turned to Anna and asked her why she did that, and why she was crying. The scenario carried on a little longer. Dr Rachel said to her that crying at everything is not a real emotion, it is a protective defence to avoid dealing with what one's actually feeling. Anna stopped crying almost immediately. It turns out that Anna felt like I was better than her, and like I had been through so much yet was this perfect achiever. Ironically, what Anna said to me made me feel like I was an awful person and not good enough.

I struggled with Anna, because my mum always used to cry whenever I talked to her about how I was feeling, which meant that I didn't ever feel heard, seen or have my emotional needs met. If someone you care about cries when you're crying, you tend to automatically stop crying and comfort the other person. I was the comforter, not the comforted, from a very young age. I also never cried because if I cried my step-dad's abusive behaviour would get worse. He would call me pathetic and a cry-baby. So, I learnt to never cry no matter what he did to me, to protect myself.

As a result, the majority of the time people didn't understand I was upset because I didn't show it in the way we've come to learn what being upset 'looks' like.

Neither my behaviour of coping – overly independent – nor Anna's – overly dependent – is emotionally healthy. They meant neither of us got our true emotions and feelings cared for by ourselves or others, which meant it was hard for us to heal and recover from our trauma.

Dr Rachel said, 'It was like a seesaw, you at one end and Anna at the other, independence versus dependence. But you actually had a lot in common. You just used ways of coping at different ends of the spectrum.'

Crying is healthy, but crying at every little thing is not; it means people will start to become numb to you crying. Never showing your emotions and not crying is not healthy; it means people think you are always okay and can deal with anything. I have gotten better at expressing my emotions and better at being able to cry; I'm still working on it. I do sometimes have to remind my family and those close to me that I'm not always okay. They see me as the strong one.

Understanding our behaviours and the way we cope is the most effective way to recognize and identify trauma in ourselves and others. They are not always that obvious, but the ways in which we cope with trauma are often the things that stop us from recovering.

PERFECTIONISM

I mentioned that Anna thought I was 'perfect' – I'm not perfect (although I am *enough*). However, perfectionism is one of the ways we cope with trauma, especially for those that have had repeated trauma and if their distressing experience involved another person.

For example, people with trauma from having a dysfunctional parent who puts them down or from being in an emotionally unhealthy or abusive relationship may use perfectionism to take control of their lives. This unhealthy way of coping can also be termed 'perfectionist over-controller'. Perfectionism is a way to deal with overwhelming feelings and anxiety – the need to be in control, with an underlying fear that bad things will happen if we are not in control, and trying to get control of others so that we don't get taken advantage of. The thinking is: 'Doing my best at everything will protect me' or, 'If I control them, they can't hurt me'. You may see this as a good thing – I did for a long time. It meant I achieved a lot because I pushed myself all the time to meet 'perfect'. But achieving and working hard are very different from perfectionism.

Perfectionism is relentless; you can never rest, and your best is never good enough. I started to develop this coping mechanism from a very young age. I figured that if I could be the best at things, it would show I was good enough, which would mean that I would be deserving of love and then the abuse would stop. I also convinced myself that if I did everything perfectly it would keep my mum safe. At the time, this helped me cope, but it became so dangerous, because being loved and feeling enough all hinged on whether I achieved. In athletics as a teenager, if I didn't win a race, I would be distraught; to me it meant that I was a failure and I didn't deserve love. And I thought not being good enough meant that I would never be able to change our situation. Before long this developed so that if I won a race, but did not achieve a personal best, I was still a failure and undeserving love. You can see how dangerous this pattern became for me. To add to what was going on in my head, my coach was also abusing me and had groomed me to fit my narrative: I believed what he was doing to me was necessary to make me the best.

Pursuing perfection meant nothing I ever did was good enough, and I didn't have a signal in my brain that told me when to stop. If I did ever stop, it would cause even more anxiety, which then made me push even harder to try and control it. Perfectionism ended up making me feel utterly exhausted and worthless, because I could never stop striving, not even for one second, and none of it was ever good enough. It was incredibly overwhelming.

The abuse I suffered was horrific, but it was the way I coped with it that was keeping me in pain – it made me suicidal in my late teens and early twenties. If I'd have got help for the abuse I suffered and understood that what I was doing to cope was harming me, I really believe I wouldn't have been struggling as much as I was. My mentally and emotionally unhealthy coping mechanisms for trauma, such as the perfectionism, were making me feel even worse. I truly believe that if Katie and Georgina had been helped to understand their pain, they would still be here.

RISKY BEHAVIOURS

While anxiety, depression, fear and perfectionism are all signs of trauma, so are self-soothing and risky behaviours.

Self-soothing and risky behaviours to avoid overwhelming and uncomfortable feelings include things like:

- Drug and alcohol misuse
- Disordered eating (controlling food or overeating)
- Over exercising
- Over working
- Excessive screen use
- Repeatedly engaging in destructive relationships and friendships
- Having risky sex or feeling unable to attach in sexual relationships
- Being irritable, easily angered or easily offended

While using these self-soothing and risky behaviours does make your feelings go away (you detach), even if only briefly, those feelings will come back quickly and often hit even harder. All these ways of coping stop us from healing our hurt.

It's not easy to admit some of these things to yourself either; it's hard to accept that some of your behaviours, even though they are because of trauma, may not be particularly nice to others as well as yourself. I definitely found this on my journey, as how I cope tends to be protectively and defensively. And it's automatic – we do all these things subconsciously. Lowering my guard to see what I was doing and how it was actually not helping me was hard to deal with – it was me doing it to myself, not the people that hurt me in the first place. We'll work through this in greater detail as we go through the book.

SELF-AGGRANDIZING

Self-aggrandizing is another behaviour from trauma when your distressing experiences have left you feeling inadequate and not enough. It comes across as arrogance – basically acting superior – but, as with everything we've discussed so far, it's another way to protect yourself from the really painful and overwhelming feelings of trauma. It's not who you are.

We may notice this in others. For example, the 'bully' that comes across as tough and arrogant is actually suffering and in deep emotional pain, yet pushes everyone away and hurts other people to stop themselves from being hurt.

I've seen this in so many children who have unstable chaotic homes and feel unloved and unwanted – they put on an angry front. Using anger subconsciously to cope is one of the hardest behaviours and symptoms to identify as trauma because it's seen as bad behaviour, and it's hard to admit to ourselves.

It's absolutely nothing to feel embarrassed or ashamed about, it's just our very clever fight-or-flight survival system. If you feel unsafe, your brain will do whatever it needs to protect you. I could be like this at times when I was younger, giving off the impression that it was best not to mess with me. If you see this in yourself, please don't blame yourself. The first step is noticing what you do to cope.

To an extent, we all do some of these things some of the time; but it's when they become a normal daily behaviour that they can be very disruptive and can leave you feeling low, unloved, lonely, and even continue the cycle of trauma. When the danger has long passed, trauma makes it very hard to understand and know what it is to feel safe.

PROTECTIVE COPING BEHAVIOURS

Below are the main unhealthy harmful ways of coping to protect us from our hurt. They are mechanisms (sometimes referred to as 'modes') to protect you from painful and overwhelming feelings. In the short term, they make you feel safer; in the long term, they keep the pain inside. They stop you from being your authentic self (the one that's underneath the coping modes and is in pain) and from experiencing meaningful relationships with others. Noticing these ways of coping in yourself can help you look underneath them to see why you're behaving that way and recognize your trauma.

It's really helpful to write these down; you can keep checking on them to help recognize how your trauma is impacting your behaviour and actions.

Detached protector: Lacks emotional connection to things and people; cut off from emotions; numbness.

Compliant surrender: Accepts and does what others want and gives in; 'people-pleaser'; subservience.

Avoidant protector: Avoids situations/not showing up; avoids making decisions; sticks head in the sand.

Angry protector: Keeps people at a distance (uses anger to do so); is agitated, annoyed, irritable, defensive.

Bully attack: Exhibits aggressive, antisocial behaviours; is mean to others to mask their own pain.

Detached self-soother: Uses drugs, alcohol, video games, gambling, excessive exercise, food as a way to avoid feelings; adrenaline junkie.

Attention seeking: Actively seeks lots of praise, attention and approval.

Self-aggrandizer: Acts superior, self-absorbed and self-important to mask underlying fear and shame.

Perfectionist over-controller: Needs to be in control; has underlying fear bad things will happen if not in control; finds it hard to relax and let go; over-achiever.

PHYSICAL SYMPTOMS AND THE EFFECT ON YOUR NERVOUS SYSTEM

Trauma doesn't just come out in emotions and behaviours, but also in physical symptoms such as chronic pain, fatigue, Irritable Bowel Syndrome (IBS), palpitations, hyperventilation, self-harm, stomach aches, panic attacks, insomnia, disturbed sleeping and flashbacks. Even skin problems, like eczema and psoriasis, a weakened immune system and, for some (both women and men), reproductive problems.

The strong emotions of fear, sadness and anger that come with trauma can show up in the body through fatigue, dizziness, headaches, increased heart rate and sweating, trouble sleeping and bad muscle tension. The body holds the stress of trauma. It can also come out through trouble concentrating and remembering, intrusive thoughts, confusion and disorientation. Using these physical and mental symptoms as signs and cues can help us recognize trauma, make changes and recover. You will use these long after you've finished reading this book.

Trauma also causes hypervigilance – think of the over-alert guard dog (see page 47) – as it makes you overly sensitive to your surroundings. Hypervigilance is an extreme awareness and alertness of everything that is going on around you. I was so hypervigilant that my nervous system was in overdrive and I could spot danger a mile off – but I was also always looking for it wherever I went.

I remember being at a 30th birthday party with my best friend. As soon as I walked in, I immediately didn't want to go near a random guy at the other end of the room. I didn't even know him and hadn't spoken to him properly. I was like a cat that had seen a dog – my spine was arched and I was ready to defend or attack. I told my friend and she was like, 'Okay, but he hasn't done anything.' She knew me well enough though, thankfully, not to judge me. Lo and behold, later that night he tried to get into the bedroom where my friend and I were sleeping. I was already on alert and shot up to fight him off. So that sense of danger can come in handy, but I was also like this even when the dangers weren't real. I would push away the good people, too.

Staying in a heightened state of prolonged hypervigilance can cause physical exhaustion, poor sleep, muscle tension and severe anxiety, and can prevent you from forming close relationships. It can lead to chronic stress and really reduce the quality of your life.

Likewise, hyperarousal is also very common. It combines some of the symptoms we've mentioned, such as irritability, risky behaviour, becoming angry very easily, being overly sensitive, having lots of physical tension all the time, and feeling panicked or 'on edge' as if you're waiting for something bad to happen. Hyperarousal is one of the core symptoms of PTSD. Initially, hyperarousal and hypervigilance are normal reactions to immediate threats. If we are in a dangerous situation, we become more alert. In the context of trauma, continuing this state over time becomes physically and emotionally harmful for us.

MINIMIZING AND MAXIMIZING

Recognizing trauma in ourselves is challenging. Keep in mind that denial and minimizing our trauma is what we do to cope. Denial is a great way of protecting us in the moment of pain, because any realization of what's really going on might just be far too much for us to deal with. We might also shame ourselves into the fact that we should be over it, which leads to further minimizing: *'It wasn't that bad anyway, just get over it.'* In the long term, this is very harmful. The brain might cleverly be denying our experience or making us feel bad about feeling this way and push it away, but the emotions are continually carried around inside without us even realizing they influence our thoughts and behaviours.

'It's very common to minimize, I'm afraid, by using critical self-talk, which actually makes us feel worse. We also maximize. Some people maximize by thinking they'll never be able to get better, and they've got to stay stuck and feeling bad forever. Staying unwell may be a way to avoid facing what we are sad and angry about – what happened and did not happen in our past. Moving on involves mourning what we have lost, so we can continue our journey through life and embrace new experiences and relationships.'

Dr Rachel O'Beney

This is a really important point to grasp: *the way we cope with trauma may be to deny or minimize what has happened to us, or even to maximize it.* There is no judgement at all with this – they are very normal ways of coping with trauma. When we minimize or maximize, we create a barrier to processing the pain we feel. To be able to process the impact of our experiences, we need to acknowledge what it is we've been through.

For example, it is very common for those who feel ashamed or embarrassed by what has happened to them – where their trauma has a stigma – to downplay or minimize it. If we minimize what we've been through, we deny ourselves of what it's made us feel, and therefore minimize the impact it's had on us. Minimizing the impact means we push our feelings away and show ourselves we don't matter.

Maximizing, which is another form of self-protection, is often a cry for validation and help. Maximizing can come from a place of distress and the need for your experiences to be taken seriously, especially if they have previously been dismissed. We may maximize our experience for the fear of it being minimized.

Both responses are valid.

It's so important to recognize if we maximize or minimize, because to recover is to acknowledge our experiences truthfully and also acknowledge what it has made us feel. So many of us search for ways to feel better without looking at what is causing us to feel this way in the first place. I very much minimized everything I'd been through because I felt ashamed and that I would be judged. Also, when I did try to tell people, I felt like they didn't understand how horrific it was. So I just shut it all away inside, and even from myself at times. The one thing that helped me begin to recover from my trauma was to acknowledge to myself and others what I'd been through and how bad it actually was.

Overcoming minimizing trauma

Minimizing is a common response to the emotional and mental trauma of physical pain, like an accident, critical illness, intensive care or serious condition. When working on my recovery with Dr Niki Snook, we used my medical history to create a timeline of some of the things that happened to me, which helped me register and appreciate what I'd actually gone through.

My mum showed both Dr Niki and I the photos of me on life support. My mum had taken photos of me in a coma because she said she wanted me to see how bad it was. This might sound counter-productive: why would I want to see myself in that state? Why would you go back over something so distressing? Why reinforce to somebody how bad something was? Why would I want to see how close I was to death? Yet this is everything right about trauma recovery.

Nevertheless, the majority of us do the exact opposite and try to paint over how horrific something is. This totally invalidates someone's experience, which is everything wrong with how we approach trauma. Devaluing just creates a disconnect to what we are actually feeling, it isolates us even more and often makes us feel ashamed for our true feelings. Minimizing what has happened doesn't make the feelings go away, it just makes you feel bad for feeling that way.

'I like to go through a timeline with patients. For example, "You came in on this date, this is what happened … we changed your antibiotics, maybe you needed some surgery …" All this sort of stuff to try and put what happened into context. Then patients can start realizing just how unwell they were, how serious it was. This also explains why it's taken so long to get better. Your experience was: you were super fit from your cycle challenge when you went into intensive care, then you get out of the ICU, and you can't even dress yourself, never mind get on a bike – you're tired beyond belief and struggling mentally.'

Dr Niki Snook

She was right. I couldn't walk up the stairs without throwing up from dizziness, I couldn't get in the shower without my mum helping me, I didn't even have the strength to lift my arms up to be able to put shampoo in my hair. I beat myself up constantly about why I couldn't do anything physically, why I felt so 'messed up' in my head, and why I was so incredibly hurt, sad and angry. Having the photos helped; and Dr Niki explaining medically how bad it was made me less demanding of myself and more forgiving of how I felt. I would say to myself, 'You nearly died; you had to relearn how to walk again; this is a lot to deal with. It's okay that you're struggling.'

Be patient with yourself, take one step at a time, focus on what we've discussed so far, and everything else will fall in place. It might make you feel vulnerable – it most likely will – but it's important to keep going.

STAY THROUGH THE PAIN

Healing from trauma is like getting into a hot steaming shower after being out in the cold. It hurts like hell to start with as the hot water burns your skin so much that you scramble to turn the temperature down and want to get out. But the only way to get warm again and thaw from the cold is to stay under the heat of the shower, which will eventually start to feel comforting. Working through your trauma will be painful at first, but if you stay with it, the trauma will start to melt away and hurt less and less.

I always kept this analogy in my mind when I was working through my trauma. In psychology it's called 'emotional thawing' – trauma is described as a frostbite, a part of the body that has been unprotected from the cold and so loses sensation and becomes numb. When you come in from the cold there's an awareness of being numb, then the numb area becomes painful as the feelings and sensations start to come back, and then it heals.

Any kind of change and facing something challenging is bound to make you feel a little wobbly. That is perfectly normal and totally expected. Be aware not to let that wobbliness make you shut down or avoid what you're feeling.

When you feel wobbly, you will need to find ways to make you feel safe to allow the feelings and sensations in (see box below).

FIND WAYS TO FEEL SAFE

Observe what's going on in your body by asking yourself these questions:

- Are you tense?
- Is your heart rate fast?
- How is your breathing?
- What is your mind saying to you right now?

To feel safe, Dr Rachel suggests finding something comforting that you can touch or cuddle, such as:

- a blanket (wrapped round the shoulders, it can feel like a safe, unintrusive cuddle)
- a cosy jumper
- a hot water bottle
- a soft toy
- a cushion

You don't have to jump straight in from choosing an object to wrapping yourself up in it or cuddling it if that doesn't feel right for you. You can take it as fast or slow as you like.

I resisted this exercise to start with because I felt it showed 'weakness', and if I let my guard down I would be unsafe. I also just wasn't used to being comforted, and whenever I was comforted, I felt like it was conditional.

In our trauma group, there was a pile of soft toys in the corner of the room. Some of the group picked one and would hold on to it for the duration. I didn't; I wouldn't even go and look.

Eventually, in an individual session with Dr Rachel, I revealed that I had an old hand-knitted rabbit ('Rabby') that, as a kid, I took everywhere with me. It was actually one of the only things that came with my mum when she was adopted as a baby and she had passed it down to me. Dr Rachel suggested I find Rabby and cuddle him. I scoffed at the idea, and thought it was silly and childish. But I did go and find Rabby, and dusted off his cobwebs. And, whenever I felt vulnerable, I placed Rabby near me; then I progressed to feel the touch of the knitted toy on my skin, then it became a cuddle. I was giving myself the comfort that I needed in order to heal that I'd never had. Cuddling Rabby did bring me comfort, and still does.

If you have anything like Rabby then maybe give it a try, or have a blanket on hand to wrap round your shoulders.

Remember you can also revisit the Safety Bubble Technique from Chapter 2.

4

The past *is* your present

AVOIDANCE

I chose to create a different life for myself – a life in which nobody suspected a thing about my past. I left my past behind. I had a different circle of friends, I lived in a different city and I was different.

Previously, I'd tried counselling, but it had left me feeling patronized, and I got annoyed with their questions. Quite often it made me feel more isolated, because I felt they didn't understand. What the counsellors said was too obvious to challenge my guard. So each time, I concluded I didn't need it – I didn't need to go into my past, because it was just that: my past.

While this is what I told myself, it couldn't have been further from the truth. But convincing myself that the past is the past meant I didn't have to face my trauma.

From now on, we are going to scrap any concept of the past being in the past. Forget Buddha's, 'Do not dwell on the past', and spiritual teacher Eckhart Tolle's, 'The past does not have power over the present moment', and even writer Mario Puzo of *The Godfather* fame's, 'What is past is past. Never go back.' These so-called inspirational quotes do not support us, they keep us in denial and in trauma.

Our past experiences do influence our present. Our past does define us. The past does have power over us. And that is okay.

By denying our past, we deny our present, we deny a part of who we are, and how we currently feel and, ultimately, we prevent our recovery. Our past is nothing to be ashamed of, whether our experiences are traumatic or not.

Allowing the idea that the past comes into our present helps us learn, helps us grow, helps us heal the part of us that has been hurt by the past, and allows us to process and make sense of the things that have happened to us. In trauma, we are reacting in the present to our emotions from the past. We have to acknowledge our past to understand why we feel like we do and work through our trauma.

Trauma therapy is, in actual fact, described as the process of focusing on the impact of the past on our life experiences and relationships. It is all about our past, because it does have power over our present. Otherwise, we'd all be robots or have had our memories wiped like that scene in *Men in Black* – excuse the reference, but that memory wiper, the 'neuralyzer', would be nice sometimes.

HOW MY PAST SHOWS UP IN ME

I had a chaotic and unsafe upbringing; as such my childhood does affect me. I can sometimes be over-protective and defensive. I now understand that those behaviours come from having to be over-protective and defensive from an early age.

I struggled a lot in my early adulthood with the normality of day-to-day life. When things were calm, it made me anxious – because I wasn't used to calm; it made me constantly feel like I was waiting for something bad to happen. I still sometimes slip back into that, but knowing this anxiety comes from my past gives me the ability to verbalize why I am behaving like that, helps me make a different choice and change the way I feel.

I can now say to myself, '*These are feelings from your past, this is your trauma. There is nothing here right now that means you're in danger; you can enjoy a calm day without being on alert.*' If I didn't understand how my past came into my present behaviour, then how would I be able to help myself make a better choice and grow? The more I see what I do because of my past and remind myself what is going on, the less it happens – because every time I catch it, I rewrite those feelings, so eventually I can enjoy a day of calm without the panic creeping in.

I was sexually abused as a child, and it does come into my present. Denying that would be ignoring the truth of how it impacted me, what the child 'me' had to suffer, and ignoring what I feel. In a nutshell, that means I would be treating myself exactly how I was treated back then: ignored and denied; so that it became a secret shame I carried for a long time. I was abused through massage and, as you can imagine, this scenario of massage and sexual intimacy has come up in my adult life. Explaining my past to a partner helps them understand why I might go from loving the intimacy to all of a sudden going rigid and pulling away. It gives them the chance to make me feel safe, and to even help me change the narrative for me to feel safe with massage. Previously, I have been in this scenario and not said anything, just rolled with it – despite during 'rolling with it' having flashbacks and feeling very uncomfortable and violated again. Knowing that your past affects your present, and why, gives you an emotionally healthier choice to do what is right for you.

My past doesn't mean I can't live a wonderful happy life and have a healthy safe relationship moving forward. In fact, only by accepting that my past does come into my present can I live a happy life. When I was denying my past and pretending it didn't affect me, I was at odds with myself all the time – struggling in intimate relationships and feeling such agonizing emotional pain. And, worst of all, I suffered in silence – I didn't tell anyone.

I spoke to a friend, Tanya, about this recently. She's been in my life for the majority of my adult life. Tanya has a long-trusted friend who does spiritual work and Reiki. He once did Reiki on me at Tanya's flat on her kitchen table. She lived in a studio then, so the kitchen table was the only place to lie down other than Tanya's bed, which wouldn't have been appropriate. I can't fully remember exactly how I reacted, because I immediately went into fight-or-flight and my brain switched into danger mode.

As soon as I laid down, Tanya's friend stood over me. I jumped off the table. He didn't even touch me – Reiki is an energy practice of hovering the hands over the body. Only a few months ago Tanya brought this up with me and apologized. This was at least 12 years later, maybe even more. She said, 'I'm sorry I made you do that. I didn't realize.' Tanya had nothing to be sorry for. At the time, I didn't say a word to her as to why I reacted so defensively – that I was sexually abused repeatedly over a long period of time on a classroom table when I was 15 years old.

On paper, it was obvious why I reacted like that, but at the time I didn't understand. I had repressed the experience so much – and never spoke about it – that I didn't connect the two. My body, nervous system and brain knew though, hence its reaction. Our suppressed or blocked memories can create a disconnect with what your body does and emotions are, to what your brain tells you. Tanya only found out about the details of what happened to me because she watched my BBC documentary *Nowhere to Run*, about my running group. Once she learnt my story, she understood why I behaved that way. At the time, I had blocked out my past experiences, but they still came out in my life.

As per the aptly titled book by Bessel van der Kolk, *The Body Keeps the Score*, we might think we can push away our past experiences, put them behind us, ignore them, bury them deep down and convince ourselves we are fine and that they don't exist anymore, but our body will remind us if we don't work through what has happened to us. The brain and the body are connected. Tanya's friend was standing over me on a kitchen table with Tanya right there – it was not a real threat, but my body didn't know that because all it felt was the very real threat from my past. My past became my present without me consciously realizing.

I know that sometimes I will be sad about what happened to me, and I'm sure I will occasionally be sad in another decade from now. My past is part of me; if I deny my past, I deny a part of myself. I did that for a long time and, trust me, all it did was keep me in pain and mean I hated a part of me. We can move away from all the things that have harmed us, and create a different life and environment for ourselves – and I did all that. But no matter what I changed around me, I still had the 'me' inside that had experienced and was hurt by the things I was running away from. I still have that 'me', it is me, so I can't get rid of that part of me.

MOVING TOWARD ACKNOWLEDGEMENT (AND A LITTLE BIT OF ACCEPTANCE)

Acknowledging our trauma is to see it as it is, whether we like it or not. I don't like that I have had to endure and suffer traumas, but I acknowledge they happened. Acceptance is being okay with the trauma we acknowledge (this is something we'll build up to and delve into as we move through the book). Acceptance is being 'not okay' with what happened, but okay with who we are and where we are now. Acceptance happens over time and comes with the more work we do to acknowledge and process our trauma. Acceptance and acknowledgement don't all happen at once.

Acknowledging that what happens to you and has happened to you affects you is the first step. The past does impact you. Frightening and painful experiences influence the way you behave now. When the pain isn't worked through and processed, it starts to influence us in an unhelpful and unhealthy way – this is trauma.

All the things that have happened to us shape how we look at things, understanding how the past impacts us and having that awareness is how we repair. Part of healing from trauma is standing up and saying, 'Yes, these things happened to me.' Admitting that to ourselves and understanding it is the very foundation of recovering from trauma. Sounds simple, right?

No! It's totally unsettling and frightening!

I was not only scared to open up; I also felt like I didn't know how to. I'd lost touch with that hurt little girl – I'd blocked her out – so how was I supposed to connect with her?

When I started working through my trauma, I was scared of what I might discover if I lifted the lid to my past and whether I'd be able to cope with it. Sadly, I was ashamed of what had happened to me and what I had endured. I say sadly, because I now know that I never had anything to be ashamed of. But at the time I didn't know any different, and I was afraid people would see me in a different light.

I hated that hurt little girl inside of me, and what she had been through, but that meant I hated a part of me – and I was so very horrible to that part of me.

I'd protected myself from my past for so long that I wasn't even sure there was anything else to me or any of me that wasn't just trying to survive and cope with my past.

It's difficult to make that shift, because the mind is very good at surviving in a state of trauma without us necessarily being conscious of it.

I spent my first few appointments with Dr Rachel just going round the houses. She would ask me questions and I would give a surface-level answer; if I did say anything vaguely displaying vulnerability, I'd caveat it with, 'But I'm doing fine, though,' and reel off my latest achievement to prove it. Like I said, we are very good at denying our feelings to ourselves, never mind anyone else. Dr Rachel challenged me after a month of playing this game: 'Why are you here then, if you're fine?' I was taken aback, but she had a point.

One of the most common symptoms of trauma is detachment even from oneself. There's a battle within ourselves between knowing that something's not okay and a resistance to accepting that – a push and pull of wanting to work through things that are so painful, but also not wanting to.

As my journey progressed, it started to click that what I was feeling and doing in my present was due to my past traumatic experiences. When that realization hits, all of a sudden you see everything through different eyes. The penny drops. You start to see what you do and why.

Letting past memories surface can leave you feeling vulnerable, and can bring up the emotions you felt at that time, which can often be distressing, painful and intense. It's important to remember to be aware of this, and that it doesn't mean you're back in that scenario or are taking a step backwards in your recovery. This vulnerability and these emotions are perfectly normal and they are actually a good sign – they mean you are allowing yourself to start processing your trauma. In trauma you are often numb, so feeling is a good thing! I know it's the last thing you want, but you do need to open up that door and look through it, at your past, in order to process trauma.

But it's all about dealing with past painful memories with awareness and under your own control; allowing our painful memories and feelings to come to the surface safely and in the knowledge that what is coming up is from the past. Allowing traumatic memories to be felt and worked through processes trauma. Unprocessed trauma often appears when you least expect it, and makes you feel a certain way with such intensity that it can grip and take a hold of you when it's least invited. In these moments, it can make you feel lost and confused as to why you are feeling this. Actively inviting in what you've been pushing down and avoiding because it's painful will ease the pain and help you connect to what you are struggling with.

Our instinct is to do the contrary, because when we have been through traumatic experiences our natural defence is to shut it all out to prevent any more pain.

Our past and present are one, they are not separate; they are tightly interwoven, like a web. The past has emotions attached to it that are very present feelings. If we feel ashamed of our past, we will feel ashamed of who we are in our present. It's important to acknowledge how those feelings affect our present. This can be daunting, but it doesn't mean we have to sit in our past. It means using our past to help us understand why we feel like we do in the present, and what we need to do to help ourselves now and for our future.

THE PAST MIGHT VERY WELL SUCK

If, after reading this, you are feeling a little unsteady, and saying to yourself, 'Well that just makes me feel even worse now; my past is something I don't want in my present,' or, 'My past is actually so distressing that if my past does have a hold over me then what's the point?' Those are perfectly understandable reactions.

The realization of the past's impact on the present is a lot to take in, and it may make us face and admit a few things that we don't actually like. That's a good sign. Saying, 'Yes, these really horrible things that have happened to me do impact me, they do hurt me and they do make me behave in certain ways', means we can actually start processing them and making changes. Think about it like this: if we don't actually admit our past to ourselves or acknowledge our trauma, then how exactly are we supposed to recover from it? We won't. The bravest and strongest thing you can say to yourself right now is, 'Yes, this happened. It was terrifying and it is affecting me now.'

In my family, I have a lot of intergenerational trauma; sadly, this is very common. For example, my biological grandma has been through some awful, really painful times, including being forced by her mum to give up her baby (my mum) under horrific circumstances – my biological grandma was sent away and my mum was taken from her at birth. When my mum and I met her, which was only about a decade ago, I could see how much hurt she was still in from the way she spoke about her life – the trauma she still carried had impacted her whole life. I felt so sad for her. She passed away recently, but I did get to meet her several times. Although she was in our lives for a short time, her having my mum so young and being forced to give her up has shaped my mum's life and through her, mine.

We do have a choice as to whether we keep carrying our trauma or process it. It doesn't mean that what happened to my biological grandma and my mum goes away, but it does mean that the pain is given a chance to heal. The same choice applies to whether we repeat our family cycles and continue to carry the pain. Studies have shown that parents dealing with trauma may find it harder to connect with their children, and the children then develop unhealthy ways of coping, like self-soothing (perhaps alcohol or drugs), and it can cause mental health and interpersonal issues, like finding it hard to trust in close relationships. The trauma gets passed down and continues. This is something my brothers and I are conscious of and have been working really hard on changing together.

MOVING ONWARD

Remember: you can work through trauma, recover from it and, in fact, grow to develop some amazing qualities from what you've been through. Keep going, keep reading.

Revisit the Safety Bubble Technique if that works for you, or think about the things that may comfort you.

There is also another exercise around the safety bubble, which I personally prefer.

REVERSE SAFETY BUBBLE TECHNIQUE

- Remind yourself of the Safety Bubble Technique (page 48).
- Imagine your bubble again, but don't go inside it. Imagine you are outside the bubble, with all the things that are troubling you – all your hurt from your past – beside you.
- Put all those troubles inside the bubble. They can be people and feelings, negative thoughts, your own critical voice in your head, the urge to harm yourself – anything that is causing you distress.
- Once all your troubles are inside the bubble, secure it nice and tight – seal it, lock it, zip it.
- Now, send the bubble away.
- Close your eyes and imagine it floating away, up in the sky, until you can no longer see it.
- Open your eyes and fill your lungs from the very bottom with a deep breath and, as you exhale, imagine that everything harmful has gone.

I know these techniques don't make everything go away, but if you can start to use them to make you feel safe in the short term, it will calm your nervous system. Calm is the opposite of trauma – trauma stresses the nervous system. Trauma makes you feel unsafe. The nervous system's job is to react to that and it goes into a heightened state. The more you can bring in the safe feelings that counter trauma, the more your nervous system will relax, and tell your body it is safe. The more you start to feel safe, the more things will start to change.

5

Flowers and stones: Repressed, fragmented memories and dissociation

It's one thing to understand trauma, how it shows up and where it's from – our distressing past experiences; it's quite another to try to access those memories and then willingly open them up.

Remember in Chapter 2 I talked about traumatic memories not getting filed in the memories filing cabinet? The ordered, logical part of the brain gets shut down in trauma, so as those memories, which are full of overwhelming emotions, form, they are left with no order or anywhere to go in the brain.

Sadly, this can make people who have gone through trauma question their memory of what they've experienced, and whether they really experienced it. And it can (wrongly) lead other people to question the person's account. We often see this happen in cases of sexual abuse. Although I do acknowledge this is a critical topic in forensic psychology due to literature showing that our memories aren't flawless, the justice system is very old-fashioned. It's based on the material rather than the behavioural; trauma is the human experience, not the 'evidential tangible proof' experience.

MY WONKY FILING SYSTEM

I found it very hard, and still do, to place exact years on my past experiences and as a result create an ordered timeline of what happened to me. My memories are like random scenes from a film or snapshots of a photograph album – all a bit jumbled with no clear chronology. I often couldn't remember what happened before or after a particular moment.

I can clearly recall to this day every little detail of my step-dad punching me in the stomach and falling to the ground when I was 15. I know exactly what the room looked like, the sounds of my mum and little brother screaming, where they were in the room, the smell of alcohol, even the feel of the cheap black dress I was wearing, but I have no recollection at all of what happened after.

Equally, I can remember being terrified when my former running coach told me off because I was messing about and trying to speak Spanish to some boys with Katie. Earlier that day I had been in the gym with my coach doing a private weights session, and I can see his face grinning down at me from the barbell I was lifting, his crotch right next to my head on the weights bench, his smell, my body tensing rigid and feeling so scared, the sports bra I was wearing, the exact position I was in; but I have a complete blank in my memory as to what exactly happened.

When I first started speaking about my abuse (which I didn't for at least 15 years) and began recovering from trauma, more memories and pieces of my puzzle started to come back to me. The fact that memories of the past are fragmented, unclear and confusing is all perfectly normal. Human memory, in general, is a tricky thing; it is complex and there is still a lot that isn't known about it.

DISSOCIATION

Not only does our memory get disrupted in trauma, but it can also dissociate from what is going on – which is what happened to me in the gym with my coach. Dissociation is when you disconnect yourself from what is happening to you in the external world – as if you're watching it happen to someone else. This is very normal if you've been through something awful. If you can't run away, fight and escape physically, your mind can very cleverly do what you physically can't: mentally escape. So, again, it's a way that your brain protects you from what is going on externally in times of distress.

And why exactly would we want to remember these things anyway? We don't. So your brain represses the memories the best it can to help you survive. Super-smart really. And I'm grateful for that, as I'm not sure I'd be here to write this book otherwise.

Unfortunately, what your brain doesn't do is get rid of the memory and the feelings of that memory; even if you can't recall parts of it, the memory still exists, it's still there in our subconscious, and so is how it makes us feel. The disassociation that helped in that moment of the awful experience is not helpful after. So, if we don't process what happened to us, the way we coped at the time will remain as the way we cope in our lives after the experience and forever more.

For the majority of the time, I was emotionally detached and dissociated from the things that I'd been through. And sometimes that disconnect is needed – if you can do it under your control. Emotionally disconnecting is a great way to protect ourselves from feeling exposed to people who don't understand, or from 'going there' if we don't want to. I have had some people make jokes about me nearly losing my life, or say things like, 'Did you not get all your travel injections?', as if they are being helpful. 'Oh! Why, thank you. If only I'd have thought of making sure I adhered to all the travel health requirements ahead of a huge transcontinental challenge that I'd spent over a year preparing for in great detail.' In such moments it is a good thing to protect yourself by detaching from feelings and being lackadaisical. Otherwise, those careless comments could have a really hurtful effect. But if I am like that with everyone and in all situations, then I'm going to end up feeling very alone – and this is when dissociation prolongs trauma, because we don't allow our feelings to be heard by ourselves, let alone others and, in turn, to receive comfort.

PUTTING MEMORIES IN CONTEXT

We can dissociate from trauma but all the while have fragmented recollections that are in photographic detail and extremely vivid. In trauma we can be in sensory overload and highly focused. When I was being abused, I disassociated to escape; I went into fight-or-flight survival mode and froze because it was too unsafe to fight or run away. This wasn't a conscious decision; this is something our very clever survival mechanism does automatically. When I was critically ill, I did the opposite: I didn't freeze, and I obviously couldn't run away, so I fought. I was highly focused, in a heightened state and had a complete sensory overload, which might explain why I have such vivid memories of that time.

I can remember the doctor pulling back the hospital curtain while I was covered in sick and telling me that I had multiple organ failure and was dying. He even wrote it on a piece of paper for me – how nice of him. Another thing that added to my upset was that hardly anybody spoke English when I was first hospitalized in Brazil. I remember my last moments before going into the coma, being intubated, and even remember when I woke and the removal of the ventilator. I can picture the room, the feel of it, the smell and everybody in it, as if I am there right now.

In trauma, things need to be put in context. I could remember so much of Rio, but the memories were like jigsaw puzzle pieces that had been spilled over the floor; and a few pieces were missing, which meant the jigsaw could never be fully complete.

'People need somebody to put their experience into context for them – human beings always want and need to know why. Some people have memory, some don't. Dreams and hallucinations get mixed up with memories. Then people have this fear that they are going mad. Expressing that this is common and lots of people have this fear is key. It doesn't mean they are going mad; it's a consequence of what they've been through.'

Dr Niki Snook

Alternative realities

Things can get very mixed up and confusing. Some people don't have context of what is really going on – patients can think they are being tortured, or have been kidnapped, or even think they are being experimented on. These confusional states can occur in a wide variety of medical situations and/or be drug induced.

When I was put in a coma and on a ventilator, the doctors needed to monitor my brain, so tens of electric nodes were attached to my head. I could *feel* what was going on, but I had no understanding of it. I was also sedated at this point – my lungs had collapsed and I wasn't breathing for myself anymore. I knew I was in hospital, but all I could feel were lots of sharp needles moving across my head and my hair being pulled. I thought that my head was being cut open. It was horrifically frightening. I could even picture the top of my head coming off. It turned out that what was actually happening was the nurses were plaiting my long, thick hair very tightly in small braids to be able to get the electric nodes to attach to my scalp. This is why it's really crucial to understand what has actually happened to you, and then make sense of it in some way.

Dr Niki works on a timeline with all her patients, explaining exactly what they've been through so they can make sense of why it felt a certain way or why they thought something different.

'A timeline helps patients accept what they've gone through and how we can support them. We explain what happened and why they feel like they do now. Medics use words from everyday life in different contexts, so we make sure patients understand what they heard and what it actually meant in regard to them. For example, we use the phrase "turning off" – "Turn off the sedation" or "Turn off that drug" – but when people hear that they think we're turning off the machine that's helping them. "Failure" is another common word we use when an organ isn't working properly – heart failure, liver failure – but the patient often think it's failed completely and won't work again.'

Dr Niki Snook

I had multiple organ failure, including kidney failure, and I was scared that the doctors would turn my life support off when I was still there inside the shell of my body. It helped seeing pictures of me in the coma with neatly braided hair, and when Dr Niki explained the electric nodes that were dotted across my scalp between the tiny plaits. The doctors weren't, after all, cutting my head open.

PULLING IT ALL TOGETHER

This is one of the problems in recovering from trauma. How are you meant to process, if your memories are fragmented, repressed and disconnected? Even working with a therapist is hard, as it requires you to explain to them what has happened in your life, and that requires you to be able to be coherent about it all in the first place.

When I first went to therapy, I was only interested in working through what happened to me when I was hospitalized in Rio, despite Dr Rachel pressing to find out more – mainly because I'd written on the intake form in the section labelled childhood, 'I don't want to write about my childhood on some stupid form.' Yes, I know, it was not appropriate, but I was struggling and I didn't want to open those wounds. I felt it was irrelevant – that was what my mind was telling me in order to protect myself from painful emotions. Dr Rachel, on the other hand, could sense there was a lot more. The cat and mouse between us – her pressing me to open up, me shutting down and not trusting her (or anyone for that matter) and my memories just all over the place – led to one of the best things I ever did in my trauma recovery work: a flowers and stones lifeline.

Flowers and stones

Interestingly, it's normal to not trust a therapist – and Dr Rachel assures me it's actually important not to pretend otherwise as it's through these areas of distrust that the therapist can tell what it is that you need. The way I was behaving toward her, and the mistrust I unintentionally showed her, conveyed to her that something had happened to me in the past where I needed to detach from my feelings, be wary and dissociate to cope.

By my friends and my family, I was seen as this tough, headstrong person because I had (without realizing) learnt to block out a lot of my painful emotions and my past. This is not an attractive way to live. Imagine a child in a cage, locked up and deprived of laughter and love; it's a horrible image to think about, and if any of us saw that in real life we would be horrified. That is effectively what I did to myself to prevent any more pain coming in. But that meant I kept my pain locked inside, and stopped any love and healing from entering.

My therapist saw me differently. She realized the strong persona was something I had created because of what I'd had to survive. My tough exterior not only masked my pain to others but prevented me from getting the help and support I needed. Dr Rachel saw through it.

To get me to open up and process my trauma, Dr Rachel got me to create a lifeline made of flowers and stones. This 'narrative exposure' technique was first developed in the early 2000s by trauma specialists Maggie Schauer, Frank Neuner and Thomas Elbert, working in refugee camps in Africa and Asia to help refugees put their fragmented and disjointed memories into some kind of structure. It's now also used to help people that have had multiple and/or repeated trauma to recollect and access horrible and devastating memories. The technique is like storytelling but with your own life – going back over your own story and putting together your memories in chronological order. The theory behind it is that working through distressing moments in chronological order can repair negative associations and responses to them.

While this may sound simple, for people that have trauma, it is the hardest thing to do. Why would we want to go back to those moments, to those horrible feelings? To that time in hospital when life felt like it was over; to what it felt like in that abusive relationship; to your childhood and the loneliness; to when you lost someone and your heart felt like it had broken in two ... or whatever it was for you. Nobody wants to go back to feeling like that. That's why many of us don't work through our trauma – ever. And it makes complete sense as to why. But unwillingly, and most of the time subconsciously, this keeps us in pain.

The flowers and stones technique provided me with an element of separation from the facts – it helped me to be able to see and order what had happened to me away from my own head.

Seeing it from the outside was pretty daunting. It was hard to face. And while doing it, I did have feelings of 'Why me? Why has this all happened to me?' But alongside those feelings, creating the lifeline helped me feel some compassion toward myself and made me want to work through my feelings. It made me pause for just a second and, rather than block it out, see that I'd been through a lot, and that it actually made sense as to why I had anxiety, depression, trust issues, was hypervigilant, had nightmares, struggled to stay in intimate relationships, was so hard on myself, had flashbacks … the list goes on.

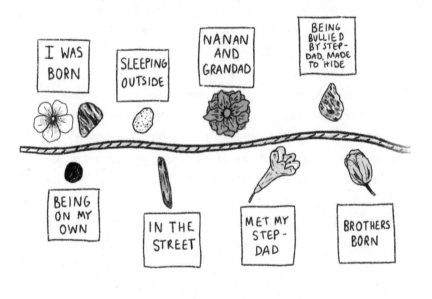

* * *

A long piece of string represents my lifeline. I place the string along the floor of Dr Rachel's office. We push the furniture to the side, and I sit on the floor next to the string with a bag of small stones of all shapes, like the pebbles you find on the beach, and another bag of small artificial flower heads and petals made from different coloured fabric.

For each major moment in my life, I place either a flower or a stone to mark that experience on my lifeline, then write what that flower or stone represents on a Post-it note. No details, just the moment. A flower represents a good thing in my life, and a stone represents a bad thing.

I start at the very beginning of my life, my birth. Was my birth a flower or a stone? I can't quite decide, so I place a light pink flower and a grey striped oval pebble at the very start of the piece of string, and scribble 'I was born' on a Post-it note and stick it next to them both. The start of my life. I am glad I was born, but my mum had me at such a young age – only 16 – that there was much instability and my mum's own trauma came into play as soon as I was born. I also feel like if she hadn't had me so young, life would have been better for her.

I move on to the next. I put a small, black, round stone with a Post-it note that says 'Being on my own'. We move up the string.

Next to a long, dark, grey stone I scribble 'In the street', which represents a memory of one of the times my mum left my dad, and everyone was in the middle of the street screaming at each other. I was three years old.

Then I place quite a big purple flower on the string and wrote 'Nanan and Grandad'; they looked after me a lot when I was younger. My grandad would make me cups of piping hot tea with sugar in (I wasn't allowed sugar), always call me by my full name Charlotte Amy Serena, and sing 'The sun has got his hat on'.

Next, I place a deep-rose-coloured fuscia and the note 'Met my step-dad'. At the time, as a child, I had initially thought meeting him was a good thing; my mum seemed happy for a short time.

This is quickly followed by a black and brown weird-shaped stone with a Post-it note: 'Being bullied by step-dad, made to hide'.

I then place a lemon-yellow, tulip-shaped flower and write 'Brothers born'. I was so happy and bursting with love when my first brother was born; and when my second brother came along not long after, I was concerned that I wouldn't have enough love *for them both. I was only nine years old, and very quickly realized that I had even more love. I doted on my brothers.*

* * *

You can get a good picture of how this went on. Make sure you take note of the flowers too. They are also important.

ACKNOWLEDGING THE STONES

Seeing the stones as the really painful times in my life made me feel sad for that person, and that person was me. That was a new feeling about myself, and a slightly confusing one. I was overly empathetic and giving to others, yet the complete opposite to myself. I was always so harsh on myself. To feel sad for 'me', the one that had gone through those things, allowed some room for me to empathize with myself. As soon as I started to feel a little bit of empathy, it made me want to do better for myself, to give myself the chance to recover from my trauma and grieve for what I'd been through. The lifeline enabled me to connect my memories with how I was really feeling and start to identify my trauma.

'One of the really good things about the lifeline is that you place a stone, to signify each traumatizing event and a flower for each positive event. With the stones, at first you just acknowledge and label the event, but you don't have to go further than that. So, for someone who feels very overwhelmed, you don't stay with the experience. You say, "This happened and we'll come back to it." Acknowledge it, but don't delve into it all there and then. The lifeline is all about putting you in the driving seat.'

Dr Rachel O'Beney

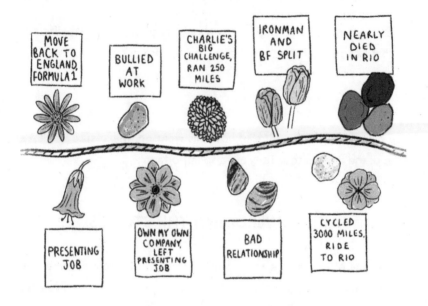

It took two two-hour sessions to finish my lifeline. It filled the room diagonally, with a bit of twisting and curving to fit. On the last stop on my lifeline I placed three different sized marbled brown stones in a pile, and wrote 'Nearly died in Rio'.

That was seven years ago, and now there is so much more to add, both flowers and stones. The lifeline will always be out of date, as things continuously happen in life. Working through trauma isn't about preventing any more stones on your lifeline – I've already had more stones, even after my trauma recovery.

Life can't be managed and controlled to stop horrible things happening. Trauma recovery is about processing all the stones you've already had to be able to keep on growing. It's about making more flowers, so that when more stones inevitably come along you are in an emotionally healthier place to deal with them and able to process them soon after. You now won't leave them to gather dust for your future self to have to carry their burden. I promise that if you face your stones, your lifeline will start to gather more flowers than stones.

The lifeline helps you see your story and start processing and making sense of those painful emotions under your own timeline and control. Doing the lifeline means we don't have to select one particular event in our lives; it makes it more manageable to reflect on our life as a whole. Our life isn't a linear straight line of past, present and future: it's a spider's web. Everything is interconnected and interrelated. Our past connects to our present, our present influences our future, and our future is created from how we deal with our past.

VALIDATION

Studies have shown that creating our own narrative can help us feel dignity and validation. It's our own testimony that helps validate our experiences and feelings. Validation is important because in trauma we are often left with feelings that aren't heard, which compounds those feelings of isolation and gives energy to all those symptoms of trauma. Validation is the opposite of trauma – it means recognition and acknowledgement that our feelings exist for a reason. Your feelings are there because of what has happened to you. They are valid. If nobody has ever told you that before, then please let me tell you. Your experience happened, what it did to you is real, and what you feel is valid, true and for a reason.

Once I'd finished making my lifeline, I took photographs and went back to the beginning, going over each stone one at a time. It started to bring me a little closer to my traumatic memories and how I was feeling. I began to connect with what it felt like in that moment – what it was really like for me – allowing myself to accept all the moments in my life that led to this, how frightening and how 'traumatic' a lot of those things were. It's not only reasonable to have the symptoms of trauma, but it's actually to be expected. That shift to not be in denial, to be accepting of why you feel like you do and how what happened to you impacts you now, is the most relieving feeling. It's like you can finally take a deep breath, let your shoulders relax and say, 'Of course I am having these feelings. Of course I am struggling with this. Look at my lifeline and the things I've had to deal with.' You have to allow yourself to accept your lifeline; ignoring it doesn't mean it's not there.

This is how you start to begin to process trauma and start recovering from it.

CREATE YOUR LIFELINE

Although the creation of a lifeline is often done alongside a professional (which is what Dr Rachel recommends), you can also do it with a trusted person you feel safe with. Dr Rachel says, 'I think it is good to do it with another person because it's about somebody having their story witnessed with another. It's about acknowledgement. You'd have minimized it if you'd have done the lifeline by yourself.'

Dr Rachel was the first person who acknowledged my story, so maybe she's right – I would have minimized it. However, now looking back at it, I even minimized it with Dr Rachel. This is part and parcel of trauma and the initial process of recovery. Even though I may have minimized it, having some of it at some level tangibly in front of me on a lifeline helped me start to accept my story more and more. The more I accepted that it happened, the less I started to minimize it.

If you don't have someone you can trust to do your lifeline with, I believe you can do it on your own, with you being a witness to your own story. I know it's not always an option to do it with someone else in a trusted space. Whether you're doing this with someone or on your own, here's what you need and how to do it. Have a go.

- You will need:
  - string – any type will do: parcel string, garden string
  - stones – from a garden, wood or beach
  - flowers – they can be artificial, real or even drawn on paper and cut out

A stone symbolizes a distressing part of your life and a flower something good. You can add both and/or more than one stone or more than one flower at each point. For example, I put two stones for an abusive relationship I'd had with a boyfriend and put two flowers for ending the relationship and another two for competing in my first Ironman competition.

- Find yourself a place you feel comfortable and place the string along the floor. I recommend doing the lifeline with actual objects in a quiet space with no distraction, but if this isn't available for you, you could try it on paper or on a computer or tablet.
- Take your time. Start with your birth and move through the next significant time in your life. Pull out the major moments of your life. Make it an active exercise and move down the string after each stone or flower. This is about laying out your timeline, not spending time on each moment. This helps make it feel a little safer rather than pulling up all the different emotions and sitting in them. If it gets too much after a while, do it in phases.
- After you've done your lifeline, take pictures of it, perhaps in sections and also in full. You can print them out or just keep them on your phone.
- The next stage of the lifeline is to write down or journal in more detail what each of the major stones in your life was and create a story/narrative of those upsetting

experiences to help understand how they make you feel now. It's about documenting what happened to you.

I spent my next sessions with Dr Rachel going back to each major stone in my life. Your lifeline is your testimony. Everything you've been through is valid and does matter.

The lifeline exercise can bring up difficult and big emotions, so be aware of that and notice how you're feeling. You can come back to it at any time if it feels too much right now. Keep in mind that some of the symptoms of trauma are avoiding what has hurt us, so your instinct may be to avoid doing this. That's completely okay and normal, you don't have to do anything about that right now; just be aware if that's what it's bringing up for you. If you do stop, you can pick up your lifeline where you left off later.

'It's a lot to take in by yourself, you need a kind person to be with you. It's the old-fashioned way of telling a story about yourself and for another person to hear it. It's an organized way of doing it. There is something so powerful about it.'

Dr Rachel O'Beney

If you don't feel ready to do this exercise, it's totally fine; you don't have to create your lifeline to move on with this book. Just thinking about it and what it could look like will help your brain think a little differently about your trauma. Move on to the next chapter, and you can revisit the lifeline exercise after you've finished reading, or further down the line when it feels right for you.

If you do feel ready to start your lifeline, but then experience overwhelm, try the following Grounding Technique to calm and centre yourself, and bring you back to the present.

GROUNDING TECHNIQUE

When suffering overwhelm or panic or anxiety, grounding can be a really helpful technique to calm and centre yourself. Dr Rachel's grounding-in-reality technique is all about labelling the here and now.

Things might feel unsafe when big and painful emotions come to the forefront, but grounding yourself in your current surroundings shows you that your outside reality is safe.

Check in with your surroundings and just look at each object around or near you and name them out loud. For example,

> 'There is my blue chair.'
> 'The wood floor.'
> 'The grey table.'

This takes your mind from its internal dialogue to external.

Dr Rachel also suggests you could:

- Look for all the red things around you, then all the blue things
- Listen to the sounds around you
- Counting in threes:
  - name out loud three objects you can see
  - name out loud three sounds you can hear
  - name out loud three things you can move or touch
  - or do three things, such as move your leg, touch a chair, nod your head.

This technique is about getting present. Acknowledge all your surroundings and root yourself where you are physically in that moment.

6

Relationships

This chapter was probably the hardest one for me to write, because the subject of it makes me feel more vulnerable than anything else. Relationships, both adult interpersonal and early attachment, are frequently at the heart of what causes trauma and how our trauma plays out. Understanding and working through this is essential for recovery.

This chapter is crucial. Before moving into it, I want to remind you that whatever you've been through, you *can* recover from trauma and have wonderful caring, loving and fulfilling relationships. It is important to know that it is not our awful experiences that cause long-term problems with relationships and connection, it's when we don't process our trauma.

Trauma can have a huge impact on our ability to have healthy relationships, because trauma affects the way we perceive ourselves and others, which has a knock-on effect on how we behave and interact within intimate relationships. Trauma can cause the following:

- issues with trust
- shame
- vulnerability
- disconnection from our own emotions, making it difficult to express love and receive it

- avoidance of intimacy
- lack of healthy boundaries
- hypervigilance
- flashbacks
- repeating unhealthy patterns of behaviour (for example, controlling another person or pursuing an emotionally unavailable or abusive relationship after suffering abuse, for that reason then perpetuating the cycle and therefore trauma).

But all of this doesn't mean we can't work through what we've been through and have healthy relationships. Recovering from trauma and being an emotionally healthy functioning adult involves making sense of our trauma and understanding the impact it has on our behaviour in relationships, including our relationship with ourselves. Once we see what it is we do because of how our trauma has left us feeling, we can change it. These difficulties are not your fault, they are what happens to survivors of trauma.

CONNECTION AND TRAUMA

'The context in which trauma happens is most often in a relationship between two people or several people. So, the site of the trauma is also the place in which we start to work to repair – that's why it can feel so tricky. Building trust, and tracking when it feels shaky, are very important.'

Dr Rachel O'Beney

In short, trauma often *happens* in connection, but trauma also *recovers* in connection. The hurt and healing is in the same place (the experience, the memory, the emotion; not a physical location). But why would anybody want to go back to the place of hurt to heal? To a place that left us feeling scared, overwhelmed, betrayed, ashamed and hurt. We don't – and there lies much of the problem.

Connections with others

Trauma almost always involves a connection of some kind to someone else – divorce, abuse, childbirth, bullying, an unemotionally available parent (neglect, mental health, addiction/alcoholism), abusive childhood, assault, death or loss of a loved one …

And if your trauma comes from any kind of relationship (friend, family, romantic), the strong emotion of shame tends to come into play. Shame is the focus of Chapter 7.

But the recovery of trauma is also through connection. We all need to have trusting relationships of some kind in life, whether it is friends, family or a romantic relationship. All human studies and research in this area collectively show that the relationships we form with others are *vital* to our mental and emotional wellbeing, and even to our survival. Relationships are where we learn, grow, thrive – and heal. One of the human universal basic needs is a secure attachment, and all that it brings with it: safety, love, nurture, care, reassurance, compassion, acceptance and a sense of belonging.

Many people with trauma may commonly avoid or end close relationships. This makes complete sense, because if the root of your pain comes from connection with another human, especially an intimate one, you don't want to risk more pain in connection. Trauma can also lead people to stay in unhealthy and abusive relationships because they feel undeserving; they may be repeating patterns they know from their past or, in its own way, this type of relationship can feel safer because it is familiar.

CONNECTION WITH YOURSELF

The relationship you have with yourself – how you feel and see yourself – has a huge impact on the quality of a relationship you can have with someone else, especially one that is romantic and intimate. It's very difficult to have an equal and safe relationship with someone external to yourself if you don't have equality and security in your own relationship with yourself.

Trauma impacts your relationship with yourself. It changes your sense of self – the way you think, see and feel about who you are.

We can destroy our own relationship and connection with ourselves by:

- being horrible to ourselves
- self-blame
- not looking after ourselves
- disconnecting from and/or avoiding our feelings
- relentless pursuit of perfection
- not allowing ourselves to have a loving external relationship.

Trauma can result in an expectation of danger, betrayal or potential harm in future relationships. It creates a distrust in a relationship and it also causes a mistrust of our own relationship with ourselves.

IMPROVING YOUR CONNECTION
WITH YOURSELF

How do you treat yourself? How do you speak to yourself? How do you see yourself?

Gabor Maté, the renowned trauma and addiction expert, says trauma literally *is* the disconnection from oneself. He says, 'It is the shut down of the self. A shame about the self. It's the disconnection of the self and from the present moment.'

Shame is dominant in trauma and affects the way we see ourselves and behave. You've already got an idea of how I treated myself; I was unkind and demanding – made myself work harder, exercised to breaking point and beyond, wouldn't eat when my body desperately needed to refuel, criticized myself relentlessly, drank to excess when I was younger, deprived myself of sleep, and so on.

SELF-TALK – OUR PARENT VOICE

We all talk to ourselves. Self-talk is the voice in your head, it's what you tell yourself about yourself.

In schema therapy, which focuses on our unhealthy patterns of behaviour and the way we cope because of our past, the voice in your head is called your 'parent' – this voice is how you parent yourself. Trauma can lead to overly critical and dismissive self-talk and harmful patterns of thinking – basically, you are not a very nice parent to yourself. This inner voice often comes from what someone has told us about ourselves. For example, if you've had a negative childhood influence, or if your parents were very critical of you, or if you've had an emotionally unhealthy relationship, you can internalize what was said to you or how it made you feel. And now, you take on their voice as your own, you repeat that language, and criticize or belittle yourself.

The voice in your head can be very overpowering, incredibly demanding and/or extremely nasty. Everyone has this inner dialogue to an extent – it's normal – but when it is consistently harmful and negative, it is very damaging.

If I was to say to you the horrible things you say to yourself, for example, 'You are not good enough', every day, multiple times a day, you'd start to take in what I was saying. You would come to believe it and start behaving differently around me. That is basically what you are doing to yourself – bullying yourself.

There will be enough people in the outside world who bully us, so the last thing you need is this nasty talk coming from inside yourself. I always felt like I was two people: the demanding, relentless striving 'me', who I thought was the strong one; and the sad childlike unhappy 'me', who I thought was weak. I thought the strong voice was keeping the weaker one at bay; what was really happening was that I was just re-abusing myself. The 'strong' voice was influenced by all the people who had bullied and abused me; my 'weak' voice was the real me in desperate pain and in need of love – so, not weak at all, just hurt and needing to heal.

When I was critically ill, I had no escape and nothing to distract me. I couldn't use any of my usual coping mechanisms, such as throwing myself into work or exercising to the point of exhaustion. It's like I was stripped raw, and every part of me that I'd hidden away was exposed. I heard my 'weaker' voice loud and clear.

Hello Charlie. I'm your past. I'm the little girl you've kept hidden away, forgotten, left in captivity for so long. Now I've escaped, and you aren't going to neglect me anymore because I'm coming for you. I won't let you rest until you acknowledge I exist.

I needed to be acknowledged – not by the outside world, but by myself.

I do sometimes wonder what kind of person I would be, or where my life would have gone if I hadn't been forced into a situation where I had to face my trauma. Falling critically ill broke me so much that I knew I couldn't carry on going the way I was.

It makes me horribly sad to think of how long I lived this way, and how long I gave myself these 'emotional beatings'.

It's unbelievably hard to stop harmful self-talk, especially when it becomes the only way you've known yourself. It can also be really scary to think about changing who you think you are, even though that part of you is harming you. I thought that the nasty voice was my driver, and that if it went away, I would no longer be driven. That was just the crafty, critical voice inside me, trying to trap me into thinking I needed it. I now know that I don't need to repeatedly beat myself up to be motivated; I know that absolutely doesn't drive me or encourage me. In fact, this voice was stopping me from being happy, because it made me feel undeserving and very lonely.

Acknowledging yourself

To heal from trauma, we need to create a sense of worth for ourselves. We can only do this by making the 'weaker' voice stronger and the 'stronger' voice weaker. For this to change, we need to acknowledge ourselves.

Where do your harmful self-critical messages come from? It's not something you were born with – we don't just decide to become horrible to ourselves. Thinking about where the critical voice originates from is really helpful. It tends to come from a parent or caretaker or influential adult; it may be a combination of people. Mine was my step-dad, my coach, some of my teachers, my relationships and some other family members.

If your trauma, or some of it, comes from abuse, the critical voice you've developed in your head continues to abuse you. Now that the abuse is just internal, there's only one person guilty of that abuse, and that is you. I know it can be hurtful to see it like that, but understanding what your internal voice is will change it. I felt really shocked and sad when I realized what I was doing to myself, but acknowledging it was the first step to healing.

Think for a moment: what do you say to yourself?

Whatever voices you notice, don't try to argue with your critical voice – you will just be arguing and creating conflict within yourself. Just listen and observe. You need to recognize what voice is your critical voice to be able to change it. The challenge is to not listen TO it, but to listen OUT for it.

Some of the things I would tell myself:

'You're a failure.'
'You're not good enough.'
'You're stupid.' (Can also come out as *'You're an idiot'.*)
'You're a fool for thinking someone would love you.'
'Of course that didn't work out for you – you didn't do enough.'
'You're worthless.'

I hope that by seeing how I would speak to myself you might begin recognizing your own critical voice. It's important to notice what you are telling yourself. When you notice it, label it, note it down. That voice is your critical, nasty and demanding parent. It's not reality, it's not serving you, and it's certainly not FOR you.

Changing your inner dialogue

I say a little spiel (speech) to my critical voice when I notice it creeping in: *'Thank you. I understand you are saying this because of the things that have happened to you. You are just trying to protect me from more pain and rejection, but I don't need you to do this anymore. It's not helpful for me now. I am enough. I am loved. I am valuable.'*

Now, I didn't remotely believe those words at first. I would say this spiel, and then my critical voice would kind of snigger to itself. It would make some comment like, *'You're an idiot for saying that.'* But the more I said the spiel and heard the nasty voice for what it was, it made me think, made me shift and made me want to do better for myself.

If you talk yourself into thinking you're not enough, you can talk yourself out of it too.

When you notice a belittling thought, try making a deliberate statement to yourself that counters it; but remember be careful not to argue with it, or it can spiral into a back-and-forth match that only your critical voice will win: *'You are unlovable – No I AM not – Yes you are, look at you, you can't even have a relationship/you have a terrible relationship, look at what they did to you, you're just an idiot – NO I AM NOT AN IDIOT.'*

The conversation will just go on and on, and the critical voice will just keep beating you in every sense of the word. It's exhausting. This is very much what my head was like for years and years. It wouldn't leave me alone. Sometimes I would think about harming myself just to try and make it go quiet. I'd often exercise so hard to exhaust myself in an attempt to quieten down the argument in my head. Arguing against it does not work. Your critical voice will always argue back, even louder, and beat you down.

To counter your critical voice effectively, you need to make a statement that is **true** and that shows the critical thought is **false**. For example, you make a mistake and your voice tells you that you're an idiot. You could say *'Making a mistake is part of being human. I actually can learn from this. Making a mistake does not make me an idiot. In fact, learning from mistakes is an effective way to improve.'*

Another way to build a strong supportive voice is to give yourself examples of reality – facts you can draw upon. For example, recalling a time when you did something well, you got a good evaluation or were praised for something you did.

Your critical voice often searches for evidence of all the negative experiences in your life that confirm that your critical voice is right. It will rerun your mistakes, or the bad things that have happened to you to prove to you *'You're not enough'* or *'You're an idiot'*, or whatever your critical voice wants you to believe. You need to develop and strengthen the opposite, the feeling of value and evidence of being competent, and all the times that you have achieved in your life.

To work through my critical inner voice, I started making a note of all the comments my critical voice would make. I then reframed these thoughts, using evidence that showed otherwise. I disproved the thoughts, and took back the power. My critical voice was telling me

I was unlovable – something that I felt as a child due to the chaos of the adults around me, and it stuck with me into adulthood. I wrote it down and then wrote all the evidence that showed otherwise – there are many people who love me in my life, so telling myself I am unlovable is a lie.

Have a go. Start jotting your inner critic thoughts down. Pick one in particular that is really strong for you and then write down another way of thinking about it. A worksheet from my schema therapy trauma group says: 'overthrow and banish the punitive parent' – the punitive parent being the nasty voice in your head.

This is the start of forming a healthy relationship with yourself. Think about Gabor Maté's explanation of trauma at the beginning of this chapter, when he described trauma as being disconnected from yourself. Connection is the opposite of trauma: it is love, calm, peace, assuredness.

TOXIC POSITIVITY

By the way, to be very clear, this is not about being 'positive'. It's extremely unhelpful and isolating when people tell you to 'be positive' when you're dealing with trauma. Positivity can actually be harmful – i.e. 'toxic positivity'. Being told to 'stay positive' can become damaging when it dismisses what we are actually feeling, dismisses the emotions attached to what we are going through and invalidates our experience. Life experience is complex – as are we – so to 'look on the bright side' or 'get over it' when we are suffering is denying part of us. 'What's meant to be will be' and 'silver lining' talk can sometimes be helpful in daily life, but not in trauma. In trauma, this can shame somebody and disregard their need for help and support. It suggests that trying harder to be positive will make everything okay, and implies that the person is to blame for what they're feeling and isn't trying hard enough.

Trauma has nothing to do with being positive or negative. Trauma responses and symptoms are a normal reaction to a distressing and disturbing experience. Telling yourself to 'be positive' will not change a thing. This language can mask what you're really feeling and can cause you to minimize your experience and response to it.

Connection Card
EMOTIONALLY HEALTHY MESSAGES

Using an index card that I recommended you buy in the Introduction (or cut a piece of card to about the size of the palm of your hand), create a connection card (or cards) with messages that can act as your emotionally healthy supportive voice.

This voice doesn't just arrive overnight, so to start rewiring the way we speak to ourselves, we need to engage in compassionate and encouraging self-talk. When we are in a state of trauma, our inner critic is very powerful, and in the moment it can be very hard to hear another voice that is more caring. The first step to accessing this supportive voice is to have those caring messages written down.

To give an example, this is the exact text from a connection card that I made (now very tatty due to its regular use!):

I'll always be with you. You are loved. It's okay to be scared. I care about you. I like you. I deserve to be cared for. I am valuable. You are loved. You are special. I believe in you. You are doing really well.

You are more than welcome to use some of the phrases I've written, or none at all.

If you find it impossible to do this task, think about the kind of supportive things you would say to people you love, or copy my words onto your own card.

As I said, you don't have to believe the messages right now. I didn't when I first wrote them down. But please read your connection card as often as you can. I would read it when I felt really low, or if I was on the way to something that was important to me – presenting a TV show, hosting an event, meeting someone new, going to a meeting, etc. I was living in London when I first started doing this work, so sometimes I would read the card while sitting on the Tube. I still have this card six years on. It's in my purse, between my debit and credit cards. I look at it a lot less than I used to, because now I say those things to myself without having to read them.

Previously, I found it very difficult to say encouraging and kind things to myself because I was struggling so much with trauma, and my nasty and demanding critic ruled my sense of self. Telling myself I was loved and valuable felt stupid and weak. That was my critical voice preventing me from getting better because I was scared.

Please try using this connection card. You don't have to show or tell anyone you've done it. However, if you would like to share it, you can share it with me on social media or via my website contact form.

If writing multiple statements on the card seems overwhelming, choose **one** critical statement that you find you say to yourself, and write something that counteracts that critical thought. For me, a key one would be, *'I am a failure and I am not good enough, that's why these bad things happen.'* Look out for this one thought and notice how often it makes itself heard and how it makes you feel. Now, write down something that counters it. For me, it's simply, '*I am enough*'. Even though you may not believe the caring phrase, read it – read it in your head, then read it out loud every time you hear your self-critical statement.

A warning: watch out for arguing back and forth with your critic – your critic will just keep arguing with you, and often even louder. Don't forget your critic is still you. Don't fall for the trap of being unkind to your critic by shouting back at it – that is you shouting at yourself. Your critic is sneaky like that!

Remember: if you can convince yourself you're not good enough, you can convince yourself you are enough.

So, grab your index/flashcards and jot down reassuring and supportive messages to yourself. It may be hard to do, and you don't have to believe them right now.

If you're not convinced that a few supportive messages will do anything, that's okay – neither did I at first! But please do it anyway, even if it's just to humour me. Give it a try.

CONNECTING TO OTHERS

Relationships after trauma are a vicious cycle. How can others connect with us, and we connect with others, when we are disconnected from ourselves?

If we have a really strong critical voice, and are nasty and horrible to ourselves, how does that express itself to others?

Dr Rachel explains one way others might experience it: 'People that are self-critical also tend to be quite critical of other people.'

This made me question whether I'm like this. I do have ridiculously high standards for myself, and was very critical of what I did. The more I've worked through trauma, the more I can give myself more manageable standards rather than totally unrealistic ones. But I feel I have projected those demanding standards on to other people in the past.

At the other end of the spectrum, Dr Rachel explains another way the self-critic can spill out into our relationships: 'It can also go the other way, where all criticism is directed inwards, at you, and you're totally compliant with everybody on the outside. You do everything another person says because you don't feel you are good enough.'

I've also sometimes done that. This is a characteristic I strongly recognized in my mum, too. She would appease and agree to anything my step-dad wanted to do. It was her way of managing danger or further criticism.

There's no escaping or separating this connection, as Dr Rachel explains: 'Inside is outside. How you are in your internal world is how you are in the external world.'

Gabor Maté puts it into context: 'If you had parents who couldn't see you, it's because they couldn't see themselves.' It doesn't mean that it's acceptable or okay, it just explains this complex relationship, and can help us make better choices for ourselves moving forward so as to not repeat this cycle.

Make sure you see yourself, so you can see others.

BECOMING CONSCIOUS OF OUR BEHAVIOURS

Sigmund Freud, the founder of psychoanalysis, talks about repeating behaviours and the need to be aware of these behaviours in order to move past them. I discussed this with Dr Rachel, as she feels Freud's paper 'Remembering, Repeating, and Working-Through', published just before the First World War, in 1914, talks about our often-unconscious compulsion to repeat.

The paper is about 'repetition compulsion', which means we repeat patterns of behaviours and emotions from the past without even realizing, even if they are not good for us. We re-enact unresolved 'conflicts' from our past in our present lives and relationships.

Dr Rachel explains its significance: 'If we don't acknowledge our experience, we are destined to repeat until we are helped to remember. Only then can we work it through. So, using Freud's language, we need to put what has happened to us into the conscious mind, as opposed to ignoring it and our trauma staying in the unconscious mind. We will just unconsciously repeat the same behaviour until it's brought into the conscious mind.'

Freud establishes the idea of 'working-through' and exploring these repetitions, so we can understand what is going on in our unconscious and process the unresolved issues and emotions related to our past.

The crux of it is, in trauma we use (without realizing) harmful coping behaviours (as discussed in Chapter 3) to protect ourselves from overwhelming emotions and challenging situations in our relationships. Think of these behaviours and protective mechanisms as our 'relationship signatures', i.e. what we tend to do in a relationship, and the patterns we play out. We can bring these signatures into our connections both in romantic relationships and friendships. And we will keep on playing out these patterns of behaviours until we *realize* we are doing them, and *address* where they came from and why. History repeats itself because we don't see the patterns we are playing out.

THE VALUE OF GROUP WORK

Group work is an effective approach for dealing with these behaviours, because you start to see your relationship signatures and patterns as they subconsciously play out with others. They may not show up so clearly in one-to-one therapy, whereas a group of people will all have their own ways of coping, just like in our daily life interactions.

This unconscious behaviour is dictated from our past hurts. It's only when it's drawn attention to that we are able to see the pattern we are repeating and our ways of coping; these could include shutting down, being avoidant, detached (disconnected), angry, defensive or complying to everything.

'We may not be particularly aware of these patterns until we get to talk with another – who *has* noticed them – and we are helped to open up about what's happened to us that has made us and start to link feelings to our behaviours,' says Dr Rachel.

When we draw attention to our behaviours, patterns and unhelpful ways of coping that we normally don't realize we're doing, we can start to catch ourselves in the moment and, over time, make a change.

Being a 'detached protector' helped me survive for a very long time – I would essentially cut off my emotions when things felt threatening – then it became problematic for me in relationships. What helped me survive now no longer serves me.

'Some patterns of coping can really get in the way of getting on with your life and forming relationships. I see signatures and patterns that get played out in group therapy, and even in myself, and I say to myself, "Oh! What just happened there?" Only when we notice what we do can we change it. It's so much easier to see behaviour patterns in another person, which is why a group is so helpful.'

Dr Rachel O'Beney

DETACHMENT BEHAVIOUR

To some extent, we all use certain patterns of behaviour to cope – like detaching, or avoiding – in our daily life. For example, when dealing with someone being rude at work, it can be helpful to switch off emotionally from them in that moment or avoid them so you don't get hurt and affected by the person's rudeness. But when you're in trauma, these protective coping mechanisms are switched on all the time, and are because of our past feelings, *not* because of the current situation we are reacting to. Detaching from your emotions or avoiding the situation will help you deal with a rude person at work, but detaching emotionally in all situations – whether difficult or not – is going to cause problems. It's very hard to form safe and healthy intimate relationships and friendships if we emotionally switch ourselves off or avoid those interactions *just in case* we will get hurt. But if we aren't aware of what we do or how we act, how can we make a change?

As Dr Rachel emphasized to me, 'All this is quite painful to discover about yourself, as you work through things.'

I realized that I had lost relationships and friendships because I had been closed off emotionally and overly self-reliant. I was scared of being hurt because I was already in so much pain and sadness. It's a vicious cycle, because being closed off made me hurt even more. I avoided my emotions, which made my depression worse; and all this blocked me from processing and healing from the traumatic experiences I'd suffered. By protecting myself, I was actually hurting myself and keeping myself in trauma. When you start to see all these things, it feels like an 'Aha!' moment, but also can be quite hard to take.

We didn't choose what happened to us or how people treated us, and we didn't really choose how we treated ourselves, because that is the nature of trauma. However, we *can* choose to take the steps to recover and relearn how we treat ourselves and others moving forward.

Make sure you acknowledge that coping the way you have was to try and protect you the best way you knew how. Be honest with yourself about the impact the way you've coped has had on your life and your relationships. Watch out for the inner critic – don't criticize yourself for the way you've coped, this kept you going and was how you've survived. We just want to change this moving forward because these behaviours don't serve us anymore.

UNDERSTAND DISCONNECTION

There is a great little exercise that demonstrates what (dis)connection and detachment from trauma can feel like in a relationship. It's good to do with someone else, but works just as effectively on your own using a mirror.

- Get a blank piece of paper that is as large as your face – A4 works fine.
- Put it in front of your face. If you're with someone else, try speaking to them – ask how they are, maybe tell them how you feel.
- Keeping the piece of paper over your face, get the other person to respond to you. If you're on your own, imagine trying to communicate like this, or telling somebody how you are feeling or what you're sad or angry about.
- What does it feel like to communicate in this way? It's impossible to connect fully; you may still be able to speak and hear, but with very little real connection.

It is difficult to connect with someone when they are detached, disconnected and guarded because of their trauma. There is an invisible wall between you and the other person. Dr Rachel did the connection exercise above with me, and I found it so powerful. It was like being forced to see how I often came across in my relationships – both friendships and intimate relationships. I would struggle to open up and say what I was really feeling, and the other person would find it difficult to really connect and get to know me. Likewise, how could they feel safe to confide in me, if they knew I was always holding back? This barrier leaves both people feeling lonely, unimportant and questioning their own worth.

My detached and guarded protector even became an issue in working with Dr Rachel. Dr Rachel explained it to me like this: 'This shows how protective you had to be in your past. You were bringing your relationship signatures and your ways of coping from the past into your present. You had to be very guarded for good reason back then. But now that really gets in the way of you building close relationships and us trying to talk and me helping you.'

A relationship signature is formed by your earliest attachments – normally from your parents or caregiver – and it becomes the blueprint of how you relate to another person romantically in your adult life.

Looking back at so many of my past relationships, I can see I closed myself off – to that relationship's detriment. I didn't want to be like that, but I didn't know any other way. Rather than seeing the love the person was trying to give me, I just saw mistrust and hurt, and feared abandonment. I protected myself from these imagined dangers within the relationship by being guarded and not getting too emotionally attached. Even when I felt the love, I questioned and doubted it because of what my past taught me about love and trust. The adults around us as children teach us how to love and be loved. I learnt that love is conditional, destructive and unreliable. I learnt that love is pain.

I see myself now and how much I've grown, and how much more open I am. I can connect with people without a fear that seizes every part of me, and without all the pain from my past flooding in.

WHAT OTHERS SEE

My detached and guarded coping mechanisms are something that came up with Dr Rachel when I joined her psychotherapy group. 'When you first came into the group, I was a bit worried that the way you detach might intimidate others – because you would look like you were all singing and all dancing. You came across as having no problems at all, so what on earth were you doing in that group? But when you began sharing your vulnerability, you had so much to give and everybody wanted to share theirs,' she revealed.

This scenario played out a lot in my life, but I could never see it before. People would see me very differently from what I felt inside because I detached and protected myself. I couldn't understand it though. In my head, I would think, 'Why do you think I'm fine when I'm feeling so awful? How could someone feel intimidated by me? I'm so depressed and worthless.' But then I realized people didn't see that side of me because I never showed it. In relationships, how I saw myself inside was so different from how my boyfriends saw me.

As it so happens, this same point came up during my discussions with Dr Rachel for this book. 'You always look bushy-tailed, and come across with an air of "So, that's all cool",' she said when checking up on how I was doing and feeling about writing my book. Note to self: showing how I feel is something I still need to work on.

Isn't it funny how we can feel so different from how we portray ourselves to others? Appearing 'strong' is something I lean toward as it's been a habit, a pattern, of mine for so long.

When I made my *Nowhere to Run* documentary for the BBC in 2021, it was something I was really conscious of and thought a lot about. At that stage, I'd done a huge amount of research on trauma and recovery. I wanted to make a documentary that not only told my story and that of my running group, but one that made other victims and survivors watching feel less alone in their experience.

If I filmed the documentary in 'detached protector' mode, disconnected from what I was feeling, then how could I connect with other survivors who need to know it's normal to feel the way they do because of what they've been through? Because I was talking about my own experience as part of the documentary, I made sure that, every step of the way, I was checking in with how I really felt, and made sure I showed that on camera. I wanted to be true to what I was feeling and what the trauma of sexual abuse looks like – and not present a front to camera, showing the real pain only to myself.

LETTING SOMEONE IN

We recover through connection. However, the long-term effects of trauma make people move away from human connection because it can be a place that is difficult to control, with feelings of unsafety and potential volatility. I would keep my distance, even in the closest of romantic relationships. So, how can a traumatized person reconnect when it can feel so unsafe?

Connection for someone who has unprocessed trauma is difficult (keep with me, it's completely possible and doable once we process). It makes a person feel like they are unsafe – even in a safe relationship – and can cause them to push the other person away.

Trauma creates a lack of trust, and experiencing trauma in previous relationships can mean that these past feelings shape the current relationship, even though that may not be reality. This can lead to acting in a controlling or standoffish, disconnected way (detached protector), or complying with everything the other person wants (compliant surrender). Trauma can leave an individual feeling undeserving of love and care. This goes back to our critical voice. People with trauma may destroy any potential relationship because of this thought pattern, and the belief that it's protecting them from getting hurt or ending up in further trauma. Trauma can also mean they stay in a relationship and tolerate bad behaviour.

Relationships are the most effective way to heal unprocessed trauma, through safe connection. Healing involves connecting and reconnecting with yourself and with others; but those of us who are dealing with trauma move away from this.

I knew somewhere deep down that I struggled in relationships, but couldn't quite admit it to myself or figure out how to deal with it. I mainly used my career as an excuse as to why I wasn't really focused on relationships, and there was some truth in that. But even that came back to my past experiences, my *story*. My mum had me when she was a teenager, and wasn't allowed to finish her school exams. I was born and then watched (and was a part of) every single one of my mum's adult relationships and close connections. I thought all relationships were what I saw – controlling, repressive and unhappy – and connections were painful and unreliable. So, striving in my career and not committing to a relationship or close connections was doing everything to counter what I'd seen growing up.

I look back now, and I can see a pattern in my early relationships. I would be 'me': fun-loving, passionate and compassionate; but, as soon as it got serious, I would change. I'd become self-critical: I'd tell myself the other person would hurt me, that I wasn't good enough and that the person didn't really love me, and even if they did, if they found out who I 'really' was and the things that have happened to me, they wouldn't love me. That was my trauma right there, keeping me disconnected and not in the present.

I'd then push that person away. I would convince myself that I'd got some form of one-upmanship over pain because they would inevitably hurt me anyway. This is a schema of mistrust/abuse. A schema is like a framework or pattern; it's effectively a way of thinking that we develop that creates an intense state of feelings, sensations, thoughts, actions and memories. The schema of mistrust/abuse is when our trauma has been caused by other people's harmful acts, and is the expectation that others will lie to you, will cheat, hurt, or abuse you, will manipulate, shame or use you – because that is what happened in the past.

This also led me to be in exactly those kinds of damaging relationships. Remember, this is all without realizing what I was doing. I would tell myself, 'I don't deserve to be loved'. Same old nasty self-narrative. This is also the schema of defectiveness, having the feeling that you are flawed, worthless, bad, incapable or useless. I also knew abuse so well that it was a place that, although not comfortable, was familiar. In familiarity there can be perceived safety, even though the safety isn't really safe. Without realizing it, I was just repeating the cycle of how I'd been treated as a child. I thought I was protecting myself, but in protecting myself from pain, I was preventing myself from feeling love, receiving love and being loved.

DIFFERENT RELATIONSHIPS, SAME REACTIONS

My trauma when I was younger came very much from a family setting and the relationships that were modelled to me, and less so from friendships.

School was a safer place for me than home. At school, I could let my emotions out, I could speak out, and I managed to form friendships. This may be similar to you, or you may find it's the other way around, or both. Some people's trauma comes through early-life friendships and bullying, rather than from family. The feelings and consequences are very much the same. Dr Rachel said that so many people she speaks to say they feel like an outsider and struggle in both friendships and relationships. My friendships have improved significantly since I started working through my trauma, but then it was in romantic relationships as an adult that my trauma really played out.

Dr Rachel commented on why that's the case for me: 'You had the capacity to make friends. It's because, despite everything, you were able to operate in the school setting and do well there. You've internalized your early life at home when it comes to forming relationships. That's why you're saying romantic relationships are the problem for you.'

At home, I had to manage every little noise, even the silences, to try and keep not just myself safe but all of us inside the house safe. At school, I could stick up for myself without something bad happening to me.

As in family and intimate relationships, bullying in friendships – especially in early life – can have a lasting impact and lead to the same trust issues, fear of rejection, lack of healthy boundaries, shame and worthlessness. When friendships become the place of emotional pain, this will impact how we form them in later life. Exactly as I struggled in romantic relationships.

PINPOINTING 'TRAUMA HOTSPOTS'

Key to working through trauma is locating the trauma hotspots – moments of intense fear. I did this through the stones on my lifeline. So: if you lost a parent young, that's your hotspot – you may struggle with romantic relationships or fear abandonment; if you were adopted, your trauma may play out in romantic relationships; if you were bullied at school and felt isolated among your peers, then you may struggle to make friends or build meaningful friendships as an adult.

My trauma hotspots were abuse at home, abuse by my coach in my athletics group, and then critical illness. By the time I experienced the trauma of critical illness, *how* I formed relationships had already been shaped. I have found connecting in friendships far easier than connecting with someone meaningfully in a romantic way, because that's where all my fear and pain came from. I had been taught through experience not to trust people.

When discussing my own difficulties as a result of my trauma, Dr Rachel said, 'It's amazing that you survived, and one of the ways I think you did this is by always being on guard and being very vigilant. It explains your hypervigilance now – we aren't criticizing you for it because it kept you safe. So now, it's about how much you tone down this vigilance. We need your healthy adult to take over from the vulnerable child part in you and really assess how much you are safe enough to relax this behaviour, which includes other ways of coping such as avoiding and detaching – so that you can start to let people in.'

It's frustrating to have to learn all these things, and it's tiring. Give yourself the chance though. Investing the time now will save so much time and emotional pain in the long run.

BUILDING HEALTHIER RELATIONSHIPS

If we can get the emotionally healthy adult 'you' taking better care of the vulnerable and neglected 'you', then that's building a strong relationship with yourself. Then, when you build relationships on the outside, they feel safer.

In a relationship, the idea is that an emotionally healthy person chooses another emotionally healthy person to relate to and then takes a risk by sharing some of their vulnerable side in a safe space. If you can be more in touch with your vulnerable self, you can then be more vulnerable with another person. Ultimately, that's how we form meaningful relationships.

'Someone who has been traumatized will repeat old patterns. They're likely to be with someone who makes them feel unsafe. It's not their fault, but unwittingly they choose what they've already known. They seek out what's familiar.

'They've chosen someone who's treated them badly, and there's a very good reason for it. It's their critical voice saying that they don't deserve anything else or anything better, and actually it's best to stay with what they know.'

'They feel they aren't worth anything, so they stay with someone who isn't good for them. And they won't leave because they are so afraid of being abandoned. We call this abandonment schema – it's something we come across an awful lot and is very understandable.'

'If you can get to a place where you understand WHY you make these choices, consciously and logically, it makes complete sense.'

Dr Rachel O'Beney

I've been in intimate relationships that have been a lot calmer and safer than previous relationships, but they have also made me feel more anxious; Dr Rachel says this is 'because you're waiting for the penny to drop'. Yes, because I wasn't used to it. I was used to chaos. The calm and safety made me feel on edge because I was waiting for the bubble to burst.

'If people are constantly attaching themselves to someone chaotic, they feel wedded to this. Giving these chaotic partnerships up is also a sacrifice and a loss, because once you do that you have to face your own behaviour in those relationships.'

Dr Rachel O'Beney

This is so powerful. To heal from trauma you have to acknowledge your own behaviour and patterns.

To make it clear, this doesn't excuse abusive behaviour or put an onus on a victim in a harmful relationship.

I had a serious romantic relationship that I stayed in for far too long. He told me he didn't trust me; he was obsessed with my ex-boyfriend, who I'd finished with just before meeting him. He found my old phone and even went to the lengths of charging it when I was out one day so he could read the messages between me and my ex from when we were together. He made me delete photos of the holiday I'd gone on with my ex and get rid of any trace of him in my house (my ex had lived with me). The more he mistrusted me, the more I distrusted him. I started to question where he was, as he did with me. I found myself acting like him to try to protect myself from the way he was treating me. He would put me down whenever we went anywhere – he said that I made him look bad because I looked too good. I wanted him to love me and be proud of me. I was falling into the same behaviours I had done as a child, and in previous relationships: wanting to be loved, so trying to 'achieve' and prove myself to gain love. He once slammed my leg in a taxi door, yet I sat in the taxi with him checking he was okay. Later that night he threw a half-empty glass of whisky at me in my kitchen.

* * *

'Who the fuck do you think you are? I've got glass in my legs. You bastard,' I shouted at my boyfriend faster than I could think.

He ignored me, looked at me with disgust, walked into my bedroom and got into my bed.

I didn't know what to do. My brain was spinning, trying to make sense of what had just happened. I could hear him crying. He knew exactly how to play me. As soon as I saw tears, my own critic went into overdrive. The behaviours I learnt as a child kick in and completely overtake any form of adult rationale.

'It's your fault she's crying,' my step-dad would say to me, about my mum.

'It's your fault I did this.' He would blame me for what he did to her and me.

'You made me angry. It's you! Look at you, pathetic. You did this.'

All I could think about was every time I had been part of this scenario with my step-dad and watched him do this to my mum.

I left the shattered glass on the floor, not even bothering to pick the stinging pieces out of my own bleeding feet and legs.

He's crying – it must be my fault.

I took my dress off, climbed into my bed and wrapped my arms round him, reassuring him and holding him tight.

This wasn't me. I was behaving just like my mum had done. I was begging for his love. I wanted to run for safety, but at the same time I wanted to run into his arms.

* * *

I couldn't seem to help myself, and the more I realized that I was mimicking my mum, the more desperate and ashamed I felt, the more I did it. I had done everything I was so determined not to do. I had watched myself scream and cry, then go to him, just like my mum used to. It hurt so much to look back and see that a lot of my childhood dictated how I now behaved. I needed to change. Why hadn't I addressed this before? Why hadn't I realized?

When I had met that boyfriend, I had been guarded, but told myself I needed to let somebody in if I was going to have any hope of having my own family. I left that relationship after another six months, but all I could think was: *'Another failed relationship. You're worthless. You're unlovable.'* My inner critic blamed myself.

When I'd moved back from living in Singapore in my mid-20s, I'd started seeing a guy twice my age. He had whipped me with a towel and threw me around his bedroom as he tried to put his hands around my neck, only stopping when his six-year-old daughter ran in hearing my shouts. Ironically, I was much stronger than him and could easily have fought him off (I'd trained in boxing and Muay Thai), but at that moment, I only felt weak and ashamed.

None of this is about putting the blame on me. Those men were abusers and had their own problems – their actions were entirely their own responsibility, and everything they did they needed to be accountable for.

However, understanding my own 'trauma hotspots' and how they play out for me – strengthening my sense of self, my own healthy adult and how I care for myself – means I won't end up in these situations again. I know what I deserve and my own worth.

People that have had family trauma at a young age will likely play out this instability and feelings of rejection in relationships in adulthood. They tend to stay in relationships that are unsafe and unhealthy for far too long, and even try and 'fix' their partner to prove to themselves they can have a successful relationship. This is sadly how unprocessed trauma can actually create more pain from trauma. But it doesn't need to be like this.

ONE STEP AT A TIME

There was a lot I needed to cover in this chapter so remember that you don't need to try and tackle everything at once. Try to break it up into small, manageable pieces. First, focus on your own relationship and connection with yourself. This has to come first – your external relationships will change from this.

I found that once my relationship with myself became more connected and present, my emotionally healthy relationships got stronger and the unhealthy relationships started to drift away. It opened my eyes to certain people in my life that were not good for me, not just romantic partners but friends too. I made better decisions about who was and wasn't in my life.

7

Shame comes from trauma

'Shame.'

'Ashamed.'

Even writing these words feels like 'shame' is coming to haunt me; they bring on such a strong emotion, the words hold that much power. In this chapter we'll work though what shame is and why we need to talk about it as part of trauma.

Notice if you feel anything just from reading the word 'shame'. If you do, there's absolutely nothing to be concerned about – just acknowledge that you feel something. If it is bringing up certain feelings or reactions, it means you do need to read this chapter.

Be aware if you feel like you want to avoid it – that is a coping mechanism to protect us from feeling those uncomfortable feelings, but it also stops us from addressing them and growing through them. Remember: you can put this book down anytime and revisit it later. Or you can skip this chapter for now and come back to it when you feel ready.

THE MOST POWERFUL EMOTION

Shame is the most powerful, detrimental and destructive aspect of trauma. Shame is a dominant emotional response to our horrible past experiences, and is part of trauma.

Shame is so dominant in trauma that it's now recognized by the Diagnostic and Statistical Manual of Mental Disorders as having a central role in PTSD's causes and symptoms.

Dr Rachel describes shame as 'one of the big drivers. It keeps a lot of pain and unhealthy coping behaviours going. It makes us feel very, very small around other people. But shame is often so hidden, it can keep things very stuck. In some cases, victims hold the shame that should belong to their perpetrators. It can also stop people accessing therapy.'

The more I learnt about trauma, the more I realized I felt the emotion of shame a lot. Not just about my past but my present, too. It was the way I felt about myself and how I spoke about myself to others.

Shame comes from trauma, but then trauma creates more shame. It's a catch-22 situation, a vicious circle.

Shame also has links back to Chapter 6 on relationships. The way I spoke to myself and interacted with others constantly made me feel ashamed. I was ashamed of the things I'd gone through, ashamed of struggling with them and, for God's sake, I was ashamed of being ashamed, and – wait for it – yes, that only continued to give fire to my trauma. Shame basically keeps you in trauma.

In my campaigning work, I remember giving a keynote speech about child abuse and neglect to raise money for the child protection charity, the NSPCC (National Society for the Prevention of Cruelty to Children). The entire room gave me a standing ovation. Despite the praise, the caring support the NSPCC staff gave me and how many people came up to me afterward, I went back home and felt awful. I had a sinking feeling and a knotted pit in my stomach like I was a child that had done something naughty. I was so alert and on edge as if something bad was going to happen. I felt claustrophobic within myself and my thoughts were racing too fast for my head to keep a hold of. I was fidgety and could not calm myself down to be able to sleep. What I had spoken about had brought all my past feelings of being worthless to the surface. I felt ashamed of what I'd been through – as if it was my fault – ashamed of openly talking about it. Despite a completely opposing truth with evidence to back it up, I made up a false truth in my head that the audience was judging me; as if they thought there must be something wrong with me to have been through all those things – and most certainly something wrong with me now because of it. I felt humiliated and inadequate – not by the audience, who did nothing but commend and praise me (many even disclosed their own abuse to me), or by the NSPCC who I've spoken for many times since this – but by my own shame.

What I felt that night couldn't have been further from reality, but that's the thing about shame: it is the most powerful and dominant emotion out of the whole spectrum of our emotions. Shame can convince you of anything it wants to, despite what is actually real. When we feel shame, it is the 'master' emotion telling us we aren't good enough and something is wrong with us.

'Shame can show up with feelings and sensations of rejection, humiliation, a sense of feeling very alone and isolated, it's low self-esteem, it can feel like people are talking about you behind your back, feelings of inadequacy … it's like that pit in the bottom of your stomach, tight and sinking. Everything is your fault.'

Dr Rachel O'Beney

That's all shame, and it's deeply rooted. Horrible, right? Yes, it is!

A TRAUMA-INFORMED APPROACH

Clinical psychologist Dr Deborah Lee has focused a lot of her trauma research on shame and the role of self-criticism. She explains that 'high levels of self-criticism appear to maintain the sense of current psychological threat.' This self-criticism comes from shame. She has written many articles highlighting the need to look at shame and guilt in relation to trauma recovery, and not simplifying trauma with just the feeling of fear being the dominant emotion.

Shame is the key emotional after-effect of trauma from agonizing and horrible experiences. Academic literature is now increasingly arguing that we have 'failed to see the obvious' by neglecting to fully acknowledge the influence of shame in trauma.

A trauma-informed approach recognizes trauma as being at the heart of victims' and survivors' experiences. In settings such as the criminal justice system, education, community organizations and, in particular, healthcare (given that trauma is a major public health issue), this approach has been ground-breaking; it is something I have campaigned for individually and as part of the Ministry of Justice Victims' Panel.

The trauma-informed approach acknowledges a person's life experiences, and aims to create a safe space of trust, care and understanding for people with trauma. This is essential for a trauma survivor to heal; it's also key to the functioning of the criminal justice system when it involves victims of crime, whose testimony is often needed for a successful prosecution. If a victim's trauma is not taken into consideration, it can lead to retraumatizing a victim again and end up with the perpetrator walking free to commit further abuse.

However, the implementation of the trauma-informed approach is still lacking and, in many respects, so is the understanding of it. This is partly because the trauma-informed approach hasn't fully acknowledged the role of shame in trauma. In fact, shame has only recently (since 2015) been officially identified as part of trauma and the diagnostics of PTSD. Shame stops people from getting help and engaging with anyone let alone accessing the healthcare or the justice system.

Studies show that many of the aims of the trauma-informed approach are more effectively addressed through the practice of 'shame-sensitivity' – understanding that people with trauma are more susceptible to experiencing shame. Shame is behind a lot of the unhealthy emotional behaviours we discuss throughout this book; including the practice of shame-sensitivity would improve the effectiveness of trauma-informed care by approaching shame and trauma as deeply connected.

Acknowledging what a person's gone through only goes so far if there isn't a focus on understanding how their trauma affects them – such as being left with self-shame. Being trauma-informed should lead to acknowledgement and understanding.

SHAME VERSUS GUILT

So, we've established that shame is key in trauma work; but let's just make sure we understand what shame actually is.

Shame is not guilt. Both are powerful emotions, but have a different impact. Guilt is like a sister emotion to shame.

'Shame is an internal view of yourself as negative and worthless, whereas guilt is associated with an external action. Guilt can encourage positive change in future actions, but shame is self-punishment and torture. Shame serves no purpose and hinders growth.'

Dr Rachel O'Beney

Guilt is an awareness that you've done something that harmed others or goes against your beliefs. It has a sense of responsibility and accountability. It is in your consciousness, i.e. you are aware of your feelings of guilt.

Shame is internally focused. It triggers emotions of self-disgust and self-loathing, with the belief that you are an unworthy person who is flawed and not good enough at your core – irrespective of any specific external behaviour. Shame is the belief that your whole self is wrong, not your actions.

Guilt can be proactive, for example behaving in a not-particularly-nice way to someone may make you feel guilty. You know you shouldn't have spoken to that person in that manner, you know it hurt them, which means you apologize and it inspires action to not do it again or to think about why you are behaving that way to that person (you may not feel comfortable with them or may need to think about whether the relationship is toxic). Either way, it's external, based on an action, and you're well aware of it.

Guilt is really common in survivors of accidents or illness. After coming out of hospital, I continually questioned why I survived, and felt guilty about it. *'Why did I survive and other people didn't?'* I also felt guilty for what I'd put my family and friends through.

'Patients realize afterward that their families have been sitting by their bedside in agony the whole time, and were told by doctors that their loved one may not survive. Patients often feel guilty for what they put their families through. Patients also start to question their own mortality – more so in younger people – and they question why they survived. This can lead to feelings of guilt as to why they are alive.'

Dr Niki Snook

I nearly wasn't here anymore. I actually died, yet I'm still alive. It's a hard concept to get your head around, especially when you hear other stories of people who didn't survive. I met a mum several years after I'd come out of hospital at a Commonwealth Heads of Government meeting. Her son had died of malaria after he gave his anti-malarial tablets to a local child. He was a strong, fit rugby player in his 20s, and he died. I felt so guilty meeting his mum. I had survived and her son hadn't. I was standing in front of her, seemingly fine, and with a full life ahead of me, whereas her son had been taken from her. She said I brought her comfort because I told her I could sense my mum was with me when I was in a coma and I felt her love. This helped her feel assured her son knew she was there by his side and loved him.

Guilt made me feel sad that he died, but I understood what happened to him and others wasn't my fault or something I could control. But I also felt ashamed – not about what had happened to me, but why it had happened to me. I felt like awful experiences kept happening to me. Falling critically ill was just another horrific struggle and fight. My thoughts kept leading to *'It must be because there is something wrong with me. I'm not deserving of wonderful, amazing and lovely things happening to me.'*

People then started to tell me how lucky I was after I'd survived: 'You're so lucky to be here.' I know people meant well, but I can't begin to tell you how devastating I found this. I felt ashamed because I didn't feel lucky. In fact, I felt so unlucky. I felt like, *'Why did this happen to me?'* I didn't feel, *'Oh wow! I survived that. I'm so lucky.'* I felt like it had ruined my life, like I didn't know who I was anymore. I lost so much work, and felt like it had sent my career rolling down a hill. Bad thing after bad thing happened, and I felt it was all because somewhere deep inside I was inadequate and fundamentally flawed.

I felt so depressed. I felt like I couldn't fight anymore. For moments, I just didn't want to be here. I had so desperately wanted to live when I was fighting for my life, then to go through all that and just want it all to end is the most confusing feeling. I wanted to die after giving every part of myself to try and live. That in itself made me feel even more shame. How could I be so ungrateful and feel this way? I should be so happy. Not feeling happy or lucky – like everybody told me I should feel – only intensified my shame and isolated me in my feelings, in my trauma.

Shame is strongly linked to depression and anxiety disorders. It can take you down a route of self-destructive behaviours – self-blame, self-neglect, perfectionism – and can quite often link to suicidal thoughts and/or attempts. All of which impact your daily life and interpersonal relationships, and all of which were dominant for me.

HOW SHAME SHOWS UP IN TRAUMA

Shame can cause people with unprocessed trauma to struggle with relationships. If your trauma came from any kind of relationship or connection with someone, including family, it is linked to the emotion of shame.

Shame is notoriously connected with sexual abuse, domestic abuse/intimate partner abuse and child abuse/neglect, but it tends to dominate across the board in trauma: childbirth, divorce, illness, community violence, war, bullying, witnessing harm to another, even caregiving and first responders ... the aftermath of all of these can lead to feelings of shame and self-blame for what has happened to you or another person, or what you've been a part of. The pain from something terrible happening is a natural reaction, but when that pain is silenced it can very often turn into shame.

Shame is the thing that continues the abuse or mistreatment – but inside our heads, in whatever form that may look like – rather than externally. In abuse, shame is also how the abuser gets power over you; shame is an abuser's friend, because shame silences you.

Dr Rachel told me about the worst kind of situation she'd worked in: 'We see people who are refugees who have been tortured; we work through their lifeline (flowers and stones) and you hear what physically was done to people, and it is appalling. But the most powerful part of what's happened to them isn't the physical, it's the shaming. Speaking to refugees, the most damaging part of what's happened to them is the shaming. Shame is the most powerful part of any mistreatment or abuse.'

Shame is like a nasty little trick to keep you in a place of trauma. It keeps you in the past, cuts you off from friends and family who could help you, and can lead to crippling feelings of despair and hopelessness. It is very destructive.

'In abuse, shame ensures that the victim keeps their abuse secret. The person it's done to feels ashamed – but they shouldn't feel remotely ashamed. The abuser should be ashamed, but the shame gets misplaced and located in the wrong person. Shame can have a big impact, even in apparently small situations, such as being singled out as a child at school for being a slow reader, or as an adult offering an idea in a meeting that is ignored.'

Dr Rachel O'Beney

Even in what seem like small situations, shaming can have a big impact on our emotions and self-esteem.

Sadly, it's also the biggest reason why people don't reach out for help. Shame makes you feel undeserving; it blocks you from recovering, and even when you start to heal it can slow down the process. Even struggling to work through your trauma can create a cycle of shame. Why can't I get over this? Why am I still feeling like this? Shame, shame, shame. It is the underlying barrier to why a lot of people struggle to recover.

BEHAVIOURS ROOTED IN SHAME

Shame influences our behaviours and keeps us in the cycle of them. Shame fuels our harmful ways of coping in trauma – avoidance, emotional detachment, people-pleasing, self-soothing through alcohol/ drugs/food, aloofness, defensive, attacking, bullying – to put the shame elsewhere. We actually shame ourselves through self-talk: 'It's my fault', 'I'm an idiot', 'I'm worthless'. Shame is never helpful or useful. Remember, these behaviours are not our character or personality, they are the unhealthy (maladaptive) coping mechanisms that we've subconsciously taken on because of trauma and feelings of shame. They are all behaviours that can change with processing trauma. Dr Rachel gave a great example of how shame drives behaviour.

'If you think about gangs, or even groups, at school, you'll hear them say, "They dissed me/disrespected me". Then the person who has been "dissed" takes action and retaliates. Of course, they feel they need to – they aren't going to stand for being made to feel tiny. The retaliation is driven by shame; in psychology it's actually called "overcompensating" – reversing the shame on someone else so you don't have to feel it.'

Dr Rachel O'Beney

I've definitely been guilty of this myself, especially when I was younger and at school. It was a case of being the big, hard (wo)man or being the tiny picked-on prey. There was no in-between in my school. I was the tiny picked-on prey at home, but at school I could, for a brief moment, push the shame away by being the bird of prey, or at least the one that the bird of prey didn't eat. I was part of a group of girls that nobody messed with. It's hard sometimes to admit these kinds of behaviours, but if we don't admit to ourselves what we do, then how are we going to change it, and change the way we feel?

'It's not excusing that behaviour, but that is the cycle of violence. We see people who have been abused go on to abuse because they cannot stay feeling small, and they have to put the shame somewhere *else. Or people that have so much shame, they are worried that they'll become an abuser.'*

Dr Rachel O'Beney

I was also worried about repeating the cycle, so managed every bit of my behaviour while wracked with paranoia that I was a bad person.

It's not just shame entangled in what you've gone through, but shame can show up in the 'how to recover' aspect of trauma. It comes up in not wanting people to know what's happened to you. Or you may downplay it, and think that everybody else is okay or goes through these things too, so *'There must be something wrong with me that I can't cope,'* or *'I'm not good enough.'* Society doesn't help either; despite some great awareness work around mental health, asking for help still has connotations of shame – as if needing support to work through trauma is weak. None of these things are true, but they are often strongly felt. I've said it before and I'll say it again, surviving what you have been through means you're incredibly strong and courageous.

PAST SHAME FUELS PRESENT PAIN

I look back now and can't remember a time when I didn't feel a dull grey cloud of shame always with me. I think it's always been there, even from a very young age. My mum tried her best, but even that made me feel like I wasn't enough. We've joked about it since, but with an undertone of pain and sadness from both of us.

When I was a toddler, my mum used to make me spell everything out that we saw on our walks; she made me read signs, street names, posters, anything with writing on it, over and over again – which, theoretically, sounds like great parenting. I mean, I could spell pretty much anything that was thrown at me in primary school. I'd also read every Stephen King book by the time I was 10. My mum got called into school and was questioned about my choice of reading material. In classic mum fashion, she told the school that they needed to challenge me more as the books they were giving me were too easy. I don't want to give you the wrong impression – I definitely wasn't a child genius – I could only read like that because my mum was so desperately trying to make sure I was clever. She was so worried that I would be 'thick' because that's what she thought she was. She wanted me to be everything she wasn't, and told me so: 'Just don't be like me.' That's hard as a child when your whole world is your mum – and I'm her daughter, so what does that make me?

Through her efforts to 'better' me, I took on my mum's own shame and lack of self-worth. This got worse. My step-dad called both my mum and I 'stupid' for years and years, and, as you know, blamed me for his actions. So, when other things happened to me, I already felt I was not enough. When I was sexually abused, it tapped into my existing self-belief that I was to blame because I was inferior and worthless. This belief stopped me from telling anyone about what was happening to me. Why would I? It was my shame and my own lacking that made all these bad things happen to me. You can see how shame compounds everything, and the cycle of trauma and shame within continues, and as such the barrier to recovery grows.

The relationship between my mum and I is now the strongest it's ever been, because we have both done a lot of work on our trauma. My mum felt a crippling shame for everything that happened to me and for not always protecting me as a mother. Her own shame got in the way of our relationship. We never spoke about my childhood – she found it too painful to talk about how things had impacted me and how they made me feel, because my pain reflected hers and her own shame connected to my trauma.

When I came out of hospital, after falling critically ill, I felt like people thought I was an idiot for doing what I'd done, and that it was my fault I was in that situation. I had cycled 3,000 miles from London, England, to Rio, Brazil. And 24 hours after arriving in Rio, I was in hospital fighting for my life. The overpowering critic inside of me said, *'You're so stupid for even thinking that you could do a challenge like that and that everything would be okay,'* *'Bad things always happen to you – how could you think otherwise?',* *'How could you think that you were actually good enough to have something go well?',* and *'You're a failure, you always were and always will be.'* This voice carried on and on. I had achieved the challenge, become stronger as the ride progressed, and raised money for charity – but the fact I was ill overrode any sense of achievement. I was tormenting myself at a time when I needed to be doing quite the opposite. The underlying shame I already had from my earlier life just got stronger. It was a breeding ground for more shame.

As I've said, shame fuels our self-destructive coping behaviours – anything to take away that feeling in the pit of your stomach. It can lead to self-injury, risky behaviour, alcohol and substance misuse, binge eating or depriving yourself of food, spending money recklessly, avoidance, and really nasty self-talk; all of which fuel the cycle of shame and make you engage further with those self-destructive behaviours. You get the picture: it just carries on and carries on.

My mum wrote me a few letters as she sat at my bedside while I was in the coma. I read them afterward. It was really painful to think about what my mum had gone through; she suffered a lot in the aftermath of nearly losing her daughter, but it was something she wrote in the first letter that stopped me in my tracks.

Dear Charlotte,

I just needed to show what you looked like from our eyes. When you are better it is your time ... no need to prove yourself anymore. We all love you so much.

Very shocking when I arrived at the hospital ...

My mum talked about the medical insurance (that whole palaver is another book in itself), the doctors, and where she was staying because it was too dangerous to stay near the hospital in Rio. And then she continued with ...

... Picture of you in my head – please, you HAVE nothing to prove.
Please be with me.
I prayed and cried.

Mum
Xx

My mum was pleading with me to stop trying to prove my worth. It made me so sad, because reading that letter I realized that I'd spent so much of my life trying to prove my worth that even on my deathbed it was being brought up. I hold on to this letter and those moments, despite the grief and sadness they caused, because I don't want to forget that I deserve better than to live my life in shame because of what has happened to me in my past. I see surviving Rio like a second chance. I'm still alive, and I don't want to keep doing the same behaviours that stop me from being happy because I'm trying to run from my past pain. Once, it was the only way I knew how to cope, but now that I have survived all these things, I don't want to keep reliving them over and over again in my own trauma.

I came out of the hospital and, despite still learning how to walk again and my failed kidneys, I tried to get back into work. I'd lost a lot of work while hospitalized, and work was a source of worthiness and safety for me. So, to try and counter the critical voice in my head and the incredibly overwhelming feelings of shame and worthlessness, I pushed and pushed myself. Challenging myself to recover quicker – try harder, do better.

'If only I achieved more, I would be worthy.'

I did recover quicker than anybody expected; and not just quicker, but better than doctors ever thought I would. My prognosis was death or, if I did survive, severe mental and physical disabilities. Even when I pushed through, the doctors still said that I wouldn't be able to live my life like before. I powered through, got stronger and made a miraculous recovery.

For moments, the sense of achievement countered the shame – but only for a fleeting minute did I feel that sense of worthiness. Then it vanished. It was all surface level, because underneath I was driven by the shame I felt, by trying to prove my worth all the time and would beat myself up over and over again. It was all under a very thin layer, because at that point all of my trauma was sitting just underneath the surface. I really wasn't okay. Fighting to keep my trauma below the surface was becoming beyond exhausting and overwhelming. I'd survived what happened to me in Rio physically, but I was still in that heightened state of fighting to survive. Every moment in every day became a battle in my own head.

SHAME AND PERFECTIONISM

To the outside world, it often looked like I was doing really well, especially with my detached protector way of coping. But it was also because of a more subtle behaviour of shame: perfectionism.

Perfectionism and over-achieving are very good disguises and less obvious signs of trauma and shame than destructive behaviours. As we discussed in Chapter 3, with perfectionism whatever you do it is never good enough.

The cycle goes like this: shame drives perfectionism, perfectionism gives power to shame, feelings of worthlessness grow so you strive to even higher standards, which set you up to fail – and you are back to square one: shame. And the cycle starts again.

If you have this behaviour of unrelenting standards, then you'll be convinced that you must work constantly to try to meet your own very high standards to avoid criticism from yourself and others.

Perfectionism is an addictive thought pattern that makes you think you can avoid shame by doing everything perfectly. Its root is fear, and it is a coping response to shame and to trauma. You try to do everything perfectly to protect yourself from feeling pain and hurt from shame; but it doesn't work. In fact, in trying to protect yourself, you end up causing yourself more pain and suffer neglect from what you actually need.

Perfectionism was the only way I knew, and the only me I knew, so it was understandably scary to make these changes – even when they were for the better. Losing my shame and gaining self-worth meant I could reach forward steadily believing in myself and what I was doing, not running toward it because I was trying to prove my worth.

SELF-WORTH TO COMBAT SHAME

Self-worth is the opposite of shame. It's important to recognize feelings of shame, and from there focus on building your worth. This is all part of recovering from trauma. Recognizing everything you are working through will mean you'll become far more aware of your thinking, your ways of coping that keep you in your trauma, and the way you talk and feel about yourself. None of this is your fault – it is all just a normal response to trauma and what we do when we leave trauma to fester. You have done nothing wrong.

Take a moment to think about why you do self-destructive things; it is because what you've been through has made you feel very vulnerable. Remind yourself that you're safe. Take your time in your feelings, rather than pushing them away, and reassure yourself. Even if you do push them away, unless you consciously allow yourself to feel them, they will remain and grow more dominant.

I found it quite hard to identify what 'reassure myself' looked like. So I started to learn a few key phrases to say to myself: *'You're okay'*, *'You're in control'*, *'You are safe'*. They may sound simple, but this is what you would say to a child that was vulnerable, upset and in pain, which is ultimately what's happening inside of you.

SELF-COMPASSION TO COMBAT SHAME

Shame can't exist in self-compassion. Self-compassion is forgiving, caring and safe – shame isn't. I had to learn how to be compassionate to myself.

Everything has a knock-on effect – if we develop and practise self-compassion, it reduces feelings of shame; if we reduce shame, we build our self-worth; and increased self-worth strengthens our voice in our head to talk to ourselves as a healthy nurturing parent would to their child.

The sad thing for those of us who didn't have somebody to reassure us when awful things happened to us, is that if we had had that, it would have made all the difference.

'If something awful happens to someone, and their family/friends straight away tell them that this had absolutely nothing to do with them, that it is not their fault, then the shame doesn't get lodged in. Those words protect you, and give utter in-the-moment reassurance. The actual act of what physically happened is far less important than the response to what happened. The response is what causes shame – and the response is what can also stop shame in its tracks.'

Dr Rachel O'Beney

If you're supported straight away, and told it's not because of you, it wasn't your fault and are surrounded with love, care and reassurance, shame may not even come into play. If it does, then it dissipates quickly because shame can't survive with compassion and empathy. Compassion and empathy are shame's Kryptonite – they zap all of its energy so it can't survive.

There are many of us who didn't have this kind of support, but we can give it to ourselves now; and by sharing and opening up, we can get support from others, too. When we've been made to feel small and frightened, we go into unhealthy harmful ways of coping so we don't have to feel like that again, and do everything to protect ourselves. But if we can, just for a moment, go back to those feelings and give ourselves the care we never had at the time of our experiences, then we can show ourselves that we are now safe.

Imagine what we could prevent if we had a society that understood shame, and a system that reflected that. A lot of trauma could be prevented if we acted immediately after a distressing experience and gave victims immediate support and help with the clear messaging it wasn't their fault. You are worthy and enough, no matter what your story is.

Everything in this book moving forward will work on reducing this harmful feeling of shame.

THE PAINFUL PROCESS OF OPENING UP

It's so very difficult to open up. We tend to internalize our feelings, and that can bring about feelings of shame. It's common for people who feel shame to suppress their emotions with the immediate instinct to shut them down, ignore them and push them away.

To work past shame, we are going to start slow. For the moment, just try to begin to be conscious of what it is you do when your emotions come to the surface. Emotions are powerful and they demand to be felt, which is why when things are left to fester and feelings of pain, hurt and shame are hidden and unprocessed, they get bigger and more intense.

I wanted to reach out for help so many times, but something inside of me fought against it. I wanted somebody to notice that I needed help for the longest time, but I was too ashamed and too guarded to reach out.

If you think back to your flowers and stones lifeline (see page 92), this is the opposite of shame. Our lifeline helps connect us and create closeness to our story. I know it's painful, I really do, but it's in the connection with what's happened to us that we can reduce the feelings of shame and isolation that are so commonly associated with trauma.

Leaving our story in the dark signals to our subconscious that it's something that should remain hidden. Even though our stories may be painful and traumatic, they are still part of us. By hiding them and disconnecting from them, we are hiding a part of us and showing ourselves that it's something we should be ashamed of. How, then, can we move on and recover?

TECHNIQUES TO FIND SELF-WORTH AND MOVE PAST SHAME

Go back to the Emotionally Healthy Messages connection card you made in Chapter 6 and read your encouraging messages.

Think about the grounding exercises we've discussed and the reminders that you're in the present.

Grounding is particularly helpful for managing and reducing feelings of shame because shame is very much internal. Shame involves getting lost in past feelings and memories with your inner critical voice, which causes disconnection from the present moment. Grounding techniques help you connect with what's around you, your reality and the present moment. By helping you be in the present, they stop you from getting lost in those intrusive thoughts and overwhelming feelings of unworthiness. Grounding interrupts the cycle of deep self-critical thought and, quite frankly, takes you out of your head and gives you a bit of a breather from your shame-inducing thoughts.

Using your senses

When we are in trauma, we feel it through all of our five senses. When I have memories or flashbacks that make me momentarily relive some of the things that have happened to me, they're experienced not just through thought but through my senses, like taste, smell and touch.

For example, even now when I'm around strong air conditioning, it immediately takes me back to lying in the hospital bed; the memory is triggered with such force that I feel the physical sensations of the tubes and a closing in my throat.

Similarly, if I'm lying down on something that's not a bed, like a massage table, I get a grip of fear and claustrophobia and all I can smell is baby oil. I was sexually abused on a classroom table, and there was always baby oil. This painful memory immediately evokes feelings of shame and critical feelings and thoughts toward myself.

But if we can discover smells and sensations that make us feel safe, we can use them to help bring us into the present and safety, and to reduce the feelings of shame linked to the past. I use lavender as my safe smell because it has calming properties. It was recommended by Dr Rachel as I couldn't particularly think of a smell that I found comforting at the time. She gave me a bag of dried lavender that I would place near me. To be honest, at the time I thought, 'How is a bit of potpourri going to help me?' Well, it did.

Smell also helped me with nightmares. Trauma really comes out in nightmares for me. I struggled with nightmares as a child, and they became ever-present as an adult. I put the lavender by my bed at night, and whenever I woke up from a nightmare, I would grab the lavender pouch and smell it – I'd literally shove it straight up my nostrils. The smell soon became a prompt for my brain that I was okay and safe, and it helped me come out of the feeling of my nightmare much quicker. I could even fall back to sleep peacefully. My nightmares used to be so vivid and overpowering that I would physically respond: my pyjamas and sheets would be soaked with sweat, I'd have palpitations, and the feeling of the nightmare would stay with me all day. Smelling the lavender would help decrease the strength and length of these feelings by simply telling my brain that I was in the present and safe. The lavender also triggered memories and feelings of my time with Dr Rachel – feelings of care, reassurance and self-worth.

Another smell that is good for grounding is frankincense – it's said to have a calming effect on the nervous system. The other aroma I like is lime, or something citrusy like lemongrass. Lime is said to encourage emotional honesty and balance, and is good for grief. Recently, I've started using juniper, also known for reducing emotional stress; it has a very woody smell, like pine, which makes me feel like I'm outside in nature – a happy place for me.

These seemingly small acts, such as smelling lavender or juniper for comfort, are acts of self-compassion, and the exact opposite to shame. The more we can do these little things for ourselves, the more we counter the nasty self-judgement and inner critic that powers shame.

These techniques aren't just to enable us to cope in the moment; over time, they can actually help our brain learn new patterns and how to give ourselves more self-compassion. Most importantly, they will tell our brain that we are allowed to be self-compassionate because we are enough.

Little actions like saying to yourself, 'I'm safe,' reading the connection card of emotionally healthy messages, wrapping a blanket round your shoulders or inhaling a comforting smell, are all acts of self-compassion, of showing yourself you are worth care. Self-compassion creates new pathways and behaviours that directly oppose the self-destructive behaviours of trauma.

SENSORY SUPPORT TECHNIQUE

This is a powerful and helpful grounding technique that uses your sense of smell.

Smell is particularly good for grounding because the area of our brain that processes smell is also the area of the brain that processes emotions and memories. Smell goes directly to the limbic system, the place of survival and our fight-or-flight response to how we react to fear.

- Choose a smell that is positive for you, that brings comfort and nice feelings to you. (Remember, smell can also bring about bad memories).
- Make sure you can carry it with you whenever you need it. For example, as well as the bag of dried lavender I had a little bottle of lavender oil that I kept with me.
- When you breathe in the smell, really notice what it smells like. Say to yourself some of the positive phrases you put on your Emotionally Healthy Messages connection card, or simply say what you're doing: *'I'm smelling lavender. I'm okay. I'm in the present and I'm safe.'*

This technique worked well for me, and I still use it when certain feelings, like shame, become overpowering. It's something I can easily do and not have to think too much about it. It works well for organized, hyper-vigilant people, like me. But everyone's different, and using smell might not be as helpful for you as some of the other techniques we've covered. It's important to try different things to find which one resonates most with you.

You might find yourself thinking, 'How's that going to work or change things for me when I'm feeling this bad?' Well, you won't know unless you try it. Be mindful of that crafty inner critical voice creating a false narrative that stops you from recovering: 'Smelling something is stupid. It's just some airy-fairy crap.' Just ensure that it's not that voice stopping you from giving it a go.

REMINDERS BEFORE WE MOVE ON

Before stepping into the next section of this book, here are a few reminders from Part I that I would like you to take into Part II.

- Identify and acknowledge where and what your trauma stems from.
- Trauma responses and feelings are normal when something 'traumatic' happens to us. These feelings can and do change when you process your emotions and memories.
- Recognize the behaviours and protective coping mechanisms you might do that are driven by feelings of shame, vulnerability and a lack of self-worth. These behaviours are patterns that think they are protecting you from further pain. Remember they are maladaptive (harmful) – they helped you cope in the moment of the traumatic experience, but don't serve you now. You can change these.
- Think about your story. Connect with your flowers and stones lifeline. Be compassionate and understanding of what you've been through.
- Remember, trauma impacts the way we see ourselves and others.
- Rather than fight your critical voice, observe it from a distance. Acknowledge that this emotional beating doesn't help you, it

will only make you feel worse and keep you down. Instead, focus on reinforcing caring and helpful messages to yourself, rather than nasty and punishing ones. Think of healthier and more compassionate responses to yourself. Find the evidence to show that your inner critic is telling you something false.

- Remember, trauma isolates us and stops connection, which is the very thing we need to heal.
- Shame is never helpful – it leads to self-destructive behaviours.
- No matter what you've been through, you can – and deserve to – recover from it.

PART II

Trauma in our lives

From the first part of this book we've got a good understanding of trauma. We've seen how and why trauma affects the way we behave, and looked at how to recognize it.

In Part II we will focus on what starts to happen as we begin to process our trauma and start to make sense of it all. Each chapter provides a deeper understanding of trauma and, gradually, you will see how it all connects in our experiences of trauma.

By the way, well done for getting to this part of the book! Just by acknowledging your trauma and recognizing how it impacts you, is part of processing it. Remember, there's no timeline to this and it's not about getting to a place where what has happened to you has no relevance in your life. Such a place doesn't exist, and the belief that it does is part of shame and your inner critic keeping you in trauma by trying to shut it all out. Your experiences will always have relevance because it is part of your story, but please don't see that as a bad thing.

Processing trauma is about getting to a place where your past story – those frightening moments and experiences – don't dominate your feelings or the way you behave now. It's still your story, but you are in control of it, you can understand how it affects you and, with that, know what you need.

Believe me, you are amazing to get to where you are, and brave and strong for reading this book.

As we start to work through trauma, we will connect with what we were feeling at the time of our traumatic experience(s) and what we are now left feeling – so things can feel worse as we process. This doesn't mean we are doing worse. We are allowing those hidden feelings to come out. We need to care for and allow those feelings to, well, 'feel'. Dr Rachel describes it as 'attending to' the feelings.

'Once we start opening up, and the protection comes down, we start feeling really frightened, as we aren't so dissociated and detached (protected from our feelings); the feelings can feel more intense than when we actually went through the awful experience.'

Dr Rachel O'Beney

Be mindful of this intensity. This is what working through trauma is. You will feel it, and that is what we want. Trauma is getting stuck in those feelings because they weren't felt and worked through at the time of the traumatic experience. When the guard starts to come down, the feelings will come in. How you feel deserves to be heard. You can do this. Stick with it.

8

Attending to emotions and feelings

Why are emotions so important? It might seem like a simple question but, even in general, people struggle to name their emotions, let alone manage them.

Trauma leaves us with overwhelming, big, fat, powerful and painful emotions. Shame, sadness, despair (feeling no hope), anger, disgust, fear, contempt (feeling of worthlessness), hurt. No wonder we want to avoid them. They are upsetting and can overwhelm us when they feel far too much to cope with.

FEELING OUR EMOTIONS

The way we feel stems from our emotions. This might seem obvious, but bear with me. Feelings are experienced consciously, so we know what we are feeling; emotions, however, can manifest themselves subconsciously. We can have an emotion but not actually realize it's there or understand it.

For example, we may have the emotion of shame but not recognize we feel shame; instead, we may feel anger. Shame comes out and manifests in other ways. Shame may present itself as feeling inadequate and sad, but we may not understand that those feelings come from the emotion of shame. Certain feelings can mask harder underlying emotions.

As I progressed through my therapy with Dr Rachel, I started to feel 'emotional' about my emotions. Because I'd previously numbed my emotions, I wasn't used to feeling so much, so it was making me overwhelmed. Dr Rachel reassured me by explaining that emotions are important because they define humanity.

Dr Rachel told me a story about a boy soldier she once worked with. What he had been through, in her words, was 'hideous'. Dr Rachel said he was so full of feelings he was totally overwhelmed by them. As a soldier, he must have had to completely disconnect and detach from anything he was feeling to survive and do the things that a boy soldier is made to do. Dr Rachel said he was really worried about his inhumanity – but actually, being so full of feelings was a sign of his humanity: love, compassion and empathy for our own kind.

Emotions define humanity.

What a refreshing way to look at all the feelings and emotions we have had in our lives so far. The all-consuming feelings of grief I'm sure we've all felt at some point in our lives mean we have humanity. When I was in a coma, the excruciating emotional pain I felt wasn't because of me, it was because of my love for my mum, my brothers, friends and family, and the thought of hurting my mum was what caused me the most suffering.

'You are not a robot, you are a human being that can interact with another human being. Relationships are about connection and that involves feelings and deep emotions.'

Dr Rachel O'Beney

We need to feel our emotions to be able to connect with others; but when you've experienced a lot of awful things and are left with trauma, our emotions can be far too powerful and painful to feel. As we have learnt, this leads us to protect ourselves from them – from both expressing and feeling emotions. This is known as the 'blunted affect', where everything is just a bit flat. This is, without realizing it, how I survived for a lot of my life. Many of us are afraid of our emotions because they feel so overwhelming at times. It becomes our imprint, our pattern, of how we then carry on dealing with our feelings. That's how so many of us come to feel numb over time from painful things that have happened to us. It's a form of survival – the 'freeze' survival mechanism – to protect our brains from the overload of big emotions.

ANGER'S DISGUISE AND THE EMOTIONS IT HIDES

I want to focus on anger because the emotion of anger is important in itself, and because it can help us understand what other emotions we are often feeling because of our trauma. Anger can be deceptive – it can conceal deeper and more uncomfortable emotions that we are really feeling. Anger can be a protective mechanism in itself – from sadness, embarrassment, shame, hurt and fear. For those that have experienced violence as part of their trauma, anger can be problematic and bring about negative connotations.

'It's quite difficult for people who have experienced violence at home to be able to be angry. They will link the very normal emotion of anger to danger, violence, to how they've experienced anger in their past. For them, being angry is not as straightforward as it may be for others, because of the early template that anger means something bad.'

Dr Rachel O'Beney

I used to struggle to recognize when I felt angry. I was asked in my therapy group to think of a situation where I felt angry, and I couldn't think of one.

***

I flippantly answer, 'I don't feel anger.' I'm not being obnoxious, I genuinely feel like I don't. Dr Rachel presses me, and asks me again if I'd noticed any feelings of anger during the week.

'Not really, no.'

I start to waffle about a 10k race that my friend and I had done; how the race had started late and that the course wasn't laid out properly and everybody ran the wrong way. It's quite funny looking back now, but at the time everybody was really frustrated.

'My friend was angry, but I wasn't. I just wanted to get on with it and I wanted to make my friend feel better.'

'Did you notice your own feeling of anger about how badly organized the race was?'

'No. I just wanted to make the most of it.' I repeat. Dr Rachel says, 'Charlie, it is important that you look at what you felt. Did you notice your own anger?'

'No, I didn't feel angry. I just wanted my friend to feel okay. I was a bit annoyed, like everyone else, but not angry.'

***

This is quite a trivial example, but it's a good illustration of how I would skip past feeling an emotion and go straight to action. That might sound super-productive, however it means the solution might not always be the right one because you don't know what it is you're actually feeling. And, if you don't know what you're feeling, it's hard to figure out what you need to help yourself.

My fight-or-flight survival system was always turned on to the max, which meant that no emotion mattered, it was just about survival. This would be great if I was in danger every day, but not so great if I'm responding as if I'm in danger from everything and everyone every day, when I'm actually safe. Remember the guard dog analogy from earlier in the book?

The group session carried on, focusing on the emotion of anger. Something was making me feel uncomfortable but I couldn't quite pin down what it was.

***

Scenes, one frame at a time, begin to flash through my mind of multiple memories from my past, as if they were being fast-forwarded, then paused, then put on rewind erratically. I am paralysed, listening to shouting and screaming in my head, but my foot is tapping away, and my leg is shaking up and down. I am squeezing my leg muscles into a cramp. My chest is rising and falling quickly, but staying in the same place with nowhere for my breath to go. My jaw is clamped tight shut, and my teeth nip at my cheeks. I want to run from the room.

I know that if I leave, I'll feel ashamed and beat myself up for not being able to deal with something so trivial. I know that feeling would be worse than staying, so I make myself stay put.

Rachel asks, 'Charlie, can you tell us what you are feeling right now?'

'I don't know. I just don't want to do this anymore. I want to leave.'

'Okay. Why do you think you feel like that?'

'I don't know.'

'Are you angry at me for making you do this? You can say if you are.'

'No.' I pause. 'I don't know. Maybe? No. I'm not angry. I just feel really uncomfortable.'

'Charlie you're having a fight-or-flight response, a panic attack. There is nothing in here though that is unsafe or making you feel bad. It's coming from inside you. What is your critic saying to yourself?'

***

It turned out it was the discussion about anger that was causing me to react in this way. Anger is an emotion that to me meant violence and being bad. I thought if I showed any anger, or even felt it, it would mean I was a bad person. I was brought up with violence in the home for as long as I can remember, and some outside the home in my community environment as well. There was a lot of physical and scary anger in my upbringing. I had trained myself to never feel anger to the point that I now had an absolute lack of ability to recognize when I felt it. My emotion of anger was masked by other feelings.

***

'I just feel really uncomfortable and bad.'

'Charlie, that's because all anger meant to you as a child was danger. Anger is a normal human emotion. The feeling of anger is normal, and we all have it. The feeling isn't bad. It is bad behaviour that is bad, not the feeling of anger. Feelings and emotions have no morals; behaviour does.'

***

The fact that I never let myself feel angry meant the emotion of anger that I actually felt inside came out in other ways. I got frustrated a lot, which I found very hard to control, but I didn't ever identify my anger around this. I would feel very sad and low, because this was safer for me than anger. I was scared of anger, and I was terrified of showing it. I thought if I was angry it made me a bad person. It goes back to the fear of becoming an abusive person because that was the behaviour modelled to me from a young age. Because of this, it was much more comfortable for me to be the person being hurt than the person hurting someone.

In reality, I was actually so angry about everything. I was angry about what had happened to me. I was angry at the people in my life who had hurt me. I was angry at myself for not helping myself. I was so angry, but I had never allowed myself to be angry, or given myself the time and space to actually work out what I was really feeling, because I never felt safe enough to allow it.

Anger as protection

Anger can also work in the opposite way. For some people, anger can feel a safer and less-painful way to react as a distraction from their real emotion. Anger can mask sadness, shame (feelings of inadequacy and powerlessness), abandonment and isolation. Anger protects us from feeling vulnerable, and that angry place can feel a better place to be than the vulnerable one. Anger can give a sense of power and control; it can be seen as 'stronger' in a society that often labels the vulnerable as 'weak'. And to be seen and known as an angry person rather than a scared person can make you feel less vulnerable.

Some people think they are angry all the time, but underneath the anger they are actually very sad and scared. But, for some people, feeling sad can feel far more scary and distressing than feeling angry.

'Emotions are often mislabelled. For some people, it's much easier to be angry, rather than sad – they don't want to feel small or ashamed. It's much easier to say, "I'm going to knock ten bells out of you," but

*really the person actually feels very frightened. It's simple and basic,
yet so complicated.'*

Dr Rachel O'Beney

There was a member of my therapy group who displayed their anger
in quite an aggressive way. Their anger was a protective mechanism.
This person was really frightened of exploring a particular exercise
in the psychoeducation work we were doing in the group. Getting
angry and disrupting the session meant they avoided having to do the
exercise they were ultimately scared of doing because it made them
feel vulnerable. This is the 'angry protector' that comes in and tries to
protect us from what it thinks will hurt us. As we are learning, trauma
makes us hypersensitive so that we feel the need to protect ourselves
from everything. The group member's anger was preventing them from
getting help and recovering from their trauma.

If you're noticing anger as something that is a dominant feeling for
you, try and look underneath it. It may feel extremely exposing and
hard to look at, but have a peak at what is really going on for you. What
is the emotion within you that is causing your anger?

Anger and trauma are intensely intertwined. Regardless of where
your trauma comes from, it creates a feeling of, 'Why did this happen to
me? If only I'd have done something different.' Trauma creates a broken
trust, whether with another person or with the world in general. It's very
hard for us to accept that horrible things can happen to any of us, so
if we create the idea that we are partly to blame then, at least in our
head, we can justify that thing happening to us. Or to someone else.
We see this a lot in victim-blaming within community violence, sexual
abuse and domestic abuse. It's a form of self-protection and a normal
instinct we all have.

It makes sense that we would feel a lot of anger. Anger is an emotion
that we all have; it arises in situations where we feel threatened,
attacked, frustrated and powerless. If we have past trauma, we can

feel like this in situations where we are not under threat, but which we are uncomfortable in. Anger can actually help us get through these moments of difficulty in our lives – it can give us strength and can drive us to carry on.

Anger is also a sign that you aren't okay with the way things are. There are times when I've felt so angry about some of the injustices in my own life and the lives of others that I've been able to actually use my anger for good. I've persistently pushed for policy and law changes, all driven by my own anger and pain. We can turn our anger into action and positive change, whether that is a change in our own lives or in our communities.

To be able to harness these emotions, we have to be able to understand what it is that we are feeling in the first place, and the only way we can do that is by really feeling them. And that is everything trauma isn't – denying our emotions is everything that trauma is.

ALL EMOTIONS ARE VALID

I want to emphasize again that emotions aren't good or bad, they don't have any morals attached to them. It's what we do with the emotion that matters. You'll notice I don't use the words positive or negative emotion either – there is no such thing. There can be a behaviour that has a negative consequence from an emotion but it's not the emotion that is negative.

My anger wasn't negative; it was a consequence of what I've been through and actually helped me survive and, even more so, create change. I would never have had the fight or energy to do certain things if I didn't feel angry and hurt by the injustice.

I've read so much literature that defines our emotions as positive or negative. This is so unhelpful when working through trauma. When I feel sad it's not negative, it's because I've been hurt – so it makes sense that I'm sad. Being sad tells me I need comfort and compassion, and it might be telling me that I need to change something in my life. All our emotions are helpful and for a reason.

RECOGNIZING AND PROCESSING EMOTIONS

It is very hard to recognize our emotions in trauma because of the coping mechanisms we use to make our feelings go away. Sometimes we are so successful that we actually make *all* our feelings go away, not just the painful ones but all of them, and we feel numb. The emotions are still there inside though.

Remember, emotions need to be acknowledged, felt and validated. The more you try to make them go away the more they will knock to be heard; the more they knock, the more our emotionally unhealthy ways of coping set in to get rid of our feelings; and the more we use those coping mechanisms (like avoiding or detaching), the harder and louder your emotions will knock.

Keeping all those big feelings that come with trauma locked away sounds good, right? Who wants to feel hurt? But keeping your emotions at bay actually keeps all feelings away, including the ones that help us get better.

Avoiding your emotions can make you feel withdrawn, spacey, distracted, empty, aloof and pessimistic toward investing any time in people or doing anything. As such, people will find it harder to connect with and be around you. So, not so good after all. The coping mechanisms may feel like they protect you, but they do quite the opposite – they limit your life.

The coping mechanisms we use, such as when we detach from our emotions or avoid them, are only meant to be used in an emergency situation: when it is very unsafe and something is happening that is so distressing, detaching from our feelings helps.

I did this a lot when I was being abused. It's our basic fight-or-flight survival mechanism. But then when I got older and was away from my abuse, I was still detached from my emotions in my daily life, because I still felt that pain from my past. And that is what trauma is.

The only way to get rid of the pain was to actually feel it, acknowledge it and grieve for what had happened to me. I needed to comfort the pain I was in, but how could I do that when I wouldn't allow the pain to come out to receive that comfort?

I know I've said this already but, as we get a greater understanding of trauma, I want to keep reminding you that processing trauma is reprocessing the pain, but in safety. To process trauma we need to access and understand our emotions, and only then can we recover from trauma.

COPING MECHANISMS TO STIFLE EMOTIONS

Detaching from my emotions was my main way of coping. This is very common and, even though consciously you may not be feeling much, subconsciously you're feeling absolutely crushed. There is a huge separation in yourself. The inside is in desperate need of help, and the outside is in isolation. The outside is numb, and the inside is full of uncared-for emotions, which grow bigger and bigger the longer they are left uncared for.

Detached ways of coping show up by not really feeling anything, a state of numbness, not caring, withdrawal, emptiness, a loss of sense of identity – you may even feel like you are observing yourself from the outside. Avoidance can show up similarly, but tends to involve withdrawing from situations that might bring on uncomfortable feelings, such as social situations and relationships.

We can also avoid our emotions by complying to what other people want. This can look like passive, people-pleasing and self-defeating behaviour.

My way of coping went something like this:

I emotionally detach myself when I feel anxious and vulnerable. I comply and agree to what people want me to do so that I receive their approval and feel worth something. I avoid things when I feel like I'm going to be hurt and I'm scared. It's how I keep myself safe.

Or, so I thought.

However, I now realize that I would also use the over-compensating coping mechanism, which can come out as anger, dominance, control and perfectionism, and the need for others' attention and approval.

I would try and over-control my life, because if I controlled it all down to a tee then I could stop any feelings of danger and vulnerability coming in. But, as it's impossible to control everything, trying to control the uncontrollable just leads to more anxiety, which leads to more controlling behaviour, and more anxiety, and so on.

These are all ways of coping developed from the need to protect ourselves, and using these mechanisms makes it very hard for us to identify what we are feeling and allow ourselves to feel it.

HOW TO IDENTIFY HOW YOU REALLY FEEL

A good way to recognize how you are feeling is to look at your physical response. Emotions change the way our body feels. With anger, your muscles tense, your heart rate speeds up, breathing is quick and high in your chest, you can feel a rush of energy that makes you feel on edge. These are all cues to tell us what is really going on underneath the surface.

Our emotions can also show up in our behaviour. Anger can cause you to get into fights easily, snap and be short-tempered at what may seem like small things; all of which can lead to difficulties with other people.

Anger is not just the stereotypical rage at someone else either. Anger can be projected inwardly, and show up as self-harm and self-injury. Your strong critical voice makes you think bad things about yourself, makes you avoid what makes you feel happy, and makes you deny yourself things like food and sleep.

Recognizing your anger can be a way to start acknowledging what has happened to you and understand you're dealing with trauma. When you feel anger, show yourself that it is okay and normal to get angry. Validating your anger is important. Tell yourself, 'Of course you're angry. That happened to you.'

When anger is really intense and overwhelming, with adrenaline pumping through the body, in the moment it can often be hard to think clearly. In these situations, the validation can come later. Over time, you may come to be able to recognize feelings of anger earlier.

Remember that in trauma your strong feelings tend to be related to the past, possibly from a very long time ago. Often, the present situation is just a trigger (we'll discuss triggers in the following chapter).

IDENTIFY HOW YOU ARE FEELING

When processing my trauma, I asked myself a series of questions to help me identify what I was feeling.

- How am I reacting/behaving?
- What's going on in my body?
- What am I thinking?
- What are my thoughts making me feel?
- What emotion is that?
- Why am I feeling like that?
- What do I need to do right now?

All these questions would lead me to the question: what is it I need at this moment?

And be able to answer it.

Get a paper or electronic notebook and have a go at answering these questions for yourself. Even if you can't answer the questions initially, or only answer some of them, this is the start of becoming more in tune with yourself, understanding what you're feeling and why you are behaving the way you are.

The more you start to do this, the more you will change the pathways in your brain from trauma to safety and have the ability to regulate your emotions. This will automatically change your behaviour, as our emotions drive our behaviour.

***

I'm sitting at my desk asking myself these questions because I'm feeling really low. I'm theoretically okay at this very moment. I'm at home, I'm safe, I have friends and family I can call on, but I just feel really depressed. It hasn't been long since I came out of hospital and got back into my life – or, more like discovering what this new life looks like.

After asking myself these questions, I figure out that I feel confused about what has happened to me. I have just nearly died. I've fought so hard to survive and to find some normality in who I am now. I feel very different, even physically I don't feel the same or recognize my own body. I've lost all my muscle tone, my hair's falling out and I have vertigo that causes me to fall over. Despite all the painful things that have already happened to me, I've always been able to rely on my physical strength. It's probably no coincidence that I've made sure I'm always physically fit and strong. I feel totally alone, like no one can relate or understand what I'm going through.

***

Recognizing these feelings and emotions didn't change my situation, but it did help me to be understanding of myself and of what I was feeling. It helped me to think about what I needed to help myself. Rather than beating myself up for feeling that way, I thought, '*It makes sense to feel like this. I'm feeling the pain and distress that I've just been through.*'

Let's look at an example of how these questions might play out. I've given multiple answers to help demonstrate, including my own answers.

How am I reacting/behaving?
Snapping at people. Pushing people away. Causing arguments. Isolating myself.

What's going on in my body?
I'm fidgeting. I have a rush of adrenaline. I'm gritting my teeth. I'm breathing faster and feel a tightness in my chest.

What am I thinking?
Everything is against me. Why always me? Why did that happen to me? Everyone else seems to have it easy. People are against me: they're going to hurt me, they're going to let me down, they don't care about me.

What are my thoughts making me feel?
Frustrated, impatient, annoyed, claustrophobic, overwhelmed, unsafe, impulsive, worthless. Shame.

What emotion is that?

I'm angry. It's anger. But I'm also really sad.

As we've discussed, getting to the bottom of the emotion can then bring up other feelings. Anger and vulnerability are different emotional states that can switch to try and cope with each other. When we are feeling sad, lonely and lost, anger can come in to try and help deal with the pain and push away the sadness. And vice versa.

Why am I feeling like that?

Because I'm struggling with the way falling critically ill has left me feeling about myself and life.

This is very personal to you, so have a think about what is driving your emotions. You may think, 'Well, I don't know. Nothing has happened today, I just feel like this,' or, 'I feel like this all the time.' That's understandable because these feelings in trauma come from the past.

What do I need to do right now?

Well, if I knew that, I wouldn't be feeling like this in the first place, would I?

It's totally normal to think this, by the way. This is very difficult to answer for people in trauma. I quite often wanted to 'attack' this question, as if it was a stupid question to ask. After I'd finished being annoyed at the question (which was quite a good indicator that I was angry), I started to take some time to try and help myself. I concocted a series of questions to help me work out what I needed:

- Do I need to speak to a family member or friend?
- What about going outside for a walk?
- What about going for a run?

- Should I go through my connection cards and give myself emotionally healthy messages? Remember, these don't mean being positive and pretending I am okay, they are about being compassionate, caring and constructive.
- Do I need to give myself a break – perhaps read a book or watch a film?
- Should I cuddle up in a blanket or with my Rabby?
- Should I rest if I'm tired? (I always struggled to do this. I wouldn't even take a bath unless I had done something to deserve it.)

Okay, so I think what I need is to speak to a friend and tell them how I feel. I also need to be more caring toward what I'm feeling by not putting so much pressure on myself today.

After working through the questions, the outcome might be that you feel conflicted – that you know you should be doing something compassionate for yourself but you feel yourself fighting against it. Watch out for that, as it is your critical voice trying to stop the part of you in need from getting the help you need.

Often, I would need to release my anger through something physical – running, boxing, screaming (great to do, but preferably somewhere private). I ran the other day and I was so angry. I ran so hard, but I also felt so depleted that in the end I just stopped running and screamed and shouted, 'Fuck!' (Luckily there was no one about.) And I cried and cried. I was angry, but underneath I was so hurt. A lot of how I was feeling was grief for myself and for the time I had lost because I was in trauma for most of my life. By letting my feelings out, they immediately felt more manageable and not so all-consuming. By acknowledging my emotions, I felt I could think more clearly about what I wanted and what I needed to do now and moving forward.

WHAT HAPPENS WHEN YOU ATTEND TO YOUR EMOTIONS?

Once we start to do things a little differently – to acknowledge our trauma, our story and to get to know ourselves – another emotional state starts to come in, one that many of us in trauma don't recognize: the happy state. Say, what? Happy?!

What does happy feel like?

Happy is when we feel everything trauma is not: safe, validated, loved, connected, protected, worthwhile, capable, understood and nurtured (cared for).

Happy is when our emotional needs have been met. It is when we have actually listened to what we are feeling and why, acknowledged what has happened to us, and given ourselves care and compassion. It is when our emotionally healthy voice is stronger than our nasty and demanding critical voice.

Getting comfortable with feeling happy

People who have had trauma from their childhood – be it at home, in the community, at school, through an illness, the loss of a loved one, having a parent that struggled with mental health/addiction, caring for a parent or the absence of caregivers (parents/family) – don't often know what is happy or playful. As such, they don't know what they enjoy doing or find it difficult to have a sense of play and fun.

All the feelings of trauma make it very hard to feel safe enough to have fun. Our bodies in trauma are full of adrenaline and our nervous system is heightened, which gives a signal to our brain that it's not safe to relax, to play and have fun – to be happy. When we do feel happy, even just for a moment, it can create an anticipation of loss, which brings a big kick of fear, vulnerability and anxiety all at once, as if being happy is too good to be true.

We have to relearn these things – and this can be a process and take a while. Everything we've covered so far are steps to feeling safer, to supporting our feelings, to acknowledge and give validation to our pain – all of which will, in time, give space and allow happiness and fun into our lives.

The happy emotion needs as much attention as our feelings of vulnerability, sadness and anger. Trauma deprives us of joy, happiness and play. Happiness can feel just as scary because, for many of us, it can feel less familiar. Trauma makes us miss out on more uplifting feelings and emotions. It's no wonder that it creates a low mood, feelings of loneliness, anger and resentment. If we have strong feelings of vulnerability, shame and fear (all trauma feelings), we tend to have an underdeveloped ability for 'happy' thoughts and emotions.

We can work on developing an openness to happy thoughts and emotions by engaging in activities we enjoy. For example, is there a hobby that you liked but gave up that you could try again? Is there something you've always wanted to try that you could start looking into? Do you have an area of your life where you can be creative? Just start thinking about ways you can learn to be more playful.

FIND YOUR VERSION OF 'HAPPY'

Ask yourself the following questions and write them down to refer back to. I've given my answers when I did this exercise to help.

- What do I feel if I'm happy?
My answer: *Loved, happy, warm, safe, cared for, connected, content.*

- What do I think when I'm happy? (What thoughts are in your head?)

My answer: Everything will be okay. I'm doing well. I am worthwhile and good enough. I am safe.

- How do I behave or what actions do I take when I'm feeling happy?

My answer: I interact with others, I engage, I'm productive, I care for myself, I cook! (Cooking might sound random, but I had a habit of not eating properly when I was feeling low. So, when I cooked for myself, I was showing I was worth looking after.)

When I first started doing this exercise, I struggled big time. It felt silly and a waste of time. I thought I should be doing something productive. Keep in mind, I got a lot of my 'temporary' self-worth from being productive and achieving. Doing something playful would, at times, make my critical voice grab a tannoy and shove it in my head on full blast: *'Oh! You think you deserve to have fun, do you? You're pathetic! You haven't done anything worthwhile today. You are a failure. You must work harder.'* All of which would stop me from exploring this part of trauma recovery. And as it is a part of recovery, I couldn't just skip over it and ignore it.

The happy child mode

When we first started learning about what Dr Rachel called the 'happy child mode', we did an exercise in the trauma group that involved doing fun, playful things and connecting to people with closeness. The session involved some kind of arts and crafts, colouring pens and scissors.

For me it was the worst session ever. I sat there like a sulky child. I reluctantly picked up a pen, but hardly took part. It was also the biggest learning curve, and showed me how hard I was on myself – how terrified I was to allow myself to just be present and do something that didn't have an end result of achievement – and how sad and hurt I really was. That session upset me more than anything else I'd done in therapy. It made me feel so sad, but it was key to my recovery. I started to grieve for all the fun and playful times I hadn't had, not because of my past, but because my trauma dominated me. Despite surviving the horrible things I had experienced, I still wouldn't let myself have fun or feel happy. I wouldn't even pick up a colouring pen!

There can be a fear around being happy when trauma has been so dominant. Our thought pattern makes us feel like something bad will happen if we allow ourselves to be happy – that's yet another harmful coping protective mechanism that disguises itself as helping us while really just preventing us from healing and feeling joy. This way of thinking is very much a part of trauma.

It may not feel like it now, but you *can* be happy. It takes practice, awareness and allowing yourself to heal your past pain. Think of the phrases on your connection card(s) – 'I am loved', 'I am lovable', 'I care about you', 'I like you'. Those messages all belong to feeling happy.

A strong happy child mode is also the biggest protector of our mental health, because it focuses on emotional regulation and expressing emotions with openness and authenticity, curiosity, learning, playfulness, meaningful social interactions and living in the moment – which are all qualities that help us manage in life. Processing our past pain allows us to feel safer to strengthen and empower the happy child inside of us, so it can play a bigger role in our life. The more we can nurture this part of us that gets so lost and squashed down in trauma, the more the happy child mode can become like a caretaker of our emotions and our minds. The happy child side of us may not fully take over, but it will certainly grow as we work through our trauma which will enable us to start to embrace happiness without it feeling like something to be scared of.

9

What happens when we work through our trauma?

This chapter is intended to create a little pause in the overall process of the book to highlight what might be going on for you as we work through trauma.

I would love to be able to wave a magic wand over you so that you don't have to trudge through your trauma to be able to recover from it. But, as you're seeing, to be able to recover, you need to process the emotions related to your trauma, and that means facing the things that you've spent your time trying to move on from.

EXITING SURVIVAL MODE

A reminder: as we need to be in the survival mode of fight-or-flight in the moment that the awful thing is happening, we are unable to process our trauma at the time. It is only in the aftermath, when we are out of immediate danger, that we can begin to process it.

If you've spent a lot of your life, like me, in survival mode, it will take some time to untangle things. Our brain adapts to survive. People can live for years and years in a state of threat, as can communities that face daily oppression, discrimination or violence – that is a long time for the brain to be in fight-or-flight. If you think about how long you've felt this way, or how long you've been in a state of trauma, it makes sense that an overnight fix isn't possible. But trust me: it's worth doing the work.

So, what starts to happen to our memories when we start processing trauma? As we work through trauma, our brain actually changes, and so do the pathways that link to our nervous system.

Let's go back to the filing cabinet analogy that we began in Chapter 2. Working through trauma helps our memories find their rightful place in the filing cabinet. They are still there but are settled and can be accessed in a safe and secure way, if and when you want to. The memories get ordered with a sense of cohesion and become integrated into your life story. This sense of order reduces their emotional power, so the feelings attached to the memories aren't as intense. This, in turn, leads to cognitive restructuring to create more accurate thought patterns and behaviours that reflect the present rather than the past. This, inevitably, reduces the strength of our inner critic.

At first, working through trauma can feel so exhausting and totally crap. Sometimes, I would feel even worse than I had before.

I felt vulnerable and upset, and my mind would keep thinking about everything that had happened. It dragged up memories that I'd long hidden in the depths of myself. I was slowly reducing the use of my protective coping mechanisms by opening up more, letting people in and telling them how I was feeling, but that left me feeling exposed and vulnerable.

It's so incredibly tough to allow yourself to feel like that and sit with those feelings. Our natural instinct – and the very thing that has led us here – has been to protect against those feelings. In trauma, we avoid and detach from feeling vulnerability at all costs.

Keep reminding yourself that by working through your trauma, these feelings of vulnerability are going to come up. It's not like they weren't there previously, they were; it's just you'd pushed them away. In processing trauma, everything that was hiding and lurking in the background will start to surface – this is perfectly normal. Feeling vulnerable and allowing yourself to stay with it means you are processing and working through trauma. Feeling safe enough to feel vulnerability means you are no longer in a survival coping mechanism. This is a good thing!

If your reaction is to run away from these memories or throw this book across the room because it's bringing things up for you, good! That means revisiting the memories is working – it's making you feel what you need to feel in order to process and recover. If you do have this reaction, that's okay, but don't run too far. Take a break, distract yourself and then revisit it. Don't give up on yourself. Let me remind you that you deserve to heal, you deserve to recover, you deserve to give yourself a chance.

When you are taking a break from your trauma work, intrusive memories will most likely still come up. Think about some of the techniques that we've done so far to remind you that you're safe and ground you to the present. For example, naming or counting objects in your current location, connecting with the smell you chose, or using the Safety Bubble Techniques or your connection cards with your emotionally healthy messages.

Our memories will remain whether they are good, indifferent or bad. We are looking to get to a point where the emotion attached to a bad memory isn't overwhelming, and that the memory is accessed safely only when we need to, not as and when it feels like it.

COPING WITH INTRUSIVE MEMORIES

After coming out of hospital, I had so many intrusive memories. Memories of being told I was going to die; of being absolutely petrified while waiting for my mum to fly from England to Brazil, not knowing if I'd ever see her again; of being in the coma and hearing my mum, brother and doctors question whether I was still there and not being able to answer.

While I was dealing with all this, I also had memories of hiding behind the bedroom door as a child, holding my breath in case I made a noise, and wetting myself because I was too scared to open the door to go to the bathroom; of being punched to the floor, of hot alcohol-infused breath and screams from my mum and brother; of wrapping my tracksuit bottoms so tightly round me after a private training session with my coach. These were some of the memories that I'd never dealt with. I'd never spoken them out loud. I'd never allowed myself to see the person that went through all this, let alone grieve for her.

So, how do you sit with these intrusive, traumatic memories and stick with it?

First off, try not to expect that you'll always be able to sit with them. As you go into your traumatic memories, keep yourself connected with where you are now, and the present moment. Initially, it's just about recognizing and acknowledging what you're feeling when you're with a memory. Notice what happens in your body, think about your breathing, and keep checking in with your surroundings to stay present. That may be enough for you at that moment. Be gentle with yourself, give yourself permission to stop and take breaks. Remember, you are in control. If you need to shut it off, then go and do something else. But make sure you come back.

The next time you visit your traumatic memories and see yourself wanting to shut off from them, challenge yourself to sit with them for a few more minutes and see what it brings up for you. Ask the questions to yourself from the Identify How You Are Feeling exercise in the previous chapter (page 165).

- How am I reacting/behaving?
- What's going on in my body?
- What am I thinking?
- What are my thoughts making me feel?
- What emotion is that?
- Why am I feeling like that?
- What do I need to do right now?

You could also tell somebody you feel safe with that you are working through your trauma so they can support you in that. Tell them how the process is making you feel and that you are thinking about the time that horrible thing happened to you.

As part of this process, don't forget to give self-compassion after exploring your feelings and memory. What is something you could do that will comfort you in an emotionally healthy way? Perhaps making a hot drink and wrapping a cosy blanket round you, taking a warm bath, reading a book, going for a walk or listening to your favourite music.

The aim is to start to be able to feel the emotions from that memory in a safe manner and to be able to acknowledge what you were feeling at the time of the experience. Remember, recovery from trauma involves processing the emotions that are embedded in the painful memory and being aware of how we emotionally understand the past. I know it's a well-worn phrase nobody wants to hear, but it takes time and practice.

REVISIT YOUR FLOWERS AND STONES LIFELINE

This might be a good time to look back at the flowers and stones lifeline you created in Chapter 5. (And if you didn't do it, give it a try now.)

The flowers and stones lifeline is *your* story – it holds your memories and it's in your control.

Try writing down some of the emotions that you feel when you look at the stones. If there is a particular stone that you just can't bear to think about, just briefly try and feel what it was like for you in that moment. Can you allow yourself to grieve for what you went through just for a minute?

There were times I couldn't bear to look back on, but at the same time I knew somewhere deep inside me that I could no longer do an edit on my life. I felt like I was operating from a concrete solitary prison cell where the walls were decreasing in size every second that went by. There was no natural light, just the same four walls staring mockingly at me. The guard dog was always barking inside my head even when I was asleep. I was exhausted from it all and I was sick of hiding. I had to address all of my trauma.

SITTING WITH DIFFICULT EMOTIONS IS PAINFUL

Earlier in the book I mentioned the word 'weathering' from Dr Rachel's research paper, 'An exploration of members' experiences of group therapy'. Weathering means staying in your strong and overwhelming feelings long enough to understand them, and sticking with trauma recovery work even when it brings up lots of uncomfortable feelings.

Trauma is going to bring up powerful emotions and, in trying to process them, it will hurt at times and you may very well feel *more* upset. This book might already have made you feel that way – indeed, I hope it does because that means you are processing trauma. You're already doing it. It can feel worse before it gets better, but it is *not* getting worse. Processing trauma does *not* make things worse. This is a normal process of getting better. You're uncovering things that you've firmly covered up for a good reason. You're working through feelings you've been afraid to go near. You are holding space for your pain in order to grieve it.

This can be exhausting and physically draining. If we are reliving memories and feelings, it can make our bodies produce stress responses, such as muscle tension, shortness of breath and trouble sleeping. For a few months, when I was working through my memories and emotions from sexual abuse, I had more nightmares, and the same ones over and over, before they went away. But they did go away. As I mentioned, I've had nightmares for as long as I can recall. Now, I hardly ever have them and I haven't had the recurring one about my coach for many years. This feeling 'worse' is short-term pain so you can prevent it from being long-term pain. Hold on to that. And remember, staying away from and remaining afraid of our feelings stops us from healing.

Becoming more attached and aware of your emotions and more connected with yourself actually makes you *feel* more. This is a good thing, but can take getting used to. Working through trauma is change – it's changing how you see yourself, changing how you feel, changing how you think, changing your coping mechanisms and changing how you behave. All this is a new awareness and it can make you question a lot of things in your life. Change is difficult, even when it's good for us.

Every time you feel like it's too much or you just want it all to 'fuck off', think about the concept of weathering. If you can just hold on and allow these emotions and memories to come out in a safe way, you will get through to the other side and things will change. These are emotions you need to release, and expressing them will eventually lead to relief. It's like a clearing out of all your suppressed emotions. It can't possibly be a quick fix; if it was, we'd all be healed. Be aware of that critical voice telling you that you need to recover and fix everything now, otherwise it's not working – it's a trap to keep you in trauma.

It takes courage to go on this journey of recovery. Keep checking in with what you're feeling, what you are thinking, what you are saying to yourself, and what your body is telling you. Rest when you need to. Move your body when you need to.

When it feels a lot in your head:

- Think of the Grounding Technique (page 95) and use all five senses to help you connect with where you are now.
- Visualize. Use the Safety Bubble Techniques (pages 48 and 78). Get inside your bubble or put everything that is hurting you inside the bubble and zip it up tight.
- Name objects you see around you; what colour are they?
- Name what you can smell, what you can hear, what you can feel, what you can taste.
- Smell your chosen smell; inhale deeply.
- Touch or hold an object (a soft toy, a small stone).
- Wrap a blanket round your shoulders.
- Clench your fists, hold tight and then release.
- Have a cold shower.
- Put on your favourite song, loud!

A SAFE PLACE TO WORK THROUGH TRAUMA

Working through trauma needs to be done in a safe environment where you can remind yourself you are now safe. I often say to myself, '*I'm safe. I am in control of my own decisions,*' and list some of the things that make me feel safe; these are things like being independent or being able to shut my door and control who is and who isn't in my home (this is a big one for me because I was brought up in an unsafe home).

Think of a few things that make you feel safe, and say them to yourself whenever you are feeling vulnerable. It's very difficult to deal with trauma if you're still going through a currently unsafe situation. You need to be able to allow yourself to be vulnerable, to feel the emotions that you felt at the time of distress, in safety.

If my brain hadn't protected me when I was being sexually abused, if it hadn't shut off my 'feelings', if I had actually felt the emotions of what was happening to me back then, my brain wouldn't have coped. Now that I'm safe from that, I can allow myself to go back to the feelings of that moment, to be able to grieve what happened to me, to give myself the compassion and care I needed back then so that I can recover from it now.

10

Noticing your triggers (and cognitive distortions)

Trauma triggers are a survival response. They can be anything that prompts our brain to recall a disturbing and distressing memory. Triggers are a common response to trauma – there is absolutely nothing abnormal about triggers or being triggered.

It's important to keep in mind that triggers are involuntary. Unprocessed trauma can re-emerge at any time, so triggers from trauma can just appear out of nowhere and with sudden intensity.

A trauma trigger is different from an emotional response. Emotions and reactions are part and parcel of life in the present – we all feel worry, anger, sadness and stress.

Triggers are a reaction to past memories, not a reaction to our present. Dr Rachel speaks of triggers as any stimulus – feeling, sensation, situation, thought, sound, smell – that brings back a past memory. It creates a matching feeling, sensation or thought in the present that was experienced in the past. As mentioned, we experience trauma through all five senses, hence why triggers can be experienced through any of our senses.

WHAT ARE TRIGGERS?

Triggers are anything that makes a past memory come to the surface with an unexpected and intense response. When you experience a trigger, you feel overwhelming emotions and physical reactions, which are frightening and can lead to extreme behavioural actions. Triggers can be both external (from the outside environment) and internal (stemming from within us). Triggers make us re-experience distressing memories or feel intense distress, anxiety and fear, as if we were experiencing this painful memory again. They can cause an emotional response so strong that it affects our ability to cope in our daily lives.

A trigger makes you feel in danger when you aren't. This is different from an instinct or intuition that might genuinely be protecting you. An *instinct* is an automatic response to a situation that comes from our innate survival and a mass of data that we process subconsciously; and *intuition* is a thought or an insight, sometimes from our past learnings – like a gut feeling about something. In contrast, a *trigger* evokes a memory from our past that makes us feel like we are right back in that memory, and so makes our body feel like it's in danger.

An **external trigger** could be a smell, a taste, a place, an action by somebody, a certain physical position, sensation, a person or even an anniversary of an event. I touched upon this when we talked about smell as a tool to help us feel comforted and safe. Because smell is processed with emotions and memories, it can pull an unprocessed memory that is floating in the brain to the forefront of your mind. The memory comes right back without any conscious thought. The body then reacts by going on high alert. The pain of the memory and all the feelings and emotions surrounding it rush back. It can make you feel like you've completely lost any sense of time or space.

The actual external stimulus isn't necessarily scary – it can be perfectly harmless, such as the smell of freshly cut grass – but the past memory it triggers is what causes the big reaction. That grass smell triggered a friend so badly she would have a panic attack. We worked out it was because behind her abusive dad's house was a field which she tried to escape across many times. The smell of freshly cut grass took her right back to those fearful moments when she was scared for her life.

There are also **internal triggers**. These come from a particular *feeling* or *thought*, rather than the external environment. External triggers can also trigger our internal triggers and keep us in a cycle of trauma.

WHY AVOIDING TRIGGERS DOESN'T WORK

When processing trauma, it's important to start recognizing what triggers you and why. If we start to notice them, we can begin to intervene – and it's essential that we do.

In the short term, avoiding triggers might bring us some temporary relief. After all, we're avoiding a situation or emotion that brings us distressing memories. But ignoring our triggers means they will carry on affecting us. Think of the 'avoidant protector' coping mechanism – the emotionally unhealthy way of coping by avoiding situations and people to avoid pain or uncomfortable emotions.

Avoiding our triggers is just that: a protective way of coping and a behavioural symptom of trauma. We can't spend our lives managing our environment to avoid triggers. I guarantee that, even if you are the best in the world at avoiding triggers and in changing your environment to avoid triggers, they will still happen because we can't control *everything* in life and other people.

Think what this means for relationships as well. I have a friend who is managing her own behaviour and surroundings to make sure she doesn't trigger her partner in any way. No matter how much she tries, things still trigger him. So, she tries harder. You can imagine what that cycle is like for them. She's walking on eggshells, full of anxiety, and he is still staying in a state of trauma. He will continue to have powerful overriding triggers because the root of them is not her, their current surroundings or anything to do with their present. His triggers are from his past, which he is ignoring, detaching from and avoiding. The environment is only triggering a stress reaction because something within it is attached to a past memory, and that same environment would be completely benign to another person.

Avoiding triggers in the long term holds the fear in place, isolates us, prevents recovery, keeps us in trauma and in shame, and perpetuates our symptoms that come with all that, such as anxiety, depression, nightmares and flashbacks. Overall, avoiding triggers limits our life experience.

NOTICING MY EXTERNAL TRIGGERS

I mentioned earlier that if I have to lie face up on a treatment table or massage bed (for example when seeing a physiotherapist or a doctor, or having a massage or a facial) and look at a ceiling, my muscles will instantly tense and my chest tighten; my brain will go to the place and moment of being sexually abused by my running coach. This physical reaction is totally involuntary. My abuse happened many, many times over several years, but always in a classroom environment while lying on a table. At first, even though I would freeze up with fear, tense every part of my body, hold my breath and sometimes tears would roll down my cheeks despite not consciously crying, I struggled to recognize the link. On other occasions I would become very defensive and remove myself from the situation.

To start with, I could feel something wasn't right – based on my reaction – but couldn't quite figure it out. I would block what was happening, and then feel ashamed about my reaction, even though I didn't understand what was causing it, but especially because the people around me would normally notice my reaction. This would make me even more defensive and either totally avoid such situations or block out any emotion. By avoiding the trigger and the memory, I couldn't do anything to help myself. My behaviour when I was in those situations was the key to letting me know that this was a trigger. I wasn't initially able to change anything; I would just notice it, but still react the same way. However, the more I noticed it, the more I became aware of what memory it kept bringing up. I could then see why I found this particular situation so triggering. I *matched* my current trigger (lying face up with a professional) with my distressing memory (lying face up as a child being abused by my coach). Connecting a traumatic experience to a trigger is called **trauma coupling**.

Your breathing can be a big clue to help spot triggers. My breathing always gets heavier and tighter; I breathe entirely from my chest, as if something external is making it hard to breathe. I also tend to clench my teeth. The anxiety also makes me need the toilet. The key is to spot what brings on a big intense emotional reaction and match it with your past.

ADDRESSING MY EXTERNAL TRIGGERS

Once I connected the dots and allowed myself to notice and be aware, I could then start to intervene. I talked to myself, to my 'scared' self and my brain that was trying to protect me.

My brain will flash to the classroom and I'll see my coach's face. I'll say to my brain, '*I know why you're doing this (brain), you always do this when I'm in this lying-down position. I know you're trying to protect me from any further abuse. But you are not in that classroom anymore. He is not here. He can't do anything to you.*'

I then say to my scared triggered self, '*You are okay. You are safe. You are in control.*' And to my brain again, '*You don't have to protect me anymore. Remember, I'm in control and, if I want to, I can get up anytime and leave. I'm here by choice.*'

I then make sure my brain connects to the present by describing the situation I am currently in. For example, if I am seeing a physiotherapist, '*I am with the physio. The physio is here to help me, I am here by choice. I can see the door and leave anytime. I have a voice and can tell them I am uncomfortable if I want to. I am not in a classroom, I'm in a clinic.*' And to my vulnerable triggered self, I would say, '*It's understandable you're scared. This reminds you of such a horrible, frightening and upsetting time. It's really sad this happened to you. You are safe now. I've got you!*'

Through this language, you'll see I learnt the ritual of telling myself that I am safe. I now tell myself that I understand why my brain is triggered, and create visual grounding cues of where I am. In doing so, my body begins to feel safe, exits fight-or-flight mode, and I start to breathe normally, as the adrenaline in my body slows down.

What your body does in these situations is a normal response to danger, and a healthy one when we *are* in danger and we may need to fight, run away or freeze and so need that adrenaline. Telling yourself you're safe and showing your body that it isn't in danger will make the trigger go away.

I still get the memory of my abuse creeping in from time to time and I feel my body wanting to react; but I now know this is a memory, and can reassure myself for as long as I need to and very quickly make myself safe again before my body starts to react as if it's in danger.

I recently had some dental work done and the suction tube they use to stop saliva dribbling down your chin triggered feelings of being back in intensive care. This was the first time I'd had dental work since being hospitalized. I was nearly sick when the dentist took some impressions of my teeth because it made me feel like I couldn't breathe. My brain took me to the hospital and the feeling of being intubated. It didn't help that I was also lying back in a medical-type chair looking at the ceiling. Double trigger.

I noticed these triggers, and although I didn't tell the dentist about the sexual abuse, I did tell her that I'd been in intensive care and was on life support so I was finding what she was doing very triggering. I had to get the dental work done, so by vocalizing what was going on for me I was able to validate my feelings. This immediately took me from the hospital in my mind to the dentist room I was actually in, in my reality. The dentist took a lot of care and because I'd told her, she did reassuring things like stroking my hand while the impressions were being taken. It made all the difference. They were all cues that I was safe and kept reminding me where I was physically in that moment.

A few weeks ago, my friend had invited a few women over to her house because she wanted to connect us all about a possible new collaboration. The conversation very quickly got onto victims of sexual abuse because one of the women had worked as a lawyer on a big case. I started to get hot flushes, my palms were damp and clammy, I felt really agitated and I wanted to leave the room. I disengaged from the conversation and held my hands tight. It came over me so quickly that I didn't know what to do. I was doing everything I could to stop myself from bursting into tears. The women had seen me in many situations where I'd campaigned against sexual abuse, so hadn't thought that the current conversation would trigger me. I sat for quite a while trying to figure out what to do and what I was feeling. I knew I was triggered, but also felt too embarrassed to say anything or leave. Previously, I would have either left the room abruptly and come across as rude, or just sat there and come across as disengaged – all the while continuing to suffer.

Despite having done so much work on trauma recovery, there are things that still grip me. The difference is the action I then took. I politely interrupted the conversation and explained that I was feeling very uncomfortable and that, as well as being a campaigner and a survivor of sexual abuse, I was a victim. I said, 'I am one of the people you're discussing, so can we please acknowledge that or change the subject?' As soon as I'd vocalized, I felt my body let go of the tension it was holding. The women around the table showed me compassion and care, and validated what I was feeling. I did have initial feelings of shame – and apologized quite a few times unnecessarily – but the feelings of shame didn't stay. Instead, I found the whole experience reaffirming and we all learnt and grew from it. Vocalizing might not always be feasible – and you don't always have to explain yourself to others – but making a decision for what is best for you in that moment is trauma recovery.

ME AND MY TRIGGERS

For the risk of spending an entire chapter telling you all about my triggers, I want to share a few more examples and how I have begun the process of changing things.

I get triggered by touch around the front of my neck in any situation, but especially in intimate ones. I don't need to explain why this is every time it happens, but I can say, 'Do you mind not touching my neck like that? I don't like it', or, 'It feels uncomfortable for me'. I've been triggered by this with something as normal as carrying children, where they hold onto your neck, especially if you're giving them a piggyback. I just gently move their hands away or carry them in a different position. Being touched here triggers feelings of unsafety for me, both from my childhood and from being in hospital. Previously, I couldn't control this; I would be right back in the moment of distress, of choking, but recognizing this happens in this situation allows me to clock it so I can do small actions to address it.

I was struggling to even go to the hospital for my check-up appointments. The hospital environment would trigger flashbacks, make me feel vulnerable and fill me with dread. I'd sit in the waiting area and feel like I was outside of my body, my mind in a fog. Under Dr Niki's advice, and with a little gentle persuasion, I went back to visit an ICU. Everything my brain and my heart didn't want to do.

I was petrified. All I could feel was what it felt like when I was ill: trapped, terrified and unable to move. I was in the hospital bed again, weighed down with piles of blankets and strapped to my bed. My heart was beating so fast it made me feel like my breath couldn't catch up and my airways were closing in. My armpits were soaked with cold sweat. Dr Niki took me around the unit to see what it was like from another perspective and to help my brain understand it, now I was physically well.

I saw the ICU as a really scary place and it haunted me a lot, but Dr Niki showed me I was now safe and that the ICU had saved my life – it had been a safe place for me even though at the time it didn't feel like it. This is something Dr Niki tries to do with patients after their experience.

'There was a patient who couldn't bear to come into the hospital, let alone go to an ICU. She was terrified because of her experience on the ICU. But after a few visits into the clinic, we got to the point where we felt she was ready. She got such a hero's welcome because, of course, it's good for the staff to see somebody that's been really very poorly to walk in, in their ordinary clothes, and look amazing; it's such a morale booster for staff, as well as a way to process the trigger for the patient.'
Dr Niki Snook

Visiting the ICU did make a difference (although before I did it, it seemed like the worst thing to do, and I was triggered from every direction). My visit reframed how I felt about my hospital stay. I also wrote to the ICU staff in Rio and sent them a gift hamper. Some of the nurses follow me on Instagram and still send me supportive messages. Going *toward* what happened to me, rather than ignoring and running away from it, helped me reduce my triggers.

How can we heal from something we won't face? Remember, we can't heal from something we are pretending didn't happen.

During the Covid-19 pandemic there were pictures of people in ICUs all over the news. Everywhere I looked I seemed to be faced with my own time of critical illness. It took me straight back to that moment. I could feel that person in the picture's pain, both physically and emotionally, because I knew what it felt like to be in that position. I made sure I turned off the news and gave myself a break from it all. Because I'd spent time with Dr Niki and worked on understanding and processing what I'd gone through, I could look at these images and not be triggered to the extent I was back there. I could have the memory, and hold it as just a memory, rather than as an intrusive moment or thought or a horrific gripping trigger.

Of course, the memory would still make me feel sad and affect me – but as a painful memory, not as a visceral moment of being back there fighting for my life. In trauma recovery, that's where we want to aim to get to.

For several years after I fell critically ill I wouldn't look at any pictures of my cycle challenge from London to Rio and avoided speaking to people who were involved. The pain was too much. Every time I saw a picture of me (they were used in the press and flashed up on socials) smiling on the bike, it triggered so much hurt and distress to think that only days after the picture was taken I would nearly lose my life. Looking at the pictures also made me so angry about what happened to me and ashamed.

I couldn't even bring myself to do one of the things I love: cycling. Just looking at my bike caused me to have a panic attack. So I totally disengaged from it all. This completely robbed me of any sense of achievement or pride in what I had accomplished, and how incredible it was to have cycled 3,000 miles and raised money for charity. It took me a while, but eventually, little by little, I started to look at the pictures and talk about the bike ride itself, rather than just associate it with the extreme distress afterward. From there, I managed to get on a bike for the first time in two years – and it happened in the most incredible way. I was in Uganda making a short film about malaria, and I cycled with a healthcare worker who delivered life-saving antimalarial drugs to his village on a bicycle. If I'd continued avoiding my pain, I would never have had this amazing experience.

In trauma, we mainly try to control everything we can to avoid or detach from anything that would take us back to the painful memories. The thing about external triggers is, because they are often from normal stimuli, we can't control them. You could be sitting in what you think is the safest place in the world, only to hear or smell something that immediately takes you back to what happened to you. So we have to face the exact thing we don't want to. The more we can show our brains that we are now safe, the more we can take the power and frequency out of the triggers.

It takes practice. To start with you may recognize the external triggers and the traumatic memory they bring up yet still have a big emotional reaction. It's a step-by-step process, and recognizing them is the first step. Be careful not to be too hard on yourself by expecting yourself to be able to stop reacting to triggers straight away.

INTERNAL TRIGGERS

From my experience, I would argue that internal triggers are harder to get to grips with than external.

As briefly mentioned, internal triggers are caused by our own thoughts, feelings and critical inner voice; they emanate from big overwhelming emotions like abandonment, sadness, feeling out of control, rejection, anxiety and stress. All of which trigger memories and associations with past trauma. For example, self-blame and criticizing yourself can trigger feelings of past shame and worthlessness.

External triggers can trigger internal emotions by giving us those feelings of fear, anxiety, shame, vulnerability or sadness. These feelings can internally trigger an escalation and self-perpetuating cycle of these emotions, which, as you now know, are the core of trauma. It's absolutely crucial to work on and address these triggers. Even more so because recovering from trauma will bring on internal triggers. Working through trauma will make you feel vulnerable. There is no way around it – trust me, I've tried everything. So, expect to be triggered. Understanding internal triggers, and what yours are, is the path to getting through, and at the other end of the path are feelings of safety, love and worth. The path is not just scary to take, but scary to stay on, but I promise you are taking the right route to recovery.

Understanding your behaviour from triggers is also fundamental. Internal triggers can lead to addictive and destructive behaviours. This can be anything from drugs or alcohol, to controlling your eating or overeating, to self-injury and overexercising.

One of the biggest and hardest internal triggers for me is the feeling of rejection. It's something I am very aware of because I still have to check in on it. My brain catastrophizes and makes me go into panic. I grind and grit my teeth, I get a headache and my body tenses, bracing as if I'm about to be physically hit. Rejection for me triggers huge past emotions and memories from my childhood.

Just a few years ago, when I was about to sign a contract for a big TV project, I got a phone call as I was walking to meet a friend near King's Cross in London on a rainy day. I was told the contract had been pulled – the board had had a change of direction. All I heard in my head were the voices of my past, *'You're not good enough'*, *'You're an idiot for even trying'*, *'You are stupid to think people think you are any good, you're pathetic and a failure'*. I hung up my phone and out of the corner of my eye saw a red double-decker bus speeding along the road, the rain was distorting everything and, for a second, I nearly stepped out in front of it. The hurt inside was so powerful and overwhelming it completely distorted any rational thinking. In that moment, every part of me – my mind, my heart, my body – was in the past. I was a vulnerable child that felt she wasn't worth anything. At the same time, my phone rang again, which jolted me from my past memories. I saw my friend's name flash up on the screen, the one who I was on my way to meet. My immediate reaction was to cancel on him. My go-to whenever I was struggling was to shut myself off from everyone, but something made me reach out and tell him I was here and about to cross the road. I often keep that moment in my mind to remind me how far I've come.

Internal triggers also come up for me in intimate relationships. (Yep, relationships again!) If I feel vulnerable, it can bring about fear and feelings of rejection (again!) related to my childhood, and make that present relationship feel to me the same as my past relationships. That internal trigger can then bring about destructive behaviour. It may make me end the relationship – even though in the present there's no reason to – as a coping mechanism to avoid those past feelings that have been triggered. Or the trigger might lead me to do more private and less-able-to-spot harmful behaviours to cope with the feelings, such as controlling my eating, working to excess and over-exercising. It would tap into my perfectionist way of coping – *'If I do everything perfectly then I won't get rejected'* – creating a relentless pressure and unrealistic set of expectations of myself. It's a vicious cycle, as these feelings then lead to self-protection against something from your past, and to isolation, when what is really needed is the opposite: connection, compassion and love.

In psychology, these harmful patterns and styles of thinking are called 'cognitive distortions'. We can all find ourselves thinking negatively at times, but in trauma these negative thoughts dominate. Think back to the critical voice we worked through, which fuels and drives these thoughts and ways of coping. Our internal triggers, our critical voice and our thinking are all interwoven and, as a result, impact how we behave – they trigger our protective unhealthy behaviours.

COGNITIVE DISTORTIONS

When I got the news of that big deal falling through – a project that I was so incredibly passionate about and had worked above and beyond to secure – I immediately 'catastrophized' the news, and my thinking was very extreme 'all-or-nothing' thinking. These are both examples of distorted thinking. Quite simply, they make us feel bad about ourselves.

Below are the main types of cognitive distortion:

- **Catastrophizing** is building something up in your mind as devastating or impossible. To me, in that moment, the news of my deal felt so devastating I just didn't even want to live. *'The deal fell through because I'm not good enough. I will never get another deal or opportunity again.'* Other examples of catastrophizing: *'I feel depressed because I am weak'; 'I snapped at my friend. They'll never speak to me again'; 'If I allow myself to feel the pain of what's happened to me I won't be able to cope.'*

- **All-or-nothing thinking** is when we think in extremes: *'Bad things always happen to me'; 'I never have anything good happen to me'; 'No one likes me'; 'I'm a bad person.'*

- **Negative forecasting** is where we predict a bad outcome will happen: *'Because this happened to me, I will never succeed in life'; 'I feel so bad now, so I will never recover from my trauma.'*

- **Mind reading** is when we imagine we know what other people are thinking which, of course, is something bad: *'People are looking at me while I'm reading my book on trauma, so they must think I'm weak'; 'My boss snapped at me – I'm going to get fired'; 'My partner is quiet – they don't love me anymore.'*

- **Should/shouldn't statements** you can probably recognize from our discussion on perfectionism: *'If I do everything perfectly, they should love me'; 'I have a family/a job/friends, I shouldn't be* *depressed'; 'I should be able handle this on my own'; 'I should lose weight to be able to find a partner.'*

With distorted thinking, we tend to filter out anything good that's happened and reject reality. The thought pattern is extremely rigid – we trust the bad and ignore the good. We put an unrealistic expectation on ourselves which makes us feel like we've failed, like we aren't enough. Cognitive distortions are created from trauma and work together with shame. Research has shown that this can cause such intense feelings of hopelessness that it can trigger suicidal thoughts. These reactions show deep triggers.

Pay very close attention to any kind of distorted thinking that you may notice yourself doing – you might recognize it in yourself straight away after reading this chapter. Try to tune into your thinking patterns now that you know that these are unhealthy ways of coping with big emotions from your past.

Once you're aware of it, you will start to notice what your critical voice is saying and what kind of distorted thinking you feed yourself with. A little reminder from me again: be careful not to beat yourself up for these thoughts – that's just part of the critic. Instead, recognize that this judging of yourself doesn't help you, and think of how bloody brave you are for working through this. Imagine how you would feel if you stopped being unfair to yourself.

I noted my various versions of this thinking and wrote them down to help me see what I was doing outside of myself:

'If I risk delving into my experiences and working through my trauma I will break down and won't be able to cope.'

I then came up with facts that showed that the distortion was actually not factually correct:

'I have survived so much. I have friends and family around me. I am learning tools and understanding trauma to help me. I am now in control and have a choice.'

This kind of self-talk doesn't take all the fear away or make the triggers disappear entirely, but it can be the difference between you reading this book and not; or doing some of the exercises in it or not; or working through your trauma further or not. It's about reassuring yourself, showing yourself the facts and building the strength of the emotionally healthy 'you' that can start to guide you out of the harmful coping mechanisms that keep you in trauma.

This was something I worked on in my trauma group. We were given a worksheet to fill in that explained that when we feel really strong emotions, we sometimes distort reality and react much more intensely than the situation warrants. This can happen because our thoughts don't match what's actually happening – this is cognitive distortion. Underneath this explanation was a space to write down your distortion, the effect it has on how you feel, and what action the distortion made you take. It then had another section for 'Your facts', and the effect of the facts on how you felt and the action you took from the facts. The worksheet questioned *'Were you more affected by facts or the distortion?'*

RECOGNIZE YOUR COGNITIVE DISTORTIONS

It's key for you to try and recognize your own cognitive distortions.

Here, we're going to consider whether these distortions are leading to really strong, difficult emotions – and how to reframe these distortions using facts.

I'll start with one of my own examples to help:

Your distortion: *If people know about my past experiences they won't love me.*

How does this make you feel? *Lonely, hurt, damaged, detached and numb.*

What action do you take? *I detached from my emotions because they hurt me (but that made me feel depressed and foggy) and I isolated myself further so no one could reject me (but this made me feel lonely).*

Facts: *I have told some of my friends and they still love me and want to spend time with me.*

How does this make you feel? *Cared for and loved, safe, accepted.*

What action did you take? *I called my trusted friend and had a lovely chat with her about how I was feeling. I was able to comfort myself and give myself some caring emotionally healthy messages. Speaking to her showed me that people do love me, no matter what has happened in my past.*

Now, in a notebook or journal, write down the below and give it a go:

Your distortion.
- How does the distortion make you feel?
- What action do you take because of the distortion?

Your facts.
- How do the facts make you feel?
- What action did you take because of the facts?
- Were you more affected by the facts or distortion?

There are absolutely no right or wrong answers. Just make sure you are honest with yourself, and from there you can practise comparing your distortion with the facts. The more you do this, the more you can start questioning your distortion and be more influenced by the facts. This is known as an experiential strategy – you are showing that you have had an experience that is opposite to your distortion.

STRATEGIES TO WORK THROUGH TRIGGERS

To be able to work through triggers it's absolutely key to notice what our triggers are and why we are triggered by them. I could only work through my triggers and reduce the strength of them because I had spent time getting to know what they were and why they happened.

All research in this area points to the need to expose ourselves to our triggers and confront them in order to process our trauma. It is a process. Notice what you avoid. Observe how you behave – your reaction and what your body does – think about what memory it is evoking. If you can't identify exactly what causes them, that's okay; it might take time, but just keep observing.

Short-term strategies

The main aim while you are identifying a trigger is to make yourself feel safe. The following strategies can help, along with the grounding work we discussed in Part I.

- Taking deep breaths slows the heart rate down and is a quick and effective way to show your brain that it's safe.
- Vocalize what you are feeling to others.
- Remember you can always remove yourself from the situation. However, be mindful of avoiding.
- Be compassionate to yourself.

'We need to set the boundary between then and now. Short-term strategies are important when confronting triggers. Grounding is the practical work in the moment, such as using comforting smells and checking in with what you can see and where you are.'

Dr Rachel O'Beney

Long-term strategies

'The short-term strategies such as avoiding can be like a sticking plaster. The longer-term work is really attending to your feelings. It's totally understandable that you feel frightened; it feels weird because feelings that belong to the past feel very powerful and are coming up in the here and now.

'The long-term strategies involve developing your healthy adult who will take care of the vulnerable self inside you, who will talk to your vulnerable child saying, "I know you're frightened. It was frightening then, but you're not there now. You are safe."' [Derived from schema therapy approach, Farrell, Reiss, Shaw, 2014]

Dr Rachel O'Beney

- Think of the self-talk narrative I used previously: 'It's understandable you're scared. This reminds you of such a horrible, frightening and upsetting time. It's really sad this happened to you. You are safe now. I've got you!' Talk to your brain, talk to the part of you that was back in that memory, scared and vulnerable.
- Notice what you're thinking and interrupt those thoughts with the emotionally healthy messages we've used. Remember to carry the connection cards you've written with you.
- Use experiential techniques from this chapter that challenge your thinking and show you the facts and positive outcomes.
- Ask yourself what it was that you needed back then in those times that were traumatic, and then do what you needed then, now. You didn't have that comfort, reassurance or care in the past in your distressing experience, so you need to give this to yourself now. It's not too late to give yourself now what you needed to be able to heal at the time but didn't get.
- Practise gradual exposure to your triggers. Remember, avoiding triggers is life-limiting and self-destructive. Avoidance is a

symptom of trauma and prevents you from healing. Remember also to be compassionate toward yourself and take breaks when you need them.

WORKING THROUGH TRAUMA TRIGGERS IS A PROCESS (BE PATIENT WITH YOURSELF)

All ways of thinking can change over time. Identify, notice and start reframing. It won't work every time, but it will gradually change things for you. It's important to identify triggers, not only to help the in-the-moment stress reaction, but also the long-term repeated exposure to your trauma. Triggers expose you to your trauma again and again, meaning you're stressing your body and mind over and over, and keeping the feelings of fear and sadness present.

I may sound like a broken record, but I want to keep reminding you that we can't erase the memory from our brains, but we *can* help it become just that – a memory that we can actually grow from rather than be all-consumed by.

The more we can be in touch and observe our thought patterns from a distance, the more we can start to intervene. Remember, we might not totally be able to eliminate all our triggers in life. While we can and do recover from trauma, some triggers may remain. I definitely haven't figured out how to be trigger-free and, to be honest with you, I don't think I ever will. I'm not sure it's really possible with the memories I have.

I have, though, reduced the frequency of the triggers. And now the emotion with them is easily and quickly worked through, and they are very rarely powerful. I can reframe them and dissipate the feeling calmly and quickly, and carry on with what I'm doing. The more I do this, the less the trigger happens.

Once you start recognizing your triggers, it will make a huge difference in understanding what you are feeling and working through your trauma. It's all about learning how to be an observer and witness of your own mind, but also of your heart. If you're hurting, it's for a reason.

We don't process what we feel at the time. Triggers show us our past feelings that are still there. Time may have passed, but our fear, hurt and upset remains if the emotions weren't cared for in our past.

Don't worry if you find you have more triggers than you realized (I have many). Celebrate every little win, even if it seems small to you. You will, in turn, learn so much more about yourself and how your past affects you. All of this will help you grow in confidence so you can cope with and manage your triggers and the emotions attached to your past.

11

Our motivations: Drive, soothe and fear

Self-compassion plays a big role in managing our triggers, and you'll have noticed it being mentioned throughout all the themes that have come up in this book so far. Compassion is crucial to trauma recovery. So let's take some time to think about what compassion is, as it tends to all-but-disappear in trauma. It's not quite as simple as just being more compassionate to ourselves, because to be able to do this we first need to understand why we aren't.

Compassion is what will help us balance and regulate our emotions and stimulate the 'soothe' part of our motivational system (which we'll go into below). To 'soothe' is not just a form of 'self-care' or something done to babies. Our ability to soothe is actually built into how our nervous system regulates itself – it's how our brains are wired. When we 'soothe' our nervous system it goes into a **parasympathetic** state; in basic terms, that means our body can rest, digest and process. When we are living with unprocessed trauma, our nervous system is mainly in the **sympathetic** state; this is the fight-or-flight system, and is a state of stress of often severe intensity.

So, what do we mean by 'soothe'? I'm not sure I had any idea before I started working through and studying trauma. Well, I knew what it meant when it came to other people – to empathize and help ease their pain – but I couldn't seem to apply it to myself. Any guesses as to why that was? Yes, you got it in one: trauma.

DRIVE, SOOTHE, FEAR

Our fight-or-flight system is a natural physical and mental reaction to danger or something that is perceived as a threat. It's our brain trying to protect us from threat and fear. But we also have three interacting emotional motivational systems in our brain: drive, soothe and fear. Each system plays a role in what motivates and regulates our emotions, and in the way we behave and respond to different situations.

We all switch through these three systems when managing our emotions, as you can see in the diagram opposite. In trauma we often have an under-developed soothe system, which causes distress and stress, and keeps us in a closed state of fear.

The original motivational system model was created by Paul Gilbert, the founder of compassion-based therapy. He described the third factor as 'threat' instead of fear. In my own therapy I worked through this model as 'fear', but it basically means the same thing.

Drive

The 'drive' system is our feelings of ambition – it aims to motivate us to achieve, to pursue our goals and go after things that lead to success. We feel great immediately after engaging the drive system because we are excited and our body produces the 'feel-good' chemical dopamine. Those of us who tell ourselves we aren't good enough rely on the 'drive' system as a way to feel better about ourselves.

Fear

The 'fear' system (threat) is there to protect us – it is our innate human instinct to prepare us to fight, freeze or run away from physical danger. In today's world these are also non-physical threats, like anxiety, being scared, shame, suffering, distress – everything we've talked a lot about in this book. When our fear system is engaged (when we are stressed or scared) our nervous system goes into a sympathetic state and produces adrenaline and pumps it round the body quickly (an adrenaline rush).

Soothe

The 'soothe' system is there to make yourself feel calm and safe – it manages our stress and connects us with others. Everyone needs this in their daily life, and even more so following any kind of upset, painful experience, shock, grief or suffering. When our soothe system is engaged we feel content, safe, trusting and have a connection with others; and the body produces opiates (feel-good chemicals) and oxytocin (sometimes known as the 'love hormone' or 'cuddle chemical'). When these natural chemicals are missing, people search for this feeling elsewhere, say through drugs, alcohol or overeating, where the effect can be mimicked. Soothing is about giving ourselves the care, the rest, the taking of a deep breath; it is about being able to slow down the mind and, in turn, the nervous system. When this happens, our nervous system is in the parasympathetic state.

OUT OF BALANCE

Let's look further into how the motivational system works.

In an emotionally healthy individual the three systems would be fairly balanced – moving from fear to drive to soothe, to fear to soothe to drive, to soothe to fear to drive and back to soothe. If we are dominated heavily by one system it is hard to have good mental health. Even staying in soothe too much would keep us stuck – we wouldn't progress, grow or get anything done.

If one system rules the others, this can have harmful consequences:

- If fear dominates, we can often feel scared, 'on guard', 'under threat' and anxious (think of the guard dog always barking even when there is no danger).
- If we spend most of our time in drive, when something stops us from achieving we become distressed, self-critical and exhausted, which leads us to bypass soothe and head straight into our fear system (think of me and my perfectionism).
- If we spend all of our time in soothe, we stay where we are and get very stuck in our life.

In trauma, fear is the motivating, dominant system, with very little (if any) switching into soothe. And, without the ability to soothe, we can't balance or cope with our emotions.

This has an impact, not just on the mind, but on the physical body through the constant activation of stress hormones while in fear mode. In a state of trauma, we often allow ourselves to anticipate other people being unkind or threatening to us, which means we are actively stimulating our threat system (often without even realizing it). Trauma keeps us in a state of threat and fear, not just as an emotion, a perception, a thought or behaviour, but as a physical neurological response that your brain and body automatically does.

Remember, it's not your fault. You aren't just being or feeling like this because there's something wrong with you – and don't let anybody, including yourself, tell you that. It's fake news that's been around far too long, both inside and outside your head. This is just how our brains are neurologically wired thanks to trauma. This is science!

It can also sometimes feel safer to be in the fear system, especially when we've spent a lot of our lives having to be this way. But if we always feel under threat, we are going to stay in this fear system and it will dominate anything else we do. The soothe system was a stranger to me, I was less familiar with it; the fear and drive systems were best friends I'd known since childhood.

I asked myself how much time I thought I spent in each of these systems. I decided that it was around 5% in soothe and the rest fairly balanced between drive and fear – I just flipped between the two. It was as if drive was a big bouncy ball that bounced me to the fear bouncy ball, which just bounced me back to drive, which bounced me back to fear, and so on. Meanwhile, soothe was a tiny, hard golf ball trying to figure out how to get involved. You get the gist!

In recovery, the more you come to understand how your motivational system of drive, soothe and fear works, the more you can help your brain and body feel safe so that they don't have to be in overdrive all the time to protect you, particularly as the threat is in the past.

STUCK IN FEAR AND DRIVE MODE

The fear system is the most powerful of the three systems, so it takes work and repetition to help it understand that it doesn't always have to be 'on' for you to be safe. Remember that the fear system doesn't just react to real threats, but also to perceived threats. Trauma makes us feel like there are threats everywhere. I was always in protection mode: threat was there at all times (even when it wasn't, the possibility of it was). As a result, I was full of anxiety, anger, self-hatred, self-criticism, fear and shame.

Even when I came out of my coma, all my brain was doing was analysing what was going on and beating myself up for ending up in this position: 'How could I let myself get like this?' The rationality of the fact that it wasn't my fault didn't even come into play. Every single part of my mind and body was on alert, all the time.

This is what I wrote in my post-coma notebook.

So, fantastic news, I could survive.

I had learnt all the necessary skills to survive danger. So maybe I should be grateful for the flashes of my past that are coming up into my present.

The ever-presentness of our pasts. Fully alive and stronger than ever.

Is that why I am having these flashbacks? Have they kept me alive? Would I be dead if I hadn't gone through all those things in my past? Have those horrors driven me to live? Or am I so accustomed to trauma that I am just able to cope? Having to survive is just normal to me.

Is it a reminder of what I had been through to drive me forward to keep on living – fear, drive, fear, drive? I'm scared, do more, I'm scared, do better, I'm scared, be more, I'm scared, be better!

I feel like all I've done in my life, from the moment I first came into the world, is fight to keep on living. In a way, lying in this hospital bed battling isn't a strange place for me.

It's what I know.

The fear pushed into my drive. The fear motivated me. It has no place else to go. My anxiety, my anger, my disgust turns into wanting, achieving, pursuing, relentless pushing, unwavering focus, outward success.

But it pushes back to make me feel unsafe again, ashamed of who I am and what I've been through, to drive me forward once more to prove otherwise. If only I achieved more, I would be worthy. You are not worthy. Achieve more.

I had completely omitted one crucial step of how we as 'normal' humans manage our emotions, like many people who have gone through what I have: to soothe. To help manage distress and form relationships. The feelings of safety, trust, protection, rest, contentment, self-love and self-care.

All just words.

It was never an option.

Constant fear means you stay there, always fighting.

I am alive, out of the coma but I feel no peace, just more torment.

Fear makes its home in every part of my body. I must be better. I must do better.

It's a pretty accurate example of our motivating emotional regulation systems of fear and drive, and the cycle of distress, self-criticism, and hopelessness it leads to. It's also a very good example of what happens when soothe is completely missing – no feelings of safety, trust, protection, rest, contentment, self-love and self-care.

I mentioned earlier in the book that before I started working through my trauma, I couldn't take a bath. Not because I didn't have a bathtub, but because I felt like I didn't deserve it. By the way, I'm talking about a warm bath, not an ice bath; I didn't have a problem with ice baths because (and this, perhaps, won't surprise you by now) ice baths are something of a challenge and bring a sense of achievement. Challenge and achieve – my place of safety. Ironically, the comforting warm bath felt unsafe to me.

On the few occasions that I did have a hot bubble bath (which was normally after doing some kind of crazy physical endurance challenge) it would make me really anxious because my critical voice would tell me I wasn't worth it. Then, the demanding part of the voice would tell me that I hadn't done enough to earn it, and that I should do more. My drive system would kick in, and make me so full of adrenaline that I'd be tapping my feet in the water like I was trapped and desperate to get out. My breath would shorten, I'd pull at the skin on my face and repeatedly swallow to try to get more air in, because I'd then flipped into threat/fear. In a supposedly relaxing bath, soothe was nowhere in sight.

The act of having a bath also came with some past triggers from when I lived at home. I was only allowed to use the shower after everyone else and for the shortest time. I rarely had a bath because if my step-dad decided at that moment he wanted to use the bathroom, all hell would break loose. This also didn't go away when I was older. I didn't live with my family anymore, but I did go back a lot, because I couldn't bear to leave my mum and brothers alone there. So, I put up with continued abuse and humiliation throughout my adulthood to make sure that I was there for my mum and brothers. This kept me in trauma, as I still felt the same feelings as I had as a child, despite appearing strong, successful and independent to the outside world.

The vicious circle of the threat and drive means we stay exactly where we are, fighting, in trauma.

WORKING TOWARD SOOTHE

Having a bath, believe it or not, was one of the big goals of my trauma recovery. For people working through trauma it's not as simple as, 'Be kind to yourself and do some self-care.' Being kind to ourselves is something we have to learn and relearn how to do, and do safely, a bit at a time, so as to not panic the fear system. Being in soothe can feel dangerous, because if you relax and drop your guard for a moment, the fear system may feel vulnerable and exposed because it's been so used to being active and in charge of you. This can feel like panic, agitation, anxiety, or a claustrophobic sensation – like you need to move. It can also set off your critical self-talk, bringing up feelings of guilt and thoughts about being undeserving of doing something caring and restful.

Self-care can feel scary and unsafe. I had to work toward having a bath and talk myself through why it was helpful for me. I had to teach myself how important it was to 'soothe', and tell myself that the scared vulnerable me was worth taking care of and was enough just as I was.

I would start by just running the bath and sitting in it for a few minutes with a book to help distract my brain. It would have to be after having done a physical activity or worked a long day, as being fatigued would help my nervous system feel calm for a minute. I gradually increased the time spent in the bath, and once I was comfortable with that, I started to take a bath on a day when I hadn't 'achieved something' or 'pushed myself' to deserve it. Again, it would involve a book; then I found that having a cup of tea helped. I love tea and find it really soothing; it reminds me of my grandad – comforting and safe. Gradually, by using these techniques, taking a bath no longer triggered my critical voice and anxiety. It started to actually become – dare I say it – *relaxing*. My brain switched off because my nervous system had finally calmed down, indicating I was safe.

It's funny looking back now because so many people, even my own family, would say, 'You don't like baths do you?', and I'd respond, 'No, not really my thing'; never acknowledging to myself or others that it was because baths triggered me so much, not just in my mind and thoughts but my physical body, too. Learning how to 'soothe' makes us more able to cope with things that get thrown our way. It makes us stronger and more capable.

HOW YOUR MEMORIES ARE LINKED TO YOUR NERVOUS SYSTEM

When we say trauma is 'in our body', it's in our memory and in the emotional core of the brain (the hippocampus and amygdala) that's part of our nervous system, which triggers our body to react as if it's in danger. That is why we need to focus on memory and emotions to heal trauma.

I cannot stress how much we need to go back to the memory in order to recover (and I know I've stressed it quite a lot of times already!). Essentially, if we change how we process our distressing memories, we can stop our nervous system from living our day-to-day life in our fear system because of our painful past experiences.

It's about *reprocessing your hurt safely*. I feel awful just writing that sentence because I know how hard it is to do, and how much you probably don't want to do it. Neither did I. As you have read, when I first saw Dr Rachel it was like pulling teeth for her. I repeatedly refused to talk about anything really, even though I had put *myself* on the waiting list for help through the NHS. I waited months, and when I got my first appointment and made the effort to go, I didn't want to talk about anything.

TRAUMA OVERLOAD

As mentioned in Chapter 4, our bodies can remember trauma, even if we're unaware of it. Normally, the first thing that happens in trauma is our body reacts. That's why observing your physical reactions is a good way to help you understand what you are feeling. The body also tries to protect the brain from 'trauma overload'.

There was a woman in my group who was struggling to cope with some of the very painful things she'd been through, and it was affecting her friendships and relationships. She had to travel a long way just to attend the group therapy as she no longer lived in the area – nonetheless she came. But every time she tried to talk about how she was feeling, tell her story and explore her thoughts, she would fall asleep. I sat next to her once – she was really upset and trying to tell us something, but her eyes started to droop open and closed, and I could see she was desperately fighting the heaviness of her eyelids. In the end, she just shut her eyes and slept in the middle of the session.

This happened every time things got too much for her. She was so overwhelmed that her brain couldn't cope so it literally shut down. After meeting this woman, I remembered how my mum used to just fall asleep. It used to frustrate me and make me feel like I had to take charge, although I was a child myself. As I got older, I used to joke with her that she was always tired and could fall asleep anywhere, but seeing how this group member responded to trauma really triggered me, and when I started to look into it, I realized my mum falling asleep was also a trauma response.

If our brain has dealt with trauma repeatedly, it will perceive a lack of control in any challenging or triggering situation, and just close down. And even though the person isn't in the terrible moment(s) from the past, the brain and body don't realize or understand the harm is no longer present because it is stuck in trauma. As a consequence, the person will be helpless to make a different choice on how to deal with their past or their future.

Physical reactions that minimize experience

One of the involuntary physical things I would do when in trauma overload was smile. You might think to smile seems like a nice thing, but wait until you see somebody smiling while talking about how scared they felt when they thought they were going to die, or talking about being sexually abused as a child. I looked like Chucky's sister, but a scarier version. Dr Rachel brought it to my attention: 'Why are you smiling when you are telling us something so awful? It's actually really sad and makes me really upset to see you do this.' It's a psychological mechanism known as the 'inappropriate affect' – a reaction that doesn't match the situation.

I remembered having a massive grin on my face while I was sharing something that I hadn't told anyone before. I was talking about what I would do after some of my training sessions with my athletics group when our coach was abusing us. Behind the back of the running track was a path that was lined with Portakabin-style rundown buildings, which I'd walk along to climb through a small hole in the railings to get to my bus stop. I would punch the side of a Portakabin without even thinking, hard enough to draw blood until my hand was numb. I'd then cry, climb through the railings and get on my bus. It's a terrible story and I was in crippling pain and depression when telling it, yet the words coming out of my mouth were not matching my expression – I wasn't just smiling, I was laughing about it.

It's common in trauma to do this. It's another coping mechanism – my brain couldn't cope with what I was talking about so my response distanced me from it. Smiling is a way to minimize the experience, to protect you from feeling the pain, indicating that your trauma isn't important because you're not important, and it can also be a sign of shame.

Sadly, smiling and laughing (or falling asleep) during a distressing recounting of an experience means we aren't processing our pain or emotions. So, the recovery and healing doesn't take place. These responses also give a false cue to whoever is around us at the time – it shows others that we are totally okay with what happened, that it wasn't that bad.

THE PHYSICAL MANIFESTATION OF TRAUMA

Trauma is most certainly not just 'in our heads'. It leads to physical manifestations that can have a significant impact on the body if the trauma isn't processed and worked through. If you think about what your body does in a state of fear and hyperarousal (the threat system) – adrenaline rushes through your body, your muscles tense up, your heart beats faster, you sweat, you hold your breath and clench your teeth – when this happens again and again and again, it's bound to have an impact over time.

It can lead to chronic stress, fatigue and migraines, as well as a greater risk of type 2 diabetes. It destroys the body's resistance to illness, increases blood pressure and the risk of cardiovascular problems, like heart attack. Trauma can cause problems with infertility and sexual dysfunction, and inflammation that over time leads to organ damage. A recent study found that people with trauma were at a 25% higher risk of developing a gastric disorder. Trauma, in some cases, can lead to substance misuse which, in turn, damages organs. There's even research on cancer patients who have experienced unexpected remission, citing that releasing emotional stress or trauma was one of the key factors in their healing. Kelly Turner, PhD, wrote a bestselling book on it, *Radical Remission: Surviving Cancer Against All Odds* (Bravo, 2015).

I saw a reflexologist recently when visiting Mexico – a woman called Nashville, Nash for short, who I met through a friend. I was lying on my back with my eyes covered, Nash at my feet (as you know this is initially triggering for me, but after a few minutes of grounding and telling myself I was safe, I could focus on the current moment). About 30 minutes into the session, Nash said, 'Can I ask you something?' I said, 'Yes.' 'It might be very personal, is that okay?', she said. I responded, 'Yes,' although slightly wary of what she was going to ask.

She pressed on a certain area of my foot, and asked, 'This hurts, doesn't it?' It was the only painful part of the pressure points on my feet, and was the part she'd been working on for the last 15 minutes while I tried to breathe and not react to how painful it was. As soon as she moved off that point, the pain went away.

'Do you get very sad?', she asked. For a second, I was taken aback by her question, but there was something about Nash that felt very safe and open. I said, 'Yes.' She said, 'You are feeling the pain when I press on the pressure point for your heart and psoas, and there is a lot of pain and sadness that you need to let go.' The psoas muscle is often called the fight-or-flight muscle because it tenses with traumatic experience. Nash had never met me before, and didn't know anything about me. She said that I was so physically strong that there was no work she could do for me, I was a picture of physical health. But my body was holding onto my emotional pain, and Nash could feel it. She told me that I didn't need to hold on to it anymore, I was safe and needed to release the sadness, which was holding me back and keeping me sad.

Touch through reflexology or massage can help people who find physical closeness through intimacy hard. These therapies can be a way to get physical closeness, comfort and touch in an emotionally safer way.

CHANGING THE WAY YOUR BODY AND MIND REACT

To be really clear: these powerful responses from your nervous system do not happen just because you've been through something. Your body reacts in this way when you continue to stay in trauma, in your fear system. If you don't give your painful memories any room to heal, the body holds on to the stress.

Likewise, the body can convince the mind it's safe by doing breathing exercises and calming the nervous system. Through breathing practices, the adrenaline rush slows down and when the mind realizes it thinks, 'Okay. I must be safe now, so no need for me to shut my emotions off.'

With greater understanding and acceptance of trauma, approaches to recovery have been developed that focus on connecting the mind to the body.

Somatic practices to heal trauma

I have spent a lot of time working through what happened to me and working through my past, my story (think back to flowers and stones in Chapter 5). This narrative exposure and prolonged exposure to our past is strongly recommended by experts globally, as is psychoeducation – understanding and gaining knowledge about psychological and emotional wellbeing, mental health and learning strategies – which we are doing throughout this book.

I also practised 'somatic experiencing', which is more of a physical or movement practice. Somatic is defined as 'relating to the body', and helps us with our mind–body connection. This practice is effectively body-centred, so rather than just focusing on our thoughts and emotions, we include our body's natural response to trauma. Somatic experiencing was first developed by trauma therapist Dr Peter Levine.

Somatic approaches are known as bottom-up trauma processing, which is focusing on the body's automatic responses to feeling unsafe – the visceral responses and body sensations – rather than just on the primal (survival) part of the brain.

Breathing

Examples of somatic practices include yoga, deep breathing, mindful walking, muscle relaxation, tai-chi and meditation, even running.

I learnt meditation and yoga with a yoga master, Neil Patel, who has a long history of yoga in his family. I'm certainly not a 'meditate every morning' type, but learning breathing techniques has helped me incorporate them in my general life, especially when I'm feeling overwhelmed and on alert.

A study from 2022 found that yoga can help with trauma symptoms because, through movement and deep breathing, it activates the parasympathetic rest-and-digest nervous system which, as you know, is exactly the opposite of trauma.

Viann N. Nguyen-Feng, the director of the Mind-Body Trauma Care Lab at the University of Minnesota (USA), which is dedicated to increasing access to holistic and trauma-informed mental health care, wrote a research paper on yoga as an intervention for psychological symptoms of trauma. The paper claimed: 'Yoga, running and other forms of somatic movement allow us to tap into the inner wisdom of our bodies and provide a method of grounding us in the here and now, rather than being stuck in our minds.'

Mindful body check

When I first started working with Neil, I was in one of the most heightened periods of my life following my critical illness. I'd walk into his bright white studio like a wound-up Tasmanian devil – not that I've ever seen one, but I always think I probably resembled the Looney Tunes cartoon character. I wasn't even able to sit down properly without tapping my foot, fidgeting and speaking at a million miles an hour. I was also suffering terrible vertigo and migraines from trauma that left me at times unable to see or speak. And then I'd leave Neil's studio a different person – no migraine, vertigo completely gone and with a stillness that had felt totally impossible to achieve an hour before. And all because I'd calmed my nervous system down by focusing on my body.

Initially, Neil got me to lie down on the floor to be able to get me to connect with my body. It was important – though triggering – for me to do this, so I could start retraining my brain to understand that every time I was in this position it didn't mean danger. I needed to learn that my brain didn't *have* to take me back to the horrifically frightening moments when I was sexually abused on a school table or when I was lying in a hospital bed fighting for my life every time I lay down like this. Imagine what that stress was doing to my body, let alone my mind.

Lying down on the floor, Neil would help me do a 'body check': starting from your feet, you connect your mind to each part of your body as you slowly work up toward your head. This gentle practice allowed me to start feeling a little safer, take down the high alert a notch and relax my fight-or-flight sympathetic nervous system.

With the body check, you don't have to do anything, it's simply about noticing and observing what is going on in your body, which helps bring your mind into the present.

I'd love to invite you to do a body check now. Even if it's just a quick one. Let me take you through it. You can always mark this page and return to it later.

PERFORM A BODY CHECK

- Close your eyes, lie flat on the floor with arms and legs spread out like a starfish.
- Focus on your breathing. Try to breathe into your stomach through your nose and out through your mouth.

- If you notice your mind wandering, think about what you are doing this body check for. Answer your mind and tell it, '*I'm doing this to help me show my body I am safe now.*'
- Now, focus on each specific body part: start with your feet and slowly move up your legs. Notice your calves, your knees and the tops of your thighs. Are you clenching anywhere? If so, relax the muscle.
- Notice your stomach. I almost guarantee you are holding your stomach in tight – let it out, let it expand and flop.
- Notice your chest. Are you holding your breath, or breathing shallowly into your chest? Remember to try to breathe into your stomach through your nose and out through your mouth.
- Notice your shoulders and your neck. Relax your shoulders. Are you tightening your neck to breathe?
- Move up to your jaw. Is it clenched? If so, unclench it. (My jaw is nearly always clenched.)
- Notice your eyes. If they are scrunched up, unscrunch them. Relax your frown.

Your mind should now be in the present, instead of completely in your own head. The body scan will have moved your nervous system from sympathetic (fight-or-flight) to parasympathetic, the place of rest, processing and digesting.

The more we can train ourselves to move ourselves out of our fear system into our soothe system, the more we can start to change how our body responds, and that allows us to work through and process our trauma.

Eventually, I'd come to Neil's studio without needing to do the body check practice with him. This meant I could begin to learn deeper meditation exercises with him, which had been impossible before as I was far too on edge. Through the body check practice, I also learnt to soothe myself whenever I was triggered by lying down. That was huge progress for me. I realized that I don't have to carry on reliving those memories.

Other somatic practices

I know it's not for everybody, but running also helps calm my nervous system and regulate my emotions. For those that know me, you know I had to get running in this book! The joke is often that wherever I am I'll have got there by running. When I feel like I have no tolerance for anything because I have all these big emotions coming to the surface at once, running releases them and calms the intensity down a notch.

There has been significant research that shows running can be used to train your nervous system into understanding that, even if your heart rate is increased and your breathing is elevated, that doesn't equal danger. Running connects your mind to your body's physical sensations in a safe way. It can help manage triggers and boost the feel-good chemicals of serotonin and dopamine in your brain.

For me, running makes me feel like my load is a little lighter, I am able to breathe (ironically) and am free to just be. Running when I was younger wasn't necessarily somatic for me, as I focused a lot on goals, times and pushing myself to self-harm.

Running is somatic when you focus on your body, your surroundings, the ground underneath you, your breathing. It then becomes about self-awareness, reducing stress and creating a stronger mind–body connection.

Other types of somatic movement that can help include dance, tai chi, breathwork or hiking (being mindful and in nature can be really positive).

The practice of reconnecting with the body could also be done through acupuncture or massage, as these practices can help release emotional pain that is held in the body's tissues. For the same reason, there is some evidence that acupuncture can help symptoms of PTSD.

FINDING BALANCE AND REGULATION

Dr Rachel describes actions like going for a run, yoga or even reading as 'behavioural activation'.

'People can do a lot themselves to help them recover and process. We call this "behavioural activation" – doing activities to release endorphins, to regulate stress. It's like pre-work to psychology. Go for a run if you are anxious. Read your book at night to comfort you and calm your brain so you can fall asleep. A lot of research shows that behavioural activation can alleviate depression.'

Dr Rachel O'Beney

Behavioural activation involves turning on a more helpful, optimistic and healthy emotional state by deliberately practising certain behaviours.

Think back to that system of drive/fear/soothe. We need to connect and strengthen the soothe element to have more of a balanced system. This is essential for emotional regulation and, in turn, key to healing trauma.

CREATE BALANCE BETWEEN DRIVE, FEAR AND SOOTHE

There are behavioural actions you can introduce into your routine that will help you work toward a better balance between the systems.

- Start by setting a goal of doing one thing that is soothing (i.e. that activates your soothe system) once a day (if that's too much, once or twice a week). Because this isn't something people with trauma naturally do, setting a goal is important; it will create an active awareness to do this and help your body to learn how to safely be in your soothe system.

- Write down a list of things (see the connection card box below) that are soothing to you and put it somewhere you'll have eyes on it regularly, like your fridge or the back of a door. You may find it difficult to figure out what is soothing, which is understandable as you haven't spent a lot of time in the soothe system. Think of 'soothe' as what is kind and caring. I started doing small things like making myself a hot drink, usually a cup of tea, but then I would progress to making a hot chocolate. Something I previously would only have done if I felt I deserved it.

- Observe what happens when you do the soothing actions. Be aware it might set your inner critic off, telling you off for caring for yourself. Remember to reassure yourself that you are enough, you are safe and you deserve to recover, and this is part of it.

- If it feels overwhelming, try it for just a few minutes and practise increasing the time and frequency.

Incorporating these soothing actions into your life will make your mind and body think it is safe. As we now know, trauma has no place in safety – feeling safe sucks the life out of trauma.

Connection Card

SOOTHE STRATEGIES

If you're stuck in fear or drive mode, the effort it takes to think of these soothe strategies can become overwhelming or create a barrier to action.

So, to give you immediate access to your soothe techniques, I suggest creating a connection card with the following activities (and add your own!).

o   Sit with a hot drink

o   Light an aromatic candle

o   Go out in nature

o   Listen to music

o   Have a warm bath (you could even add some comforting smells by using bath oils)

o   Draw/paint/colour in

o   Use a diffuser with essential oils

o   Get an early night

o   Cook your favourite meal

o   Wrap a blanket round you

o   Knit/crochet/embroider

o   Cuddle up to a hot water bottle

o   Read a book

o   Buy yourself some flowers

o   Engage in any of the physical activities we've discussed earlier in the chapter

Keep this card alongside your Emotionally Healthy Messages connection card to use in your wallet or bag, so you've always got them to hand and so you can use them together.

Remember, activating soothe doesn't replace drive. It won't make you ineffective, unproductive or weak. In fact, soothe is essential for drive to be effective, productive and strong. You will be able to enter into drive feeling energized, safe and connected, rather than exhausted, scared and disconnected.

Spending more time in soothe and discovering safe practices that work for you will help you soothe with care, rather than with self-harming 'disordered soothing' through things like drugs, overeating, gambling, over-exercise, alcohol or risky behaviour.

I think a lot of us do these soothing behavioural activations already, without even realizing. Once you understand what they are, and how our wonderfully complex mind, brain and body works, you can start to do those things (and others) with consciousness, and incorporate them into your learning about trauma recovery.

I want to encourage you that, armed with the right tools and understanding, you can start to heal yourself using 'behavioural activations'. If you've got this far into this book, you are already doing this. You should be proud of yourself for getting to this stage. I spent years trying to figure all this out, and even more years trying to apply it.

SQUARE/BOX BREATHING TECHNIQUE

A deep breathing technique I would recommend you try is square breathing, sometimes called box breathing.

Research has shown that this is an effective treatment for trauma, and has even been labelled by medical professionals as an 'exceptional treatment' for trauma and everything around trauma, including anxiety, depression and general daily stress.

This is a technique that Dr Niki gives all her patients. She said some people can't believe she's saying a breathing exercise

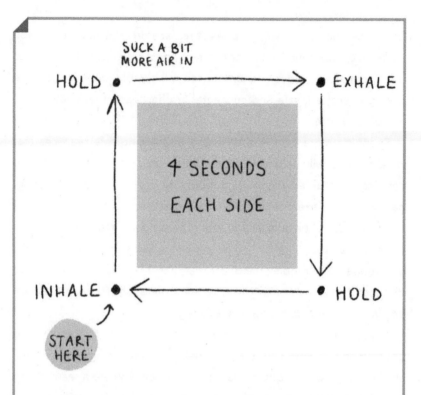

will solve their problems. I get that. I felt like everything I was going through and had been through was so much bigger than a breathing exercise. But in this chapter, we've discovered breathing and somatic practices tell the nervous system it's safe, which is the opposite of trauma. So, give it a go.

Square breathing involves making a square with your breath. Notice it's not called rectangle breathing, so make sure you keep all sides even so it forms a square. You can do this anywhere.

- Take a deep breath in through the nose from your lower belly, feel it expand and count to four. This is the 'up' arrow.
- Hold it along the top of the square, suck a bit more air in and count to four.

- Slowly with control, breathe out for four evenly – the 'down' arrow.
- Then hold at the bottom of the square for four, and repeat.

If the four count is too long to start with, reduce it to two, and then you can build it to four, or even longer. When I was working with Neil, after months of practice I managed to get it to 12 counts each side. If your mind wanders, don't worry about it – that's just what minds do – just go back to the count.

12

Letting go

The thought of actually getting better made me feel scared and unsafe. How would I protect myself from getting hurt? How would I push myself through the process? How could I be strong?

My protective mechanisms had become very much a natural part of who I was. My past was ingrained in my identity. My independence, drive and strength were built on my hurt. My voice came from my feelings of injustice. If all that went, who would I be left with?

FUELLED BY TRAUMA

I was good at being in trauma. Actually, I wasn't just good at it – I would go as far as to say I was the master of all masters of it.

I could detach from people who loved me so I didn't get hurt. I could push myself to the limit, and then some, because I didn't think I was enough (and I felt better when I was harming myself). I could get myself back to work after being in a coma with a big smile on my face, despite throwing up through exhaustion and crying all night, every night, when I got home.

I even held on to the fact that my difficult past experiences were why I survived my critical illness when the doctors said the odds were minimal. And I do still believe there's some truth in that. The doctors said that I was incredibly strong, not just physically but mentally. I did fight. Fighting is one of the things I had mastered.

I am really good in tough situations. I have an ability to survive, and I'm a great person to have around in a chaotic emergency-type situation. Why? Because it's what I know best. I'm already in fight-or-flight all the time. I'm already in trauma and ready to fight and survive. I mean, I find running across the length of England – which I have done – easier than caring for myself and having a loving relationship. I know that sounds like a great achievement – and it really was, I'm not taking anything away from that – but I can't do that every day. And even if I thought I could, my body would eventually break, and so would my mental state.

At the time I took on that epic run, I was very much 'not in trauma recovery'. I pulled my shin muscle on the first day and had a gastro virus which led to a few dodgy situations and multiple toilet stops – even in a kebab shop, much to everyone's amusement. Running on a torn shin put me in hospital at 3am three days into my run; against doctor's advice I carried on for the remaining four days. I made it to the end of the run, despite damaging my body, and attended the party and live auction that I'd arranged the very same night. All I cared about was raising enough money for the amazing charity Women's Aid. It meant everything to me that I did that, but I didn't care for myself. In fact, I actively ignored my pain. Everybody celebrated and partied into the night, while I went home and collapsed with exhaustion.

I was scared of getting better because I was scared of letting go of that relentless drive system that dominated me. I was scared of letting my trauma go because I didn't know who I was without it. But I also didn't know *how* to let it go. All my efforts of letting my pain go – extreme exercise, overworking – kept it front and centre, because I was trying to let my pain *go* without having *let it in*.

You can't let go of something you haven't let in.

Our trauma influences our behaviour subconsciously and involuntarily. Part of that behaviour for me was to avoid and detach from my emotions and any emotional pain I was in. As we now know, this is very common in trauma. But that person who is avoiding and detaching is not who you really are. These behaviours are protective responses to pain and fear, but by blocking the emotions, you can't actually let them go.

Letting your trauma in is to allow yourself to feel and experience the emotions associated with the traumatic thing(s) that happened to you. Only then you can let the pain go. By refusing to grieve for myself and the emotional pain I was in, it stayed inside of me, pushed deep down but seeping out through protective behaviours that, in a vicious cycle, kept it in place.

For as long as I'd known, I'd been trying to survive. I called myself a survivor, and very much felt like I was *still* surviving. I never thought that I might have actually survived, so didn't need to keep holding on for dear life every day.

SURVIVOR

I have made it through all of the really awful things that have happened to me. And so have you. The struggle comes from what those experiences have left us with.

I'm alive, after being technically dead at one point due to critical illness. I'm alive, after the many risky situations I put myself in because of my trauma. I'm alive, after the times I hurt myself because I didn't want to live. I'm alive, after the dangerous household I lived in where every morning we weren't sure if today would be the day that it all went too far and ended life for all of us. I'm alive, after the teenage girl, my mum, fought to keep me and fought to raise me. I'm alive, after being abused by my running coach.

My coach got convicted and put in prison. I'm no longer living with or in contact with my step-dad – in fact, none of my family is under his control anymore; my mum left after 29 years of marriage (with a Lidl bag of belongings and £40) and divorced him.

I survived the heartbreak of my grandad's death, who was like a father figure to me. I've survived all the things that have been thrown at me in adulthood, including abusive relationships and additional family trauma as a result of the years of abuse we all suffered. I've even survived my most recent heartbreak from unsuccessful IVF attempts, which is triggering for me in all directions. I didn't try for children earlier because of my past trauma. It has definitely been challenging to not allow the critical voice to start growing in power again – *'This is your fault. You're a failure.'*

Thankfully, my healthy caring self is much stronger – *'You are enough, whether this happens for you or not. You can try again. You can adopt.'* I spent the majority of my most fertile years avoiding getting pregnant. Once I'd got through to a place of trauma recovery, I realized that it was me that was preventing myself from having a family of my own, because I was scared of repeating our generational family trauma.

I've survived …

… but, damn, it's so hard letting go.

It's actually scary to be without all my pain.

LETTING GO IS NOT GIVING UP

Letting go doesn't mean giving it all up so that you won't be able to protect yourself emotionally or physically if the need arises. As life is, we can't avoid painful experiences, so we might as well live in a place of emotional and psychological wellbeing rather than in a place of trauma everyday trying to protect us from something bad happening. If and when it has to, your brain will do what needs to be done to protect you automatically.

Letting go will create a 'healthy adult you' who can balance your needs and responsibilities. This 'you' will know it's safe to feel emotions because it will comfort your vulnerability and reassure you that it will take care of you. It won't abandon you when you're feeling sad and hurt. This 'you' will be able to sit in a feeling without running away from it. This 'you' will enjoy you having fun and seeing you laugh and smile, rather than criticizing you for it. This 'you' will know you have value, no matter what past experiences that have caused you trauma.

A SIDE NOTE ON PROGRESS

Although I've structured this book so that one chapter will feed into the next learning step, it doesn't mean that I expect you to have aced that step by the time you've finished the chapter!

You might want to go back over and revisit elements we've covered, especially ones that you feel are particularly sensitive to you.

Be aware of the chapters you want to *avoid* going back over, as normally those are the ones you need to work through more.

This chapter is about letting go, but all the earlier chapters are part of the path to letting go.

EMOTIONAL CONNECTION TO TRAUMA

In trauma, we hold on to our protective coping behaviours because they make us feel safe by making us think we are protecting ourselves from experiencing any further pain (although it's a false feeling of safety); we respond to past hurts by trying to prevent and avoid future hurts.

Despite all the horribleness, we still have a deep emotional connection to what we've been through. We might not like to admit that – I don't like to admit it – but it's an uncomfortable truth. We can't help it, that's just the way we are all wired. We get comfortable with our pain. And so, losing our pain is still an emotional loss.

In the process of reprocessing in order to let go, we may feel some self-blame, which may make us feel shame. Be mindful of those avoiding and detaching protective coping mechanisms kicking in. Remember that these mechanisms work in the short term to block the pain, but the pain is still there and it will keep us in trauma. This is very normal and part of the 'non-chronological' aspect of trauma recovery. Remember, you now have more understanding and knowledge than you had before; you now have tools. So every time you feel like the process of recovery is pushing you backward, you're actually moving forward ten times more just by engaging with the process.

LETTING GO MEANS CHANGE

Just as the emotional connection we have with our trauma makes it hard to let go of it, it's also hard to let go because that means change, and with change comes uncertainty. Even though the change will take us to a safer place, as we let go and heal, the healing feels scary because it's unfamiliar.

Familiarity is predictable – we know what we're going to get. What if the letting go creates more painful experiences? This is untested and untrodden ground. The way you are currently feeling is well trodden, so at least you know what you are going to get, even if it feels awful. It seems self-contradictory, but we cling on to what we don't want. Trauma keeps us in dread, yet the thought of losing it gives us dread too. It's absurd, I know!

It's important to understand that this fear of change is not a conscious decision – we are responding like this unconsciously. Sticking with the status quo – even if it's not good for us – is a learnt response to what we already know, and we don't know any different. As Freud said, we are destined to repeat our behaviours and emotions, and create situations based on our past experiences, until we remember and work through these unresolved memories.

'There's a repetition of feelings in your present that you should have had back in the awful moments but repressed because you had to, to get through it at the time.'

Dr Rachel O'Beney

FINDING A NEW IDENTITY AND GETTING YOUR BASIC NEEDS MET

Our experiences were painful but they are part of us, and they are why we are who we are. Letting go can feel like we are letting go of some of our identity. That protection part of us that doesn't want us to be hurt again will try to grip on. It will ask, *'How can you possibly survive if I can't constantly protect you from danger and the hurts that come with it?'* This is our learnt experience.

Survival is our first instinct. As humans, we are wired to avoid pain and do everything to have the best chance of survival, but not necessarily to thrive. This was all well and good when we were being hunted by predator animals and in a world where we had to catch our own food.

Survival is based on how we best adapt to our environment. If we are in distressing and disturbing situations, we engage the coping mechanisms we've covered in the book – we detach, avoid, defend, comply with everything and everybody, even bully or attack others to protect ourselves from anything that may feel like a threat. Again, this is great if you face imminent danger, but these behaviours in our current environment are more often harmful than helpful.

Our protective coping behaviours work amazingly in awful situations, but are not so useful when our survival in society is based on human connection, love, belonging, relevance, self-fulfilment and autonomy. These basic needs are 'universal' – a term used in psychology that means it applies to all of us, no matter what our demographic, culture or personality, and sits across all theories and practices that we share. These universal needs are as important as shelter, food and water due to the complexity and ever-changing world we live in. They play a crucial role in our mental health, in social connection, in our ability to adapt, our cognitive development and how we navigate challenges.

Self-Determination Theory in psychology states that to psychologically survive we need three things to be able to thrive and grow:

1. **Competence** (to be effective in something)
2. **Autonomy** (the ability to act on our own values and interests, and one of the many reasons why domestic abuse is so detrimental)
3. **Relatedness** (to have close affectionate relationships with others)

Schema therapy, which is what I studied, defines five emotional and psychological needs that we all require from childhood:

1. **Autonomy/a sense of identity**. The need to have the independence to make and influence your own choices and behaviour, to take responsibility and be accountable for yourself, and to feel a sense of control over your actions and the consequences of them. It is about knowing your values and

aligning them with your life. For example, being in a relationship or a workplace that reflects your autonomy. The opposite would be a controlling relationship or toxic work environment that limits your autonomy and therefore your identity.

2. **Secure safe attachment**. The need to have trusting, supportive and healthy relationships (friends, family, partners/romantic) that create emotional safety and support.

3. **Freedom to express your own feelings and needs**. The need and ability to say how you feel, to feel your emotion, to say what you're thinking and what you need without judgement or something bad happening, like punishment or retribution. It's about having emotionally healthy communication and wellbeing (which is impacted severely by trauma).

4. **Spontaneity and play**. The need to have fun and feel joy! This is about doing playful activities that are creative, stress-relieving and engaging. Cue dancing, painting, being silly with friends, playing games (board games, sports games) – anything that brings you joy.

5. **Appropriate self-control**. The need to understand and manage our emotions, impulses and behaviours in an emotionally healthy way. For example, if you're feeling angry, this would be about being able to identify that you feel angry, understanding your anger and where it's coming from, rather than screaming at somebody and taking your anger out on them. It's not about 'controlling' your emotions but letting them out in a healthy way. I'm not a fan of the term 'self-control', as it has negative connotations for me. It triggers me to feel like it's about holding in our self-expression and feelings, which is everything I've spent a long time undoing because of my trauma; but the key word here is 'appropriate'.

Connection Card

BASIC NEEDS

It might be helpful to write the five basic needs on pages 240–41 down on a connection card to keep alongside your Emotionally Healthy Messages and Soothe Strategies cards.

While each need is defined in detail in the book, on your connection card, pick a few key words to remind you of the needs and their definitions.

For quick reference, I put my Basic Needs card on my bedside table (so it now has plenty of tea stains on it).

Don't worry if you feel like some of these basic needs aren't a part of your life yet. Living with trauma often means a life without these basic needs! Meeting these basic needs is recovery from trauma. If you notice, they all link into everything we have been working on so far: healthy relationships; understanding, feeling and expressing our emotions; growing through our past to be able to feel safe enough to have fun and bring joy into our lives. Keep checking in on these basic needs.

We need all of these things both as children and adults. We may officially be grown up, but we all have that 'inner child' in us. Our inner child is the part of us that holds our emotions, memories and beliefs from the past, as well as our hopes for the future. And if you didn't have your basic needs met as a child, then you won't expect to have them met as an adult.

Sometimes the idea of the inner child is relatable, and sometimes it can put people off doing the work, as it makes them feel a little silly. That's totally normal. But see it like this: your inner child is your subconscious that has learnt and picked up messages and behaviours as a kid and stored them in your brain before you've been able to process mentally and emotionally what they are.

Our subconscious influences our actions and feelings, but it is not fully aware it's doing this. Hence why we have to go back in order to move forward. We can't let go of and heal from upsetting emotions and memories if those memories are sitting in our subconscious that our conscious mind doesn't recognize. Makes sense, right? This is the same as Freud's unconscious mind that we covered in Chapter 6.

What we are doing in this book, as hard as it is, is bringing our difficult memories and feelings into the conscious so they don't dominate our present and future without us realizing, and so we can let them go.

Remember, you deserve these universal basic needs. You deserve healthy, supportive and safe relationships. You deserve to grow and feel fulfilled. You deserve to have the ability to decide what is right for you. All this defines letting go.

THE PAIN IN LETTING GO

I know how much this hurts. Sometimes working through my trauma made me so sad. Other times, it would make me so angry that Dr Rachel told me to punch the cushions, which did actually help. I also did a lot of boxing during that time, and the punchbags got a real hammering. At times, I would just sit and cry after being so angry. I never cried so much in my life as I did when I was working through my trauma.

Letting go is also grieving. You're grieving for yourself, for your hurts, for what you've had to deal with, and for the things you've missed out on because of trauma. If your trauma comes from the loss of someone else, you are also grieving that loss. Grief is prominent in trauma recovery, no matter where your trauma has come from. Grieving is the process of letting go.

Think about whether you had your basic needs met when you were younger. It can be upsetting if you didn't have these essential needs fulfilled – it feels really hurtful. Let yourself be upset about it. You need to grieve the fact that you didn't, and understand what you do now because of that. I might sound like a broken record, but I'm going to say it again: we can only make emotionally healthier choices for ourselves if we understand the impact our trauma has on us and the hurts we carry.

It will feel hurtful, crappy, annoying, frustrating, and it can make you feel sad and angry as you process this. I'm sorry you have to. It's totally shitty – not exactly a technical psychological term, but I'm making it one. It's totally shitty that you've had to go through what you've been through, and now you have to put all this work in because of what it's left you with. There's no shine you can put on it – and any literature that does so is irresponsible. Yes, we can heal, we can grow, we can recover. I want to be clear that we can love, we can laugh and we can actually do really quite amazing things. It's just shitty that we have to work through the pain to get there. It's okay to feel upset and angry about it, and quite rightly so, because what you've experienced is upsetting and unfair. This is all part of letting go.

FORGIVING YOURSELF IN ORDER TO LET GO

Forgiveness is another reason why it's hard to let go. When I say forgiveness, I am talking about forgiving *yourself*, not others. There are different schools of thought around whether it's necessary or not to forgive others for trauma recovery.

Forgiveness can mean different things to different people, and I know there is a sentiment about forgiving to move on. I do not believe in any way that it is necessary to forgive someone else to move on. You can move on and recover from trauma without forgiving a person that has hurt you. Forgiving a friend for a mistake is very different from forgiving someone who abused you.

Forgiveness of *yourself* is what's important. I forgive some of the people that have caused my trauma, but only because that is a positive and beneficial thing for *me* and I want them in my life. My mum is one of those people. I chose to forgive her and work on our relationship. What happened to us wasn't her fault, she was a victim of domestic abuse; but some of her decisions, like staying with my step-dad and abandoning me in order to move to another city with him when I was just a teenager, hurt me more than anything he ever did to me. I found out about the move when I walked home from school to see a For Sale sign outside of our house. Yes, I can understand why she did those things, but that doesn't mean they hurt me any less. I felt rejected by the person I love more than anything, and I was deeply isolated. My mum was and still is everything to me.

I also blamed myself, both as a child and as an adult, for what my step-dad did to us. If I thought rationally in my conscious mind, I knew it wasn't my fault, but the past emotion from my memories still made me feel like it was. I had to work on forgiving myself; part of that was reminding myself I was just a child and validating what happened to me. (See the flowers and stones activity in Chapter 5.)

I *don't* forgive my step-dad or the coach that abused me. What they did to me is unforgivable. And I don't *need* to forgive them in order to recover from what they did to me. Their actions are theirs alone; what they did is their burden to carry, not mine.

It's not your responsibility to forgive others. It's your responsibility to forgive yourself. Forgiving is about loving yourself, being compassionate and caring for yourself and forgiving yourself for anything you blamed yourself for in your past. I felt ashamed and I was angry with myself for not speaking out about our coach. So I needed to forgive myself to heal that part of me.

Of course, you can choose to forgive others if you feel it's right for you – but don't feel like you need to. I promise you, you don't. 'Forgive and forget' is a nice concept, but it doesn't apply to each and every situation. Forgiving when you still feel so much pain is just masking how you really feel. It's okay to be angry, it's okay not to forgive someone. Your recovery is about forgiving yourself.

Self-forgiveness is the opposite of shame. Shame gives trauma all the ammunition it needs. Once I got to this stage in my own journey, I felt angry at myself for not helping myself earlier; angry at myself for ignoring how I felt and for putting a lid on all my painful memories. Which had subsequently meant putting a lid on and shutting off the hurt part of me. That cycle again! I blamed myself. I wouldn't blame another person for any of that, yet I blamed myself. I felt ashamed of the mistakes I'd made; ashamed for the people I'd hurt and let go of, even though they loved me and I loved them; ashamed for the hurt I'd continued to cause myself, even though the actual harm of my experiences was over. I needed to forgive myself.

Forgiveness in trauma can be particularly hard if you feel like you've done something that goes against your own moral values. This often comes up with service members and veterans. As part of their job, they participate in and witness horrendous acts, often with repeated exposure. Think of the boy soldier that Dr Rachel worked with: by his own moral standards and by society's, he would have had to do some awful and shocking things to survive – none of which were his fault. He was a child and would have been killed if he'd have gone against the grain and fought back against his leaders (groomers), yet he felt ashamed and questioned his own humanity. It makes me think of the book by Ishmael Beah, *A Long Way Gone*, which is a heartbreaking-yet-beautiful read. By the time Ishmael was 13 he had committed and witnessed a lot of violence. He felt like it was a part of who he was, that he was violent at his core. To be able to allow himself to heal he had to forgive himself for what he'd done.

The need to forgive yourself is also important if you witness something distressing that goes against your values, causing what's known as 'moral injury' – I'm going to call it moral trauma, as injury makes it sound like a physical act. You may blame yourself for not intervening, believing you should have done more. A defining attribute of moral trauma is guilt, which can turn to shame, so forgiveness is absolutely necessary to be able to let go of this shame.

A psychiatry paper from 2022 on forgiveness and moral trauma (injury) stated that a 'violation of one's deeply held morals and values can be profoundly distressing and shatter one's sense of self at the deepest level.'

The same concept is prominent in family trauma. A child often blames themself for abuse in the home, whether emotional or physical; blames themself for their mentally unwell parent or for the death of their family member, or for the fact their parents divorced, or blames themself as an adult for their own divorce. Shaming yourself only keeps you in trauma.

This is also prevalent with first responders. When I spoke with Dr Niki I know this is something she felt as a doctor, especially during the Covid-19 pandemic. She said, 'The whole two years were awful for every intensive care doctor, nurse, worker and for the patients. I just don't ever want to go back there. We lost a lot of nurses from the ICU sadly.' One of the biggest causes of trauma in first responders is guilt (which, with repeated exposure, can turn inward to shame) and feelings of helplessness. Dr Niki told me she put posters all around the ward of Charlie Mackesy's illustrations and quotes from his book *The Boy, the Mole, the Fox and the Horse*, to keep reaffirming there was hope and strength in what they were all doing. If you've got Charlie's book, you'll notice some emotionally healthy messages in there that we've covered on our connection cards: '"I am enough as I am," said the boy.'

WHO YOU ARE NOW

Being clear on what your morals and values are *right now*, rather than what they were in the past will help you forgive yourself and let go. Whatever you feel like you were a part of in the past, leave it behind and focus on what you value now and what your intentions and decisions are now based on. Your morals and values *now* are what matters. You are in control *now* of your behaviours and actions.

Your difficult memories will still be there, and they will still, to some extent, influence you and your actions, but in a safe and considered manner rather than in a fearful and protective way.

Letting go happens gradually with care and self-compassion. It's not about yanking yourself away with force or 'breaking' the cycle – as we so often hear. If you try to deal with everything all at once, you will feel defenceless and panic, and end up straight back in trauma.

Letting go is processing, connecting, rewiring and reshaping – it is not breaking away.

Keep listening out for your critical voice and what it's saying to you, especially as you start to let go. It will most likely get scared and want to shut down what you're doing with phrases such as, '*This is stupid, it won't work*', '*You're too old for this*', '*You've had trauma all your life*', '*You don't deserve to get better*', '*You're too damaged*', '*You're unhealable*'. Remember that's your critical voice that you've taken on over time – it is not who you are now. And none of it is true – you do deserve to heal, and you can.

You *can* recover no matter what you've experienced, what you've done, what's happened to you, how long you've been like this and felt this way or how old you are. Memories don't change, but people do.

Connection Card

LETTING GO

Alongside your connection cards of Emotionally Healthy Messages, Soothe Strategies and Basic Needs, we are going to create a Letting Go connection card. The ideas here may include some of the things you already have on your soothe list, but think about how they feed into meeting your basic needs.

This is what is written on my Letting Go connection card:

Remind myself of my basic needs.
It's my responsibility to care for myself and show myself I am worth care.
Strip it back to the basics.
Eat properly. Regular and full meals.
Recognize in what situations I detach, comply, avoid, push people away – and with whom. Think about why I'm doing that. Is it triggering a feeling from the past?
Express how I feel and practise doing so.
Go outside.
Exercise.
Meditate.
Check in with how I can comfort myself, lavender, Rabby, blanket, hot water bottle.
Talk to a friend.
Socialize.
Be compassionate to myself and forgive myself.
Remember self-punishment is never helpful.

Write down what you think would help remind you of meeting your basic needs, and some strategies on the process of letting go. These statements should be pointers to remind you of your recovery and everything you've learnt so far.

You can put the connection card on your bedside table, in your purse, wallet, bag, or stick it on your wall, door, fridge. Just don't put it in a drawer – if you're anything like me, it wouldn't see the light of day again.

You could also add the phrases 'I forgive myself', 'I deserve to heal', 'I deserve a life where my needs are met' to the Emotionally Healthy Messages connection card, or start a second connection card with more messages on it.

PART III

Growth through and after trauma

'Growth? Through trauma?' I hear you ask.

It is possible! Actually, it's more than possible – it's downright doable, and happening in you as you read this.

As I started to work through my trauma and face what I was feeling, rather than running away from it, I began to notice little things within myself and my life that were different. I still heard my critical voice, but it was more of a conversation than an outright civil war. I could show myself that what it was saying wasn't true.

When I first began to understand my trauma, I thought this would be impossible. I thought others may be able to do this, but for me, my nasty and demanding voice toward myself ruled; it was the only voice I felt I had, and I didn't believe I could change that. Yet, lo and behold, I started to hear my emotionally healthy voice telling me that I was doing well, that I could rest, that I was a lovable and kind person.

I still played out a lot of my pain through my protective coping mechanisms, I still got consumed by my feelings, and I still got triggered. This may not be what you want to hear, but, as I said from the start, I will only be honest. To tell you it all just disappears, just to sell the dream, would be a lie, and that is not why I'm writing this book. I hope that hearing that, while in growth, your past, your feelings and your ways of coping will still crop up, will help you heal even more. And that when you still feel the effects of your trauma through growth, it won't be a shock or make you feel like you've failed and aren't enough – all of which would risk taking you back to a state of trauma again.

I would catch myself, as if I was a fly on the wall, doing many of the things we've discussed in this book. The difference is that now I would say to myself, *'Oh! I recognize what this behaviour is!'*

At first, I could only observe what I was doing, but not quite *stop* myself from doing it. Then I found my inner dialogue gradually shifted. For example, I was having a conversation with a new person in my life, but I was feeling upset that day. I started to notice myself emotionally detach, and then want to avoid any further conversation to protect myself from any rejection. Instead, I stayed and carried on talking with the person, opened up (a bit), and that was enough. The person didn't think I was pathetic, but instead comforted me, reassured me and actually shared some of the things they were going through. We connected. I felt better. Rather than judging me, they felt closer to me. Before, I would have ended up on my own and not felt cared for or understood.

The conversation in my own head went something a little bit like this:

'Oh! I recognize what you're doing here: you are suppressing how you feel – you're in detached protector behaviour.'
 'I can't cope. It's too much, so I'm going to shut off.'
 'Why are you doing that?'
 'I don't know, maybe because I feel scared and vulnerable?'
 'That's okay. It's understandable you feel like that. You've been through a lot, you are working through things.'

'I just feel off and don't want to talk. I just want to leave and be on my own.'

'But you feel upset?'

'Yes, but if I show them I'm upset, they'll think I'm pathetic.'

'Will they?'

'Yes, because I'm not enough.'

'Let's think about this. You are enough. The "I'm not enough" comes from your past.'

'Hmmm, yes it does.'

'Remember, you are safe now, and I will look after you. You don't need to shut off from this person. They seem like they are being genuinely caring. Remember, you deserve people to care about you. Stay a little longer and give it a try.'

From this awareness I made a different choice than I would have done previously when I was right in the middle of trauma. Previously, I wouldn't have even had the conversation with myself. I would have clammed up, snapped, changed the subject, and most likely walked away. Instead, I stayed long enough to make a connection, and in opening up, the person actually felt safer with me.

This is growth. Growth is making different and emotionally healthier choices for yourself. Note: this is not *past tense* 'grown' – meaning fully developed, fully progressed. We are 'still growing', *present, active tense*. We are learning and recognizing the impact our past experience has had on us; we are understanding it, and adapting to this change. We will never be done growing, and that's okay.

13

Understanding (post-traumatic) growth (and what it's not)

One thing I want to address when we talk about growth, is the term post-traumatic growth (PTG) – positive change that can result from adversity of trauma – and all the perceptions and expectations that come with that term.

I hear and see inspirational quotes like 'Adversity is the key to greatness' and 'If there is no struggle there is no progress.' Such quotes make me break out in sarcasm: *'Oh! So there's a silver lining to all the horrible things that have happened to me. Great!'* One thing's for sure: it's nearly impossible to 'motivational quote' our difficult feelings from trauma away.

I accept what I've been through and I am proud of who I am, but, damn, I wish I hadn't had to deal with quite so much and face so much adversity. As much as I've gone on to do impactful things with my story, it's important to acknowledge that it's also hindered me. My trauma stopped me from receiving the love I needed. My trauma kept me feeling isolated. My trauma kept me in abuse – not just from other people but because I also became my own abuser. My adversity set me back in the early days of my career because I had such low self-esteem. My trauma means I have lived with depression for as long as I can remember. My trauma means every day in some way I'm reminded of the pain of my past.

THE ISSUE WITH POST-TRAUMATIC GROWTH

This brings us to post-traumatic growth and the possibility of transformation, the focus on positive changes and the potential to find meaning in our trauma. The theory of PTG was developed in 1995 by psychologists Richard Tedeschi, PhD, and Lawrence Calhoun, PhD. It seems to have been popularized recently alongside more open dialogue about trauma and its impact. PTG theory suggests personal growth, resilience (I hate this word, and I'll explain why shortly) and transformation can come from trauma, and that people who 'endure psychological struggle following adversity can often see positive growth afterward'.

We hear this jargon so often, but sometimes I wonder if the words and phrases 'resilience' and 'transformation from trauma' are actually just another way of masking and diminishing trauma. I get sick of society putting a shiny polish over adversity and trauma. There is universal evidence that we achieve more when we *encourage* ourselves and are encouraged by others, as opposed to when we degrade ourselves and are degraded by another.

We shouldn't dismiss adversity and trauma's impact just because good *can* come out of it. Good doesn't always come out of it. I have seen too many lives destroyed because of trauma, and lost too many loved ones to suicide. It's important not to pretend. It doesn't do anyone any favours. I spent far too long pretending I was okay, and that kept me exactly in the place of pain.

We have to be very careful how PTG is perceived and interpreted, to ensure it's not just another pressure to put on a trauma survivor, and to ensure it doesn't trigger shame about how a person should be recovering. The idea that we should be growing and transforming when in reality we may feel isolated and stuck can trigger protective coping behaviours like avoidance and detaching and, as we now know, this stops us from processing our emotions and memories and keeps us in trauma.

Toxic positivity

I mentioned toxic positivity in Chapter 6. In our search for post-traumatic growth, we might focus on the positive, and in doing so downplay or ignore what we really feel. Remember: processing trauma is about allowing *all* the emotions associated with it to be heard, not about being positive. The fact that we have a full and complex range of emotions, including the ones that hurt and scare us, gives us our humanity. Avoiding those emotions suppresses them, and stops us from processing our feelings and connecting with others – we stay stuck, which is quite the opposite of growth post trauma.

Cognitive dissonance

Focusing on PTG without doing all the work we have focused on from the start of the book – acknowledging our trauma, making it part of our story and validating our experience – could lead to cognitive dissonance. I've seen a lot of people struggling with trauma do this – I even did it myself. Cognitive dissonance is where you reframe or reinterpret your experience to align with what you want it to be, which is 'not actually that bad' – you put a positive spin on it. This goes back to the minimizing of our pain and of the distress what happened to us caused. Recent research and studies suggest that when the idea of PTG is used in this manner it is just an illusory defence.

Reframing PTG

I do want to be cautious about the concept of 'post-traumatic growth'. The use of 'post-trauma', makes it sound like, once we've done the work, we are out of our struggle and everything is hunkydory. We have to be very careful to acknowledge that the painful memories that bring about trauma don't disappear – they just get less painful and we get more able to cope with them; our painful memories move from the present and become just that, 'memories'. But our past is still part of us, and I want us to be proud of that, no matter what our past looks like.

For me, PTG is about being able to adapt, accept and 'find rest' in our past. The positive growth is engaging in recovery and sticking on the continued road of it; and if you leave the road, growth is getting back on the recovery road, no matter how many times you come off it.

To grow and heal through trauma is the 'positive growth' and shift. This is recovery.

PTG is commonly called a *phenomenon* because of the notable positive changes observed after trauma, but the same experts have also warned that not everyone who experiences trauma will experience PTG. I beg to differ. Anyone who is working through trauma is recovering, and anybody who is recovering is experiencing growth. Even when at times things feel worse, and you feel full of emotion and 'weathering' the storm is goddamn awful, that's still growth.

GROWTH AND REPAIR

Growth *is* what we are working toward and what we are actively doing in trauma recovery, but it's important to keep checking that emotionally unhealthy coping behaviours aren't creeping in.

Growth is about honesty, reconnecting with yourself and feeling safe enough to explore vulnerability in what you are feeling.

Dr Rachel doesn't use the term or concept of PTG; she prefers to focus on repair. She says repair *is possible*.

'Don't give up on the possibility of repair. You can come back and revisit something another time – again and again – for another opportunity to repair. Although it can feel awful at the time, it's an immense opportunity. If anything, that IS post-traumatic growth. The moments that are most difficult give us the opportunity to understand more about ourselves and so, to repair.'

Dr Rachel O'Beney

RESILIENCE IS NOT THE AIM

Over the years I've been asked to do numerous talks on the topic of resilience, both in corporate and education settings. Resilience, meaning to rebound or recoil, has become a recent buzzword, even though it has been around since the early 17th century. As I mentioned above, I really hate this word.

'Resilience is an old-fashioned word for managing and coping,' explains Dr Rachel. 'You've managed and coped, but been neglected on the inside. Resilience is just coping for a bit more and a bit longer.' 'Resilience' is a word that now goes hand in hand with 'tolerance' – we tolerate awful situations because we 'should' be resilient. We tolerate our pain and depression because we should be resilient through it. We tolerate our trauma, we just need to build more resilience.

Whenever I get asked to do a talk on resilience, I always ask the client what they mean by resilience. Do they mean mental toughness? Strength? The capacity to withstand? Getting through and enduring something difficult? I couldn't disagree more with all of these definitions or with how we speak about and teach resilience in our society.

In my talks about 'resilience' I teach how too much resilience can keep us in harm and suffering. I teach that we need to understand and connect with our feelings and emotions, to learn how they influence our behaviour and actions. This is how we should be teaching and explaining resilience, especially in schools.

Imagine how emotionally well-equipped the next generation would be with this kind of psychological, emotional and behavioural understanding. When distressing things do inevitably happen, they would be able to process their trauma rather than just endure it. Early intervention is key to preventing the consequences and impact of trauma on people as individuals, families and as a society.

We should be aiming for growth, which involves learning about ourselves and our feelings, and adapting so that we can not only overcome tough situations but can emotionally recover from them.

A sticking plaster and a mask

Dr Rachel believes that 'resilience can be just another sticking plaster. If big things happen, we should be upset and hurt – healthy responses that enable us to get help. If we are in touch with our vulnerabilities and know how we are feeling it is a barometer for what we need. Resilience can be just another label and a quick fix. How are you supposed to measure resilience?'

When my mum left my step-dad, I had to call 999 as I feared for my mum's life, my life and even his. He was threatening to kill us, but also saying he was going to kill himself. It was terrifying. I hated what he was doing to us, but also didn't want him to hurt himself. He got arrested and the mental health services came. It turned out his threat of killing himself was a way to emotionally manipulate my mum. He sniggered at us behind the backs of the mental health support workers and police. It's sadly a very common tactic in domestic abuse, as the abuser wants to stop the victim from leaving by any means. We had a family friend who left her husband in the years previous, he threatened suicide and insisted she came to the house otherwise he would kill himself. She went to the house; he killed her and then himself.

We managed to get away and find a safe place. Victim support phoned me the next day as a routine follow-up. On the call I asked them for help. They said to me that they could offer a lesson over the phone on how to be resilient. It almost made me laugh out loud, despite my situation – I was shocked. I'm very resilient, I wouldn't be here if I wasn't. In fact, I'm probably one of the most resilient people I know, but I suffered because of it. I built resilience, not out of choice but out of survival. I had to. I coped and built more resilience, but I lived with depression and PTSD *because* I was so resilient. I was so resilient I could tolerate anything. How is that a happy and fulfilling way to live? Part of the reason my mum stayed in her abusive marriage for so long was because she built up so much resilience – she kept going and withstood the abuse. Hardship was our norm, that's how resilient we were.

If you've survived anything challenging or distressing, you're already resilient. Fuck building more resilience!

What my mum and I needed in the aftermath of her leaving her abusive husband was help to not be *more resilient* but to actually *process* everything that was far too overwhelming. I didn't get that help, and so I shut off all my emotions in resilience. I was so good at being resilient that I was flat, numb and empty – perfectly emotionless to survive anything that came my way. I was so resilient I found it hard to open up, to connect, to love myself or be loved. As we've already learnt, this makes us depressed, feel isolated and alone.

Resilience masks vulnerability and prevents us from caring for ourselves, allowing care from others and recovering from trauma. The emotional detachment we've worked through earlier in this book is a good indicator that resilience is overtaking growth and healing. Sometimes there is a time and a place to detach from your emotions – for example, if someone is irritating you in a meeting and you just want to get through the agenda – but resilience is not a good way to permanently cope with life, never mind deal with trauma.

GROWING THROUGH TRAUMA

Recovery is growing through trauma. Just the act of reading this book, of processing what is going on for you, is growth. It's already happening and will continue as long as you keep working on yourself.

You don't need to wait for a 'phenomenon' to embark on growth – to enter PTG with a fanfare – and you don't need to be more resilient. You are already strong enough to even be here and reading this book. All of this is part of the process, and it takes time.

To experience growth in and through trauma you don't have to use your trauma to do good, or to make meaning out of your trauma, and you certainly don't have to find the 'silver lining' in it. You can say it like it is: it was shit – no ifs, no buts. Taking the journey of trauma recovery – learning, processing, adapting and living with a more emotionally healthy approach – is more than enough. That is PTG. Surviving what you already have and being here today is courageous enough, strong enough and valid enough. You don't need to make it anything else.

I'm still coping with my trauma; it still likes to throw me a curveball once in a while, but having the awareness and understanding of how I react, of how it impacts me and knowing what helps me, all lead to continued growth. This is my definition of PTG.

14

Ongoing recovery: Techniques for healing

Social scientist Roy Baumeister and journalist John Tierney wrote a book called *The Power of Bad*. It was based on Baumeister's research paper on the negativity bias in psychology. In summary, it says that bad events have far more power over us than good events, because it's our evolutionary history to be better attuned to bad things in order to help us to survive.

'Survival requires urgent attention to possible bad outcomes, but it is less urgent with regard to good ones. Hence, it would be adaptive to be psychologically designed to respond to bad more strongly than good.'

Roy Baumeister and John Tierney, *The Power of Bad*

Baumeister and Tierney also argued that there is no opposite to trauma:

'Psychologists have long known that people can be scarred for years by a single event. The term for it is trauma, but what is the opposite? What word would describe a positive emotional state that lingers for decades in

response to a single event? There is no opposite of trauma, because no single good event has such a lasting impact.'

Roy Baumeister and John Tierney, *The Power of Bad*

Why would I start a chapter with something that seems so dismal – so discouraging and hopeless – at first glance? Well, let me show you why I believe that this approach to trauma is what we should be recognizing in order to feel encouraged and full of hope!

Bad things hit hard and for a long time, and, as Baumeister and Tierney found, they give out a longer lasting and stronger emotional response than the good stuff. I remind myself of this all the time – that feeling the impact of bad things for a long time is perfectly ordinary. What a relief it would be for us all if we could be honest about that as a society. The brave face and pretending keeps us alone in our pain. You are not alone – you are feeling just like me and many others.

Recovery is *ongoing* exactly because of this. Putting an unrealistic expectation on yourself to miraculously feel better will only harm you and stop your progress. Believe me, I am the queen of unrealistic expectations – it's how I coped for a long time, but it's also one of the things that kept me in trauma. I was 'coping', not 'living'. Be aware of your recovery becoming a thing to beat yourself with.

THE PRESSURE TO RECOVER

In early and ongoing recovery of trauma, unrelenting standards and expectations can creep in. I have included the quote '... designed to respond to bad more strongly than good' from *The Power of Bad* to remind you that what you've been through will take time to heal.

A boatload of our continued pain comes from beating ourselves up because we are struggling with the bad things that have happened.

This beating up devalues the power of what we've been through, and therefore denies a part of us – the part that needs help.

***

I wake up, having done years of therapy, having completed group therapy and my own psychoeducation study, and I feel so low. So much so that I don't want to get out of bed and face the day. I feel empty and numb, yet overwhelmed by emotions: lonely, sad, hopeless. Straightaway, my inner critic finds its voice, telling me I'd failed in my recovery.

'What's wrong with me? Why do I feel like this? It's in the past. I should have moved on by now. I should be over it! I understand it now but I'm still getting anxious so I've failed. I'm a failure. I'm never going to get better.'

Despite having all this amazing knowledge about mental health and trauma, here I am, at the bottom of the pit, telling myself: 'I am a waste of space, I am never going to feel better' (ignoring the fact that I did feel better – and on a daily basis, too), 'I am useless, I will always be depressed, I am unhealable.'

At that moment, due to the expectation I put on myself to not allow myself to feel sad (telling myself I shouldn't feel sad given all the recovery work I'd done), I use my recovery to shame myself. I immediately fall back into my familiar coping behaviours – I detach and avoid. I shut myself off, ignore calls, self-soothe (self-harm) by exercising until I feel pain and am physically sick, and spend the entire day degrading myself. My inner critical voice is alive and well.

I can, to an extent, see what I am doing, but how I am feeling is controlling everything, and with such intensity. The expectation that I should never feel like this ever again because I know better is making me worse.

After a while, I look at the connection cards with my emotionally healthy messages and the one with some of my strategies.

'Phone a friend', I read. No, reaching out to anyone feels like too much.

'Have I eaten?' I realize I haven't. So I make myself a cup of tea and some toast. It's all I can face.

I also realize I haven't washed my face all day – basic self-care has gone out of the window. It feels like the biggest effort in the world, but I wash my face – forcing myself to realize I am safe and deserving of care.

I get into bed, put Rabby on the pillow next to me, cry (which is a good thing – I am allowing myself to feel my sadness and let it out) and read a few pages of a book. Gradually, my racing mind calms down enough to let me sleep. I am exhausted from the pressure I'd been putting myself under. I get through the day.

The next day I feel able to give myself more of what I need.

***

The stress of expectation

The expectations of our own recovery and healing can activate the same stress system as the trauma itself, and trigger the emotional systems in our brain that lead us to feeling anxious, angry and depressed. We go into the fear system, and this activates our old ways of coping by protecting ourselves.

I want to make sure you know that you *will* feel low sometimes, but that doesn't mean you aren't recovering.

When I have low days now, I say to myself: *'This is normal.'* I've spent a long time in trauma, but now I know how to be compassionate to myself. I know what emotionally healthy ways of coping look like.

I know that the feelings will change because they already have. I know that I am enough. Feeling like this happens from time to time, but now I can care for and help myself.

WHAT GROWTH AND RECOVERY REALLY LOOK LIKE

Recovery, growth and change involve understanding, gradually facing and validating your traumatic experience, the painful memories and the emotions that come with it, and the impact it has had on you.

Recovery and growth mean fewer and less-intense symptoms. It's feeling more understood and understanding yourself more. It's understanding your triggers and feeling more in control.

Growth and recovery allow you to have a fuller life. You manage to connect and relate to people in a healthy way. You know when you feel upset, and help yourself or ask for help when you need it.

Trauma recovery is knowing who's good for you and who is not. It is feeling safe, with your body being in a less-heightened state, and having a stronger sense of yourself. It is empowerment.

A reminder of the use of the word 'ongoing' in the chapter title: your recovery and growth is in progress, and always will be.

Recovery is adapting and learning how to make emotionally healthy decisions through our life.

What recovery *isn't* is putting it all behind us, forgetting our past experiences (forgetting a part of us), deleting our memories, pretending those things never happened and never feeling any emotional pain or overwhelming emotions again. Don't be mistaken in thinking that's recovery. If you do, when those things don't happen you will only use them as another thing to beat yourself with. What that *actually* is, is harmful ways of coping. It is trauma, not recovery.

'YES, BUT ...' – UNDERMINING YOUR GROWTH

Starting a sentence with 'Yes, but ...' was my go-to way of dismissing just about anything that I did well or any praise given to me: 'You spoke so passionately!' 'Yes, but I should have said this ...'. I found it so hard to receive praise that I would not only dismiss it, but actively counter it.

For some people in trauma, hearing praise can make them feel like something bad is going to happen because they have an internal narrative that someone is only nice because they want something from you. This can be particularly strong for those who have suffered any type of abuse, bullying or mistreatment. It's a reaction that can be very deep, automatic and feel ingrained. However, if you notice this in yourself, that's great, because even just being aware of it is active growth through trauma.

'Our internal critic is undermining; it's trained through negative experiences and past disappointments not to believe in the positives that happen to us. Yet there is a painful longing to believe and trust when someone reaches out to us. It's such a longing that we don't know how to deal with it. If we, all of a sudden, get loads of praise, it's like being starved and then being given so much rich food at once – we sick it up, unable to digest it. We need to be given little bits at first, learning to digest it. We learn through understanding the process that we are locked into, and by building up trust slowly, through repetition.'
Dr Rachel O'Beney

As a starting point, I would challenge myself to say thank you to the praise I received. I might still be dismissing the compliment in my head, but not dismissing it out loud or arguing against it was a start. I am now much more able to praise myself and receive praise, but sometimes when I'm in a stressed situation my 'Yes, but ...' still comes out.

ACCOUNTABILITY IN RECOVERY

It's important to be accountable for ourselves as we move forward. Accountability does not mean responsibility for the past or your trauma – watch out for that inner critic coming in offering self-blame or judgement. It was not, and this *is* not, your fault. You're not accountable for your past and what has happened to you, but you are accountable for what you do from this moment onward.

Remember the basic emotional and psychological need of autonomy/a sense of identity that we discussed in Chapter 12. This is about being responsible for yourself and your actions now and for your future. Accountability is taking the time to understand, to recognize and to make better decisions that serve and fulfil *you*, and not your trauma. Trauma makes you feel out of control. Having a sense of agency over yourself is vital for your mental and emotional health.

You didn't have a choice before, but with the knowledge and skills you are gaining, you do now. It is now your responsibility to give yourself a chance to heal. You can help yourself, and are capable of doing so. Being independent and accountable is the opposite of the trauma feeling of helplessness – that is empowerment, not self-blame. You are in charge.

KEEP GOING – YOU'VE ALREADY COME SO FAR

As Dr Rachel puts it, this is 'change-focused work. It is about looking at what is possible now. What are you going to choose to do differently?'

When we are right back in the feelings of hurt, it all feels very intense: low mood, anxious, full of anger, mind racing ten to the dozen and telling us competing things. Even when you *can* see things with perspective but can't seem to change what you're feeling or the way you're reacting, it can be hard to step in and actually *do* all the things we've discussed. It takes practice, and you may not always be able to immediately implement your learnings and strategies.

In these moments when you are overwhelmed with your pain, give yourself *time*. Even if it takes you all day – or all week – for you to recognize how you are feeling and what your needs are, that is progress, that is recovery.

TECHNIQUES FOR MOVING FORWARD

I want to share with you some techniques that can help you move out from a difficult period as you continue to recover and grow. We have covered some of these in the book, so you will recognize many of the strategies. Here, I'm showing you how what we've learnt so far plays out in real situations.

Alongside the techniques are examples from my own journey. Some you may relate to more than others, and you can adapt them to be more specific to you.

The techniques include a range of:

- **Cognitive statements** to say to yourself that contradict your inner critic, your nasty and demanding voice. Think of your Emotionally Healthy Messages connection card (see page 107).
- **Experiential strategies** that will help you recall experiences that contradict the way you are feeling. Think about the Recognize Your Cognitive Distortions exercise and the facts that showed what was real (see page 200).
- **Thinking and behavioural techniques** such as the behavioural activation exercise, Create Balance Between Drive, Fear and Soothe (see page 226).

Detached protector behaviour

Situation: *I don't want to open up or talk. I'm coming across as unapproachable and detached because I feel no one can be trusted. Why am I doing this? This happens to me when people get too close too fast; it triggers childhood memories and feelings of fear, pain and rejection.*

Experiential strategy: *Remember that if I take control of the interaction by allowing myself to control any physical closeness and take my time to feel safe rather than push them away, I will feel better about the situation. Reassure myself that they won't criticize and reject me.*

Behavioural strategy: *Go outside. Go for a walk (perhaps with a person to talk to) or a run. Take some slow breaths/practice box breathing. For me, this alleviates the claustrophobic feeling I get in this situation.*

Avoidant protector behaviour

Situation: *I'm avoiding picking up the phone, or applying or going to an interview for a job/role.*

Experiential strategy: *I ask myself why I'm avoiding it. It's because I have a fear of feeling rejected. I remember when I have done things that have gone well in a job/role before; I recall a positive fact.*

Cognitive technique: *Think of reasons why I would be good at the job, why it would be good for me to go for the interview, and why nothing horrible can happen to me there. Remember my feelings do count. Try to express how I feel and how I will get my needs met. Phone someone and tell them how I feel about it. I am not alone. People do care.*

Overwhelming emotions

Situation: *It's first thing in the morning and I have so much to do I start to get overwhelmed. I won't make it. I am a failure. I am stupid. Everybody else is cleverer and more capable than me. I will never amount to anything. I can't cope.*

Experiential strategy: *Remember I have managed times like this before – many times – and got through. Remind myself that good things have even happened on these days.*

Cognitive strategy: *I can do it again. I know what you (the critic) are trying to do by putting me down to protect me, but I am capable and I can cope.*

Behavioural strategy: *I can write a list and start to work on one task at a time. Breaking it down will make me feel more in control.*

These are all examples of recognizing what you are doing and feeling, and different ways to strengthen healthy thoughts and feelings. Keep practising the techniques and strategies; unfortunately, just doing it once won't change months or years of self-judgement and harmful coping responses to your pain, but repeating these new ways of thinking and doing will start to impact your behaviour and reduce the grip of your past feelings.

Noticing healthy coping strategies

We've focused so much on our unhealthy protective coping behaviours that I want to also make sure we now recognize when we *are* using the healthy coping strategies that we've learnt. The examples below are, again, examples from my own recovery work, but here the strategies are starting from the place of a healthy emotional mind that is in recovery and growth from trauma. It's important we recognize what our thinking looks like when we are using healthy strategies.

- **Setting a limit or boundary**. *I am using healthy coping strategies and behaviours when I manage to set a limit or boundary without feeling guilty about it. I can say, 'No, I can't help you right now, but I will try to get back to you when I'm feeling better. I have a lot to deal with.' I can allow myself to do something that is good for me to replenish myself. I can tell myself: 'It's okay to care for myself, and focus on what I need to do. I am still a good friend.'*
- **Keeping calm**. *I am in a healthy coping strategy when I can keep calm in a stressful situation, despite feeling big emotions, and do not lose trust in myself. I can think of situations when I have managed to give myself encouraging messages and instructions like, 'You will do really well, it's just a challenge. You've faced and got through many challenges, you can meet this one and get through it.' I can ask, 'What is making me feel this way and why?' I can tell myself: 'I can be compassionate and understanding to myself. I am enough and I deserve care.'*

You can add these to your connection cards or notebook. See if you can write your own set of statements that help you access the healthy coping strategies we've discussed.

Connection Card

RECOVERY/GROWTH GOALS

This connection card focuses on your recovery or, if you prefer, growth goals.

I keep this connection card in my handbag as I quite like coming across my recovery goals by chance when I'm rustling through my bag trying to find something else. I appreciate the handbag part may not apply to you, so again have it somewhere you will come across it regularly.

My mum lived with me for two years when she left my step-dad – he took everything initially and left her homeless. She had her connection cards of healthy messages and her goals stuck on the wardrobe and the back of the door of my spare room. She told me she found them really heart-warming to see, and they showed her how much she was growing. The repeated action of reading them every day helped reinforce them, and reduced the strength of her critical voice.

Remember: the connection cards are what you will take away with you after you finish reading this book. They are not to be put in a drawer, never to see the light of day. The connection cards are for you to reflect, to keep revisiting and rereading, way after you've finished reading this.

This was my Recovery/Growth Goals connection card, written exactly as I wrote it back then:

Continue self-care – meditation, sleep, relaxation time. Try to focus more on the positive and things that have gone right. Prove that things do go right, rather than focusing on what hasn't.

Concentrate on what makes me happy and keep exploring what I like and what is good for me, what I want for my life rather than fixing and sorting everyone else and my family.

Work on making myself feel safe.

What makes me feel safe?

Talking to my vulnerable self. I am enough.

Remind myself that I am safe.

On the other side of the card I focused on things I was still particularly struggling with and wanted to focus more on. Again, exactly word for word as I wrote it back then:

Rejection. Fear of abandonment. Remember I am loved. Loved by friends.

It's okay to feel sad and upset and hurt about this.

Updating – reminding myself that I have done good things.

Done well list!

Have fun.

Positive things have happened to me.

Watch how I criticize myself when I answer with 'Yes, but ...'

Dr Niki uses a version of the Recovery/Growth Goals card with her patients. She gets them to write their goals down so they can see how they are progressing, and realize that they are already doing what they are aiming for. It's a way to look back on your progress, especially if things are feeling frustrating or you're being down on yourself – you will see that you have come a long way.

TRANSITIONAL OBJECTS

When I was in group therapy, I was given a pencil case for my transitional objects. In the case, I placed a small bottle of lavender oil, a teabag, a pen, a selection of small pieces of coloured card, a feather, a pebble and some fluffy material.

The pencil case of transitional objects was for us to use to self-soothe when on our own and keep that connection to our recovery. A transitional object gives you a helping hand to remind you of all the things you've learnt about supporting and caring for yourself, and a little reassurance that you're not on your own. It's something tactile that you can carry with you that reminds you of the work you have done and what you've learnt. It will prompt you to calm, comfort and attend to the vulnerable feelings inside. It's like a good trigger to encourage you!

The lavender smell was grounding and brought me back to the here and now, as did holding the smooth, cold pebble. It was actually one of my stones from the flowers and stones exercise, and it reminded me of everything I've been through, in a good way, because I've survived and come so far from that stone. The teabag reminded me to care for myself. The fluffy material is like a comforting soft toy, and stimulated my underworked soothe system.

Just because we become adults doesn't mean we don't need that same soothing and comfort that we do as children. Transitional objects are used a lot with children to help them make the emotional transition from dependence to independence. Dr Rachel explains: 'We don't lose that need [for transitional objects] as adults, we just dress it up. Smoking. Drinking. We just disguise them in adult-acceptable ways. They are unhealthy adaptations in need of transitional objects.' Holding a cigarette, a drink or a phone can bring comfort and stability, but these are all dysfunctional transitional objects.

I kept this pencil case by my bed and only very occasionally looked at it and used it, but I always knew it was there. For me, its mere presence represented that I was courageous and cared enough about myself to understand my trauma and allow myself to heal some of my pain. It showed me I was worthy, and that gave me comfort and safety. I even took it with me when I was working on different projects abroad. It normally sat under a pile of clothes, but just knowing I had it with me gave me comfort. I knew if I was struggling, I could go to it and remember what I had learnt: that I've gone from being dependent on my trauma to being able to let my trauma go, and that when I'm struggling I'm equipped to help myself.

CREATE A TRANSITIONAL OBJECT

I'd like you to create a transitional object that will remind you of this book and everything you've learnt and discovered about yourself. The object will help you to keep moving forward and know that, even though the book has finished, the work continues and that I am there with you.

If you can, find or buy yourself a little pencil case or a small toiletry/makeup bag that you can put a few things in. Here are a few ideas of what to include:

- Something to do with smell, like a small bottle of essential oil or dried flowers.
- Connection cards – either blank ones or ones you've already written on, or one with a message specifically reminding you of something you're working on.
- Grounding objects, like a piece of marble, a stone or a crystal.
- A teabag.
- A Lego figure or small action figure.
- A stone or flower from your flowers and stone lifeline.

- Soft and fluffy fabric or small object.
- A word or phrase from this book – or even a page from this book.

If you feel a bit uncomfortable doing this, try putting the objects in the case or bag and then leave it somewhere private. You don't have to go back to it unless you want to, but just know it's there and that you have created it because you care about yourself. All of this is in your control.

15

Barriers: What to do when you hit one

In Chapter 14, we looked at techniques to support ongoing recovery. This chapter is like a 'part two' of that chapter, as we delve deeper into what might stop us moving forward with our growth in recovery.

We've already discussed many of the barriers to starting this journey and continuing on it, such as avoidance, detachment, fear of overwhelming emotions, being scared to go back to a place of vulnerability, and feelings of shame.

Now that you're here, in Part III of the book, well done, for continuing to overcome those barriers. You are on a courageous journey. But I'm sure they won't have completely vanished. This is trauma recovery, after all.

In this chapter, I want to spend a little time exploring what your barriers to recovery might look and feel like now that you are working through your trauma.

You may feel a little nervous and unsure of this newer version of you and your new ways of thinking. Even though it's a much safer and emotionally healthy you, it's still unfamiliar and different. Change can be intimidating, even if the old way is debilitating. Trauma makes you feel out of control, and recovery can trigger feelings of vulnerability and fear of losing control because you are now letting yourself feel and show your emotions. Feeling vulnerable can be very uncomfortable. But being vulnerable is part of the process – it's expected! So, hold steady.

RESISTANCE TO CHANGE

Barriers can come from your own resistance to change. Working through trauma is change; everything you do differently in your approach to your feelings and thoughts is you changing. Remember: you are still you, just an adapted you. The fear of becoming overwhelmed by all this and the new feelings that may be coming in can lead to resistance to the recovery process.

Your resistance isn't your fault, and you might not even be aware of it. It's not like you're standing there with your hand in the 'STOP' position, shouting, '*No! I do not want to feel better or come to terms with my trauma. I want to feel this way.*' It's more likely to be you standing there with your hands clasped slightly nervously or maybe your arms crossed in a protective position, saying, '*I feel really anxious. I've got all these feelings on the surface now, and it's making me feel really vulnerable and/ or angry. So I'm going to hide behind the person signalling 'STOP' so I won't feel so exposed and overwhelmed. Thank you. Goodbye.*' In the short term, doing that might actually make you feel a little bit better, but if you stay like that in the long term it will feel worse. You've already been there and know it doesn't make anything feel any better. So keep peeking out behind the person signalling 'STOP', and slowly keep edging out.

SELF-DEFEATING FEELINGS

Self-defeating feelings and self-sabotage are all part of recovering from trauma. Self-defeating behaviours are patterns of thoughts like *'I will never feel better'*, *'This won't work'*, or, *'I should be happy'*. They can lead to you talking yourself out of doing the recovery work.

I'm sorry to say, but working through trauma does take work – continual work. I know it's annoying, frustrating and unfair, but you have to be honest with yourself.

Remember, you *can* be angry about what happened to you, what you've been through and the work you're having to put in now. Let it out. I was angry, and sometimes still am. I went for a run recently and stopped half way through and shouted 'For fuck's sake!', and swore and growled a bit more. That's okay. It felt good to let it out. Whatever you do, don't let this anger stop you. By expressing this frustration you will feel better and go on to make more caring and healthier decisions, which will allow some room for happy feelings to come in. Remember: you have the ability to take these actions. Your trauma has ruled for long enough, now it's your time to take control.

SELF-INJURIOUS ACTIONS

Self-injurious actions may be taken if it all feels too much. You may drink to excess to make it all go away, or overeat or exercise until it hurts. If you do, that's okay. Don't use the action as a stick to beat yourself with – that's just self-sabotage. You did it, accept it; tell yourself it's part of healing, but you aren't going to do that tomorrow and you're not going to hate yourself because of it. Be compassionate and understanding of why you took that action. Just keep reminding yourself there are emotionally healthy ways to soothe yourself.

Feeling the pain again can make us revert to old patterns. All the self-protective ways of coping with our painful emotions can link to bodily and emotional memories. These memories can drive our unhealthy ways of coping, like avoidance, aggressiveness, closing down or compliance/submission, and stop us from learning, growing, developing and balancing our emotions from trauma.

AWARENESS IS KEY

The important point about the barriers that may arise at this stage is being aware of them, so when they do happen they don't take you by surprise and set you on a road back to where you've just come from.

If you start having self-defeating feelings, label them as that, and recognize they are a part of trauma recovery. If you start feeling particularly vulnerable, recognize it as a part of trauma recovery, and remind yourself that vulnerability is an essential part of processing trauma. Remember: how can you let go of trauma if you can't let it in in the first place? Vulnerability and feeling your emotions are a sign you are recovering from your trauma, you are healing and growing. This takes strength and courage. Vulnerability and feeling our emotions are how we connect with ourselves and others; it's not a bad thing or something to be feared. Keep reminding yourself of this. We will keep repeating without realizing until we repair it.

At first during my recovery, I convinced myself that 'better' and 'recovery' meant that all my more challenging feelings, my emotional pain and my trauma would disappear. I wish I'd have accepted that these roadblocks do come up, are normal, and are actually how we repair. We learn more every time these things happen.

Understanding and knowing that barriers pop up in recovery and growth will help you keep an eye on them. You can say to yourself, *'Oh, I know what this is. This is just a bit of anxiety because this all* feels very new, and feelings have arisen that I've spent a long time trying to get rid of or have seen as a bad thing. It's understandable that I feel anxious, and I get why I'm telling myself that it's too much and I can't do it. I'm going to choose to be compassionate and give myself some reassurance.'

Keep reminding yourself that you don't have to hold on to past trauma to protect yourself. Think back to the very start of this book where we learnt what trauma is and what it causes – hypervigilance, a heightened state and self-protective behaviours. These symptoms won't just disappear overnight. The main difference between then and now is that I am aware of what I am doing and why.

CONSIDER WHO YOU OPEN UP TO

Something that happened to me as I was making better choices for myself was that I continued to overprotect myself with other people. I struggled to open up, so when I did do it, it could be really crushing for me if I felt like the person I was talking with didn't understand or downplayed what I was going through and didn't give me the reassurance I needed. That would make me clam up and stop me opening up to others.

However, this did make me analyse my relationships. It made me think that perhaps the people who were making me feel like this actually weren't being supportive and didn't understand. I brought this up with Dr Rachel, and she gave me some valuable advice which has stayed with me. She said, 'Think about whether that is the right person to open up to about what you've been through.'

Consider whether perhaps someone is stuck in their *own* trauma, maybe they are struggling themselves, maybe they don't have your best interests at heart. If so, they are not the right person to talk to. This doesn't mean *not* 'opening up' at all. This just means picking the person that you think is the right person to speak to about what you're feeling. Also, the fact that someone is not able to be there for you is not about you or because of you; it's about *them*.

I would try to speak to my mum about my trauma, but she was in her own trauma and struggled to listen to me. My trauma was also partially her trauma. Once, we had an argument about it and she told me to stop bringing up her past. I was so hurt and angry. I told her that it was *my* past too, and I was entitled to ownership of my own story. It was the first time I'd ever stuck up for myself with my mum; I never told her how she made me feel because I didn't want to hurt her. This was a pattern I'd developed from a young age – I took on the role of protector because I saw her being hurt by others. I couldn't bear to see her hurt.

I was really sensitive to feeling not listened to by my mum because I never felt heard by her when I was younger. I know that was because we were all in a domestic abuse situation, but it didn't mean that my feelings weren't valid. I noticed that speaking to her about my trauma work and recovery was not helping me. So I decided to tell her things on a surface level when she asked, but open up more to a few key close friends who listened to me and gave me the validation I needed.

This is a good example of using a coping mode in a healthy way. I was still getting my needs met, but also protecting myself against something that I knew wasn't helping me.

Likewise, I struggled sometimes to listen to my mum talking about her pain and trauma because it was also my life, so it could be quite triggering for me.

I now open up to my mum, as she has also done her own trauma recovery work. Sometimes the 'I'm not being listened to' feeling still comes up. When it does, I can tell her how I'm feeling and what's making me feel like that, and she can acknowledge and reassure me without either of us feeling defensive and getting upset at each other.

CONTINUOUS COMPASSION

If you see what you are doing and can't, in the moment, make a different choice or soothe yourself, that's okay. We can't expect our trauma to just disappear.

Sometimes I could help myself, and sometimes I couldn't. I found that I got frustrated when I could see what I was doing but couldn't seem to change my behaviour, reaction or feelings. I felt like I wasn't getting anywhere, despite now noticing and understanding what I did.

Dr Rachel reassured me that this was all part of the recovery process. It may help to revisit Chapter 11 and look at your Soothe Strategies connection card (page 228).

Check in with what your inner voice is saying to you – are you starting to criticize yourself? Remember that critical voice is not helpful in your recovery. The voice you need is the compassionate, understanding one. Get your Emotionally Healthy Messages connection card out to remind yourself you are enough and are doing the best you can right now. Remember to recognize the expectation you put on yourself.

ONGOING TRIGGERS AND BEHAVIOURS

Recovery from trauma works in stages. We can't change how we feel or what we do unless we first recognize our feelings and actions and why we do them. And we have to recognize them not just once, but repeatedly until new pathways start to take over the old.

Everything we do in trauma is habitual – small actions that we've taken over and over again and, for some of us, for a long time. Recovery is essentially recalibrating – slowly but surely, and with safety, starting to change those habits.

Recovery does not mean we will never feel anything to do with our past experiences again. The painful memories don't go away, but they do become less present, less all-consuming and easier to deal with.

Triggers will still happen, but try to see them not necessarily as something to fear or to shame yourself with, but as little signs that you need some reassurance and comfort in that moment. Triggers are trying to protect you from danger, they are just a little confused and overactive in trauma, when they come about because of a memory rather than the current moment. If you ignore the triggers or dismiss them through fear or shame, you are rejecting what you need to work on – as a consequence, keeping yourself stuck. That feeling is coming in for a reason and is creating a stress response. It's not you 'overreacting' or 'being silly'. It's basically knocking hard on your door, saying, 'Hello? I'm in danger here. Help me. Stop ignoring me. Please protect me.' The more you ignore the feeling the more it will panic and create more fear, and make you even more heightened and frightened, and make you react even more strongly to the trigger.

Some people in trauma can't always consciously remember everything that happened to them. The subconscious knows though, and triggers will show you. Reframing the way we feel about triggers will help us listen to what we need.

My mum would trigger me every time I spoke to her about my therapy and my psychoeducation work. I noticed what was going on and changed the situation so I would feel heard. I also know I get triggered by lying in certain positions. I no longer avoid those situations; instead, I reassure myself and acknowledge the memory of why that happens. I use cognitive strategies, telling myself the current situation is safe. And I stay, so that I am not depriving myself of something that is safe and actually really beneficial, like a massage.

Exposing myself (safely) to these triggers also shows me I need to keep working on my pain from my sexual abuse and keep talking about it. Ignoring it and never speaking about it kept me in pain. The more

I see and experience love and care, even though people know I've been sexually abused, the more it reinforces to me that I am lovable, worthy and proud. I was scared that if people found out about my abuse they would think there was something wrong with me and not want to be in a friendship or relationship with me.

A WORD ABOUT RECOVERY FROM SEXUAL ABUSE

If you have been sexually abused and haven't 'told your story', I want to make it clear that you absolutely do not have to do that in order to be in recovery from it.

I got asked recently by a sexual abuse survivor if I thought he should speak openly about it in public. I said, only if you think that will help *you*. He said he saw me speaking and felt like it was his duty to. I told him categorically that it wasn't his duty.

It absolutely isn't my duty or his duty (or your duty) to speak up. *I* do it because it feels right for me. For me, the more speaking about my abuse has a positive impact on others, the more it diminishes the negative of it.

It's the duty of society as a whole – the system, the government – to prevent abuse and to protect victims and survivors. I speak about my experiences because I want to, but it doesn't come from a place of shame or feeling that somehow this is a responsibility of mine.

It's not a victim's duty to protect other victims. Victims and survivors are already *more than enough* by just surviving. If you are a victim or survivor of sexual abuse, then you should share your story in your own time and only disclose it to someone who can be trusted as a safe person.

I do believe that sharing what happened to you helps. It's not your burden or something you need to hide. The shame is not yours to carry. Telling a trusted person shows you that you don't need to be in silence, in the place shame likes you to be.

TECHNIQUES FOR WHEN YOU'RE TRIGGERED

Part of recovery is honing our ability, over time, to control our response to triggers. With this, they will get less frequent and less powerful.

Remember: triggers bring with them strong emotions and they can come out of nowhere, so you won't always be able to control them.

When you are triggered, try a Grounding Technique (pages 95 and 148). These are proven to be highly effective, so keep practising them! Here's a recap of some grounding ideas:

- **Smell**. Inhale an essential oil, like lavender or peppermint.
- **Focus**. Count objects around you, e.g. name four objects that you can see, or touch three objects, or name two things you can hear. Or, label objects you can see (this really helped me), e.g. 'I see the blue carpet, the comfy chair, the tree outside.'
- **Present-moment awareness**. Remind yourself who you are and where you are. What can you smell?
- **Box breathing/square breathing**. Inhale for four, hold for four, exhale for four, hold for four, and repeat.
- **Body scan**. Notice and mentally work through each part of the body.

- **Music**. Listen to a favourite song and turn the volume up. I'm not sure the volume level is necessary for grounding, but my grandma does this a lot and swears by it. She normally has Queen's 'Bohemian Rhapsody' blasting out of her speaker.
- **Connection cards**. Use the messages to ground you, e.g. 'I am safe'.
- **Somatic movement**. Engage in mindful walking and running, breathwork, yoga or meditation.

Once you feel a little safer, the strength of the memory will lessen and the emotions will feel a little bit more manageable. This is when you can move on and use the Recognize Your Cognitive Distortions exercise to think about where the trigger came from and why (page 200).

Working through trauma, having all these realizations and even reading this book may make you feel like your trauma dominates you. I felt a lot like this. Opening your eyes to it all can be empowering and show you that you aren't 'crazy', but it can also make you feel like this is all of you. It certainly made me take a step back and say, 'Shit! This is me.' It hurt and made me feel bad about myself. I saw all my coping mechanisms and behaviours because of trauma. But they are not you – they are your symptoms because of what you've experienced, and you are not your symptoms. Seeing your symptoms, although upsetting, is how we repair. You can't repair something you refuse to see.

16

Acceptance never judges you

Acceptance is where the big shift really starts to happen. This is what began to make all the difference to me.

This isn't just some therapy jargon that we say outwardly but don't remotely feel inside. 'Acceptance' is pivotal in human psychology and is the final stage of the trauma response. It's also critical to the healing process that we 'accept' that the trauma has happened and that it has had an impact on our life.

WHAT IS ACCEPTANCE?

We can interpret acceptance in many ways. At first glance, how does the word 'acceptance' make you react? Initially, I construed acceptance as a bad thing. It made me want to hold on to my anger and actually made me even more angry: How can I accept what's happened to me? Accept what's been done to me? What? Just accept that it's all okay? Just give up? Don't fight anymore? Accept that I'm always going to feel like this? Why even bother then? Acceptance felt passive, stagnant and weak.

Acceptance felt like an injustice to myself. I thought, if I accept all this, I am just giving up on myself and handing myself over to a life of pain, sadness, depression, anxiety and loneliness. If I accept all of this, will I be someone destined to always be unhappy? That thought was really tough to stomach.

This is where my head went – and maybe where yours is too – but stick with me.

Acceptance doesn't mean any of the above.

Acceptance doesn't mean condoning what happened to you, or accepting living with how you feel now or being stuck in your pain. It's not a case of acceptance versus change – these are not opposites; rather they feed into each other. Acceptance leads to change. *Accepting* our stories and having our stories *accepted* (validated by others) leads to a change in our ways of coping.

Acceptance is a word akin to acquiescence, which is derived from the Latin *acquiēscere*, which means 'to find rest in'. Acceptance is described as agreeing (assenting) to the reality of a situation, recognizing a process or condition – often a negative or uncomfortable situation.

Dr Rachel prefers to use the words and phrases 'grieving', 'mourning' and 'working through our pain', rather than 'acceptance'. Acceptance is looking at what is possible now. I feel like grieving and mourning *are* acceptance.

THE ROLE OF ACCEPTANCE IN RECOVERY

Research has shown that developing acceptance of emotional experiences is an important component of recovery from trauma. There's even a form of psychotherapy called Acceptance and Commitment Therapy (ACT), which focuses on mindfulness and acceptance.

According to ACT's underlying theory, mental health disorders result from attempting to *avoid* a past experience; so, a goal of treatment with ACT is to develop more accepting, mindful attitudes toward distressing memories and negative conditions, rather than avoiding them. I haven't had this type of specific therapy, but similar concepts were integrated in the schema therapy I did. Studies have shown that in survivors of interpersonal trauma (pain caused by others, such as strangers, acquaintances, friends or loved ones), ACT reduced symptoms of PTSD and depression.

For as long as I can remember, I've been in a continuous battle with myself. This is because what I've experienced is a part of who I am, and is the part of who I am that I hated. I tried to run away from that part of me through my career, through living in different countries, through achievement, through leaving relationships with people that loved me and literally through running until it hurt in order to overpower the emotional pain. I denied and rejected the things I've been through and, as a consequence, denied myself. I wouldn't allow myself to feel my emotions, even though deep down I felt all of them with such strength that my heart would physically ache. I wouldn't allow myself to grieve. I rejected the validity of what I'd been through. I excluded the part of myself that had gone through distressing things from love and from joy.

Denial, rejection and exclusion are all factors of trauma, and are the opposite of acceptance.

The stages of acceptance can be compared to the framework of the five stages of grief developed by psychiatrist Elisabeth Kübler-Ross; both are a process of emotional healing. The five stages are denial, anger, bargaining, depression and acceptance.

Although there is some kind of linear order, it's very normal to flip-flop back and forth between the stages.

In trauma the stages often look like this:

- **Denial** – being unable to acknowledge that the distressing experience happened as a way of protecting yourself from the pain and overwhelm.
- **Shock and disbelief** – finding it hard to process what has happened; feeling numb, detached from your emotions, and possibly confused.
- **Anger and resentment** – feeling angry with yourself and/or others about what happened.
- **Bargaining** – trying to regain control by protecting yourself and vowing to yourself you won't get hurt again; think of the cognitive distortions (page 200).
- **Depression and despair** – this is where the pain sets in through sadness, feelings of hopelessness and mourning for what you've gone through.
- **Acceptance** – a recognition and acceptance of what has happened to you, its impact and that it's part of your story.

The stages of change that run alongside the above are:

- **Precontemplation** – not acknowledging there's a problem
- **Contemplation** – recognizing/acknowledging
- **Preparation** – understanding and learning
- **Action** – making changes
- **Maintenance** – continuing with your trauma recovery work

As mentioned previously, it's very normal to keep going back and forth through these stages. For example, to continue our recovery, we may go and learn more, and that learning may make us acknowledge our traumatic experience on a deeper level or bring up something else that happened; we then contemplate and feel our feelings, understand, learn and make changes again.

Acceptance is staying with yourself, rather than avoiding and running away. Acceptance is allowing yourself to feel how painful things have been for you. Acceptance is to recognize and give validity to past experiences that have harmed you. Acceptance is to be self-compassionate and know that it wasn't your fault.

Acceptance is *acquiēscere* – to find rest in what's happened to you and in yourself.

MY JOURNEY TO ACCEPTANCE

I often get asked if surviving critical illness and near death has changed me and, if so, how. My answer is always: I don't know how going through something so awful can *not* change you, I think it's impossible. So, yes, it has changed me. To start with, it triggered all my previous harms, pain and fear.

When I was in the coma, it seemed like every scary and distressing thing that had happened to me was coming to the surface at the same time and I had no escape. It was absolutely horrific and terrifying. However, when I began to recover from my illness, I couldn't stop thinking about why everything was now coming to the surface. I knew I had never dealt with any of this 'stuff', and it would seem that my critical illness stripped me of my armour and my barriers and left me in a red raw state. I was scared, but I also knew it was a wake-up call to deal with it all.

Now, I'm not saying I'm glad Rio happened because it meant I started dealing with my trauma. I'm not going to go that far and say it was all meant to be. Being so very ill was itself horrible, and it caused my family and friends huge amounts of upset and pain. It impacted my career and my personal life, and I feel like I lost a good year or two of my life. I spent a significant amount of my time during my physical recovery resenting what happened to me. I wish I didn't have those memories of my lungs closing in on themselves and not being able to breathe, of sobbing on my own in the most unbearable pain, of hearing the doctors say I was dying. But worst of all was being in the coma on life support and hearing my mum and brother upset and wondering whether I was still there, and not being able to reach out and tell them I was fighting, I was still alive and to not give up on me.

It hurts my heart so much just writing about it. The pain is still there. It will always be there. I still find it difficult to talk about, and I can be very sensitive if I feel like what happened to me is minimized in some way. You wouldn't believe that some people make jokes about it when they talk to me – not out of spite, but out of their own way of coping with it. Previously, I would laugh along, despite it really hurting me. I now say, 'Please don't joke about it.' I don't allow myself to be made to feel like that anymore whether their intention is good or not; it's not okay for me to be made to feel like that.

I am a new version of myself. There's the pre-2016 me (2016 was the year I fell ill), and the post-2016 me. Many things are the same. I still push myself to achieve. I still feel sad. I still feel angry. I still have depression. I still have painful memories. I still get overwhelmed. I still get triggered.

So what are the differences?

I now push myself to achieve with self-care and compassion, through a love and passion about what I do and strong self-esteem, rather than through fear and feelings of not being enough. I can run without self-harm, without needing to break myself; I can run just for running's sake, instead of running with gritted teeth and unrelenting standards. I can run with a smile on my face.

I feel sad because I am human – I have humanity, I have empathy.

I feel angry because that is a normal healthy emotion that we all have.

I have depression and I accept it. I understand it and I know where it comes from. I don't hate myself or beat myself up because I have depression. I live well with it. I can be happy and still have depression.

I accept that I have a painful past and that my memories sometimes hurt and make me sad, but they stay in the past as exactly that –

memories. I am no longer constantly and involuntarily reliving those distressing times.

I can use healthy coping strategies when I get overwhelmed and I can calm my nervous system down. I can comfort myself and allow myself to grieve, which makes me feel cared for, valid and seen.

I can connect and get close to people without being dominated by fear.

I know my triggers and I can make myself feel safe; and I continue to work on the things that set them off.

This is my acceptance.

Accepting is hard, but I can't emphasize enough what a key component of recovery it is.

ACCEPTANCE IS POWER

Remember that acceptance does not mean you have to be okay with what you've been through. I'm not okay with what's happened to me. It's about accepting how awful it was and accepting how it's (quite rightly) impacted you.

I am proud of myself for doing all the things I've had to do to survive. It's remarkable what we can endure. As I've said before, the way I coped kept me in trauma but it also kept me alive. I am grateful for that part of me. I say thank you to that part of me – not for what happened to me but for the amazing me that survived it. I now help myself to feel safe and to let what happened to me go, because that is the least I can do for myself.

The 'me' that has had to fight so hard for so long deserves at least that much. Acceptance does not mean that you have to forgive or excuse anything that happened to you in any way. It is about accepting you, *despite* what has happened to you.

Acceptance is a continuous process, so take your time with it. It is never judgemental or critical; it understands your struggles and accepts you as you are. In acceptance there is no home for shame.

Everything in this book works toward acceptance. We have gone from a lack of awareness of our trauma, to an awareness of our suffering and pain, to an awareness of the impact it has on our mind and our behaviours subconsciously, to an awareness that we don't have to act on our past feelings (they are from our memories), to helping ourselves observe our mind and what it says to us, to accepting ourselves (and our trauma) so we can develop a sense of self that is compassionate when we have troublesome emotions so that they are calmed and heard.

In acceptance you can stop fighting all the battles that you are never going to win. Stop fighting what has happened to you – you can't change that, no matter how hard you try. Put that energy into fighting for yourself now – fighting for your life, for your future, for your recovery – and not fighting against the past.

17

Reconnecting
with yourself

Being seen and heard by someone is often talked about in the context of dating and relationships. The fundamental need for validation, empathy, respect, active listening, open communication, trust and feeling valued by the other person is essential for a fulfilling relationship and a strong bond. Reconnecting with yourself after trauma is a little bit like building a healthy trusting relationship, but this time with yourself. In trauma, we don't see or hear a big part of ourselves; we lose touch with what we are experiencing inside, and with that we lose trust and safety in ourselves and in the decisions we make.

Reconnecting with yourself means validating your experiences, being empathetic and respecting your feelings without judgement; remember, all your emotions are valid and serve a purpose. Reconnecting involves actively listening to yourself, paying attention to your needs and treating yourself with kindness and compassion. Most importantly it's about learning to feel safe within yourself, knowing that you trust yourself to take care of you. It means embracing your entire self, *and* the scars left by your past.

Once we have started to accept what we have experienced and how it's impacted us, we can now start to 'self-accept' and build a genuine connection with ourselves.

RECONNECTING WITH MYSELF

I wanted to share something with you that I wrote when I finished my group therapy work and saw Dr Rachel for the last time as a patient. At this point, I was well on my way with my psychoeducational journey.

***

I walk into Dr Rachel's office for the last time, my shoulders back and open, my mouth naturally turned up into a half smile, thinking about the first time I walked through these same heavy-set doors.

Back then, I felt so vulnerable, but I never looked like a person 'in need' by society's standards. I had refused to sit in the waiting area, and instead hovered at the security door between the reception and the consultant rooms. I made myself as unapproachable as possible – a form of protection that, without realizing it, limited the amount of help and love I allowed myself to receive from the outside world. My legs would shake uncontrollably, my fingers would scratch at my scalp while I'd flick my nails with my other hand. Today, I wasn't that person anymore. I still don't like sitting down to wait, but I can do it without a gripping in my throat that makes me breathe and sweat as if I am running through an overgrown forest where I can't see my way out. I breathe easily now.

I say 'Hi' to the guy in reception, whose beaming smile makes his round cheeks touch his dark eyes. He picks up the ringing phone as he buzzes me through the security door with his other hand; he knows my face so well he doesn't bother to check my name or ask who I'm here to see.

Dr Rachel stands in her doorway and ushers me in, her tall commanding figure matches my own. We sit opposite each other in our usual position, in the same blue material office chairs, like we've done for the past two years. What was once a face-off, is now a warm and trusting check-in. The blue carpet, the blue chairs and the white walls so ingrained in my brain as a reference that I'm safe and in the present.

'You're in my office. You can see and feel the blue carpet under your feet, the white walls with the pictures, my desk in the corner ... you're safe and you're a healthy adult that now has the tools to make healthy decisions and care for yourself.'

This was the way all our sessions began and ended.

I smile openly at Dr Rachel as she starts to speak.

'This is our last session. How are you feeling about it?'

'I actually feel fine. I mean, I'm a bit worried. I know that I won't be able to come and speak to you, but at the same time I know that I can deal with things myself. I know I have a healthy adult inside me that can care for me. I never thought I'd get here. There was one point where I couldn't ever imagine quieting my critic, being able to relax without telling myself that I'm failing, I'm not good enough.'

Dr Rachel is staring wide-eyed, leaning forward in her chair, inviting me to carry on.

'And ... well, I feel like I can actually have a healthy relationship now, and feel safe enough ...'

'You can, and deserve to have that. You've done so well, Charlie, you have really taken all this on. What you've been through is so awful. But that's not your life now. You've allowed the vulnerable child inside you to start healing. You're safe, and you've grown into someone who can parent yourself. You've learnt to love and

care for yourself. Now you know that you can put boundaries up that protect you, you know that you will be able to recognize when something isn't okay for you. You nearly lost your life in Rio. It was only a matter of time before something happened again and with a potentially worse outcome. I was worried about your safety. I can see you walk out of this door and know that you have the ability to keep yourself safe. You are valuable and important.'

***

Out of everything that I've worked on with Dr Rachel, the thing she was always most concerned about was my drive to push and push to prove that I wasn't a failure, the overarching message in my brain that constantly told me I wasn't good enough. Honestly, it didn't matter what I achieved, as I would pick it apart. It was never good enough; in my head I'd failed and hadn't achieved enough.

Dr Rachel was concerned that my constant need to prove my worth was so dominant that I didn't ever see danger or notice when I needed care. Yes, it is also one of the reasons why I've done so well in terms of career achievements; I was tenacious and worked above and beyond, never accepting that I couldn't do something. It also served me well when I was younger, as it led to escaping it all and creating a life that I'd always dreamed of. But because I'd never allowed myself a moment to heal from what I'd been through, no matter what I achieved, I still felt like I was trying to escape.

***

'Yes, I know ...' is all that comes out of my mouth. Compliments are becoming more comfortable, but I still feel a little unsure of how to respond when somebody says I've done well.

It makes me sad sometimes to realize how much I've cut my feelings off, rejected people's help, withdrawn, worked and exercised to an excess, to harm myself.

'So what have you written as your goals?'

I lean to the side and pull a bright white piece of A5 card (my connection card) out of the top of my bag, full of biro scribbles. I start reading.

'So ... well ... I want to continue self-care – like getting enough sleep, creating relaxation time and meditation. I'm getting loads better at this ...'

I look up at her and then back to the card, realizing that I want her reassurance and praise – a familiar habit. I continue.

'Try to focus more on positive things that have gone right, rather than focusing on what hasn't. Concentrate on what makes me happy, and keep exploring what I like and what is good for me, what I want for my life rather than fixing and sorting everyone else's. Work on making myself feel safe. Ask myself what makes me feel safe? Talking to myself, that I'm enough as I am. Remind myself that I'm safe.'

I turn over the card and see the word 'rejection' glare at me in black ink, but I smile knowingly.

'I've written "rejection" basically to give myself healthy parent messages when I feel rejected and tell myself I am loved. It's okay to feel sad, upset and hurt about this.'

***

I really struggled with rejection. It was such a big trigger for me. If I didn't get a job, or something didn't go right or happen for me when I'd put everything into it, I would catastrophize it as if it was the end of the world. I hated not getting the result I'd worked for. I just wanted the pain inside to stop. I felt like no matter how hard I tried, I would always be a worthless little girl, because the hurt inside was so powerful and overwhelming.

***

I carry on reading my connection card. 'Updating ... reminding myself that I have done good things and things have gone right in my life. Positive things have happened to me. Keep an eye on my demanding critic. Have fun!' I laugh.

Dr Rachel uncrosses her legs, and glances at me with what feels like a gentle affection. She stands, moves a few steps to her desk, my eyes follow as she picks up a crimson red folder and hands it to me.

'These are my notes that I've typed up from your lifeline that we've gone through. It's got everything in it.'

I open the folder and read the first lines on the page.

> I was born on 9 November 1982 at Jessops Hospital, Sheffield. My mother said she had to keep me. I was special. When I went to nursery, I didn't want my mum to leave me. I cried so much that I retched. I was fighting to escape and find her.

I scroll down with my eyes.

> The house was quiet and unfriendly. I sat in a corner of the living room alone. I was scared of being noticed.

And reach the bottom line.

> When I was eating, I had to make sure I didn't bang my fork on my teeth. I had to be silent. I was terrified.

I flick through to the last page of 18 and read the final words.

I was taken to a normal hospital room out of the ICU. I made it.

I close the folder tight, my palms warm and sticky. I don't need to read anymore.

'It's up to you what you want to do with it. I can keep it, or you can take it with you, and do what you like with it. You can keep it; some people like to get rid of it or burn it.'

'I'd like to keep it. This is my life and I've gone through all this. I don't need to run away from it anymore, and I'm not ashamed of it. I want to keep this.'

'Okay. I think that's helpful for you. Remember, Charlie, that you used coping behaviours, particularly detached protector, as a way to survive all your life. You now know that this detachment was useful to survive, but it stops you from getting your needs met and developing relationships now. You've worked so hard at changing this and using good parent messages to quieten your critic and reduce the fear that you've carried with you from childhood. It's been a privilege to witness your progress.'

We both stand up for the last time together. I bite my bottom lip and tell myself that it's okay to feel the array of emotions that are sweeping across me like swirls of paint on a canvas.

'Thank you, Dr Rachel. I'm so grateful.'

I hand her an envelope with a thank-you card inside, walking out of the door away from her, not wanting to stand still and make a big deal of it. I walk out of the door, but pause and turn back to look at her. The familiar block clenches my throat to try and stop me from showing how I feel – but I can now recognize it and move it gently out of the way to allow myself to let go.

'You've literally saved my life. Thank you.'

***

WRITING AND DOCUMENTING

A good way of reconnecting with yourself is to look over any writing and documenting you have done through your recovery. I still have the folder with the notes of my lifeline and a notebook full of my own scribbles. I suppose this notebook could be called a journal. I never called the notes I made, the writing I did, a journal as it felt too formal and just another thing to beat myself up about if I didn't get a chance to write in it. For me, there's also a fine line between journalling and overthinking everything I did each day. Because of how trauma internalizes our feelings and thoughts, being too much in our own heads is not particularly helpful.

If I had a notebook nearby or in my bag, then I could just write stuff down when I felt like it. This didn't feel like a pressure, it was more of a release being able to do it whenever I felt like it and whenever I needed it. Writing notes about how I'm feeling or what's going on in my life is something I've always done. Without realizing it, I'd developed a strategy that is now widely recognized for our mental health. I have found pages from my school exercise books that I'd ripped out to write on from the age of 11 years old. They were painful to read, as I was distraught and crying out for help, even then. Despite the fact they hurt to read, they were good for me to see, to make sure I don't keep that little girl in hurt anymore. I've spent far too much of my life feeling that way and keeping myself in trauma. I will not allow that for myself again.

I recommend you write and keep writing, adding to and reading back over the notes you've made. If you haven't already done it, consider creating a flowers and stones lifeline, if you feel able to. You don't ever have to look at it again, but keep it so at least you have the option. I like to keep all these things; it's comforting to know they are there if I ever need reminders. Also, for me, throwing them away or burning them feels like getting rid of a part of me, and I feel like I've spent a lifetime doing that. I have been through what I've been through, and I want to continue to grow to love and accept all the parts of me, including those that were hurt so badly and remind me of painful times. They are still me, and deserve to be loved.

CONNECTION CARDS

Revisit the various connection cards that you've made throughout this book, which I hope you now have dotted around your home or in the bags you use day to day.

In trauma recovery it can be hard to give ourselves those caring, supportive and emotionally healthy messages, especially when we are feeling overwhelmed, so use the connection cards as references.

Remember that, even though your self-critic might tell you the opposite, the emotionally healthy messages will still have an impact. Your critic isn't your only voice, it doesn't own you and it certainly isn't the only part of your brain. If you can tell yourself that you won't feel better and are not enough and believe it, you can also tell yourself that you *can* recover and *are* enough and believe it.

RECOGNIZING THE WHOLE OF YOU

In Chapter 6, we talked about our relationship with ourselves and how trauma can eat away at our sense of identity. In trauma, a big part of who we are walks through life in disconnection and detachment. I mentioned that I often felt like I was two people – one strong and one weak. The strong was relentless at hating me for what I had been through and did everything to keep the weak part of me at bay. The weak part of me was constantly crying out to the strong part of me to be heard and taken care of.

Trauma splits you into pieces. Reconnecting with yourself through trauma recovery is putting all those pieces together, so you can be as one – to not be in constant conflict with yourself, to feel safe in yourself and trust that you will take care of you.

I have a lot of parts to me – we all have many layers to us. Reconnecting is about tapping into all of these layers, bringing out their strengths and working together, rather than being at odds. Sometimes I am protective, sometimes I'm vulnerable, sometimes I feel like I can take on the world, sometimes I just want to cry and shut it all out. Before I worked through trauma, all of me would be in one big fight. I am still all of those things, but now they all care for each other. Now, when I do just want to cry, I care for myself so that once again I feel like I can take on the world. When I'm vulnerable, my protective side can come in and be compassionate and make me feel safe. When I'm protective, my vulnerable side can check to see if I'm okay and ask why I'm being so protective and check if I need to be comforted.

Connecting with yourself is repairing, restoring and reclaiming – which is the opposite of disconnection, avoidance and detachment.

WRITE A LETTER FROM YOUR HEALING SELF TO YOUR PAIN

I have one last thing I'd like you to do: write a letter from your emotionally healthy self to your hurt, scared, vulnerable self.

This isn't one of those 'What would you say to your younger self?'-type letters. What I'd like you to do is write from your emotionally healthy self that is in trauma recovery in the present to the hurting you inside that is in pain from your past. The process is about connecting those two voices, those two parts of you. This is reconnecting with yourself.

As Dr Rachel explains, this letter is connecting 'your emotionally healthy voice to your vulnerable scared self and listening to what it needs. Talking to yourself is a sign of emotional health, not the first sign of madness. Talking to yourself means you're thinking, and thinking is the key to emotional maturity.'

In trauma you can't be yourself as you are too busy protecting yourself from further pain, being on guard, shaming yourself and putting yourself down. In your recovery, you now have room for yourself, to be real, be open and be true to who you really are. You are shaped by what happened to you, but who you are is *not* what happened to you.

Find yourself somewhere quiet. It's really important that you're honest with yourself. Nobody else ever has to read the letter, so please try to be open and honest. It will be upsetting to do, but it's okay to let yourself cry, to feel the emotions that will come out. This is the grieving process, and a promise to yourself that you will continue your recovery and care for yourself. It's an ongoing journey that we will always be on, but it will get better.

My letter

I'm a little nervous, but I want to share my letter with you. I've never shared this before outside of Dr Rachel and my trauma group. I hope it helps you write your own and know that you are absolutely not alone. I am with you.

Dear Charlie,

I want you to remember that I am always here to protect you, be kind to you and love you – how you deserve to be loved. You are lovable and wonderful just the way you are – and more than good enough.

What happened to you was NOT your fault. You were just a child that had no choice and did the very best you could to survive. You did incredible to survive all of the abuse you suffered – you don't have to do this on your own now or ever.

I am in control, we are together, and we can make our own choices and decisions. We have the right tools to care for ourselves. I am a healthy adult that will and can take care of you.

I am so sorry that I have let you suffer for so long, but that's because I needed help to understand how to care for you. The horrible critic was too strong because I thought that was the only way I could protect you from harm.

I'm so sorry, because I've now realized that I was the one doing you harm. You are not a failure. You are worthy of love.

And you are not a bad person. You are a normal human being that is allowed to have and show your emotion. We don't have to hide anymore, and I don't have to have the critic or angry protector in charge anymore, only if it's helpful and I want it to be.

I want you to feel and tell me how you are feeling.

If you are sad, feeling vulnerable and scared, I'm going to reassure you, be kind and give you what you need.

You are more than enough.

You can love.

You can accept love.

Because I am here.

I'm your healthy adult.

I love you and care for you.

I'm always here.

Charlie

It's up to you what you do with your letter. You can keep it somewhere safe. You can reread it when you feel you need a reminder of that promise you've made to yourself. You can share it with a loved one if you feel it will help; but only do this if you feel safe with that person and it's the right thing for you, and not because they've asked you to. If you would like to share it with me, you can also do that.

I read mine out loud to my group. I felt like I wanted it to be heard, and I knew the group was a trusted and safe environment for me to do it in. I cried while writing it and I cried while writing it out again in this book. A good cry though, a cry that helped me grieve for the things I've lost in trauma, a cry that allowed me to process my feelings and a cry that gave me the opportunity to soothe myself and get care from others. A cry that made me want better for myself.

Final words

Working through the many challenges that have been part of my life makes me empathetic, understanding and relate to people. I have a strength (through processing what's happened to me) that I've used to be a voice to those that are going through some of the things I've been through; and with that voice I've helped to change numerous laws and policies and raised money for charity.

I now have a deep connection with myself, which means I question how I feel and what I am doing in my life. I have a self-worth that means I have healthy boundaries in friendships and relationships and can give so much more of myself. I appreciate my life and myself, and my relationships are healthier and more meaningful. I've lost all the relationships that were not good for me.

I found that the more I grew and recovered, the more my circle of friends changed. Friends who felt disempowered by an empowered me (ultimately unhealthy relationships that kept me in trauma feelings) distanced themselves. I, in turn, started to see the adverse impact they were having on me, and worked on developing a stronger support system. As I reduced my own unhealthy behaviours and grew, I was able to do that.

None of this takes away from how horrifically distressing what I've been through was, and how I still sometimes feel the hurt; but feeling the pain allows me to make a choice for myself for what support I need in that moment, whether from myself or others.

I chose to write this book because I know how hard it is to work through trauma. I know some days it just feels too much. I know how much it hurts.

I also know that you can get through. I know that you can work through trauma and feel better. I know that you can love and receive love. I know that you can smile genuinely with joy in your heart. I know you can find rest in what's happened to you.

I wrote this book because I've walked this path and am still walking it. I want to share my knowledge and experience and the support of the people that helped me with you, because I know the pain and I also know that what I've written can help heal it.

I often felt like I had no control over large parts of my life, which made me seek control in an anxious way. Throughout my life, I have felt worthless and been consumed by surviving trauma after trauma to the point where I became so heightened it was my normality. I can't change what has happened to me, but I can change how I deal with it. Realizing that I do have a choice, even if the choices aren't necessarily the ones I want, means I have agency over my life.

Sometimes I find myself slipping into old patterns and behaviours; even when writing this book I could hear some of my old critical messages toward myself come in. It's understandable because those messages are trying to protect me from disappointment and rejection, preempting the worst outcome. But – and this is an important 'but' – the power of them in my head is much less today. I can catch them before I take them in, and I can change the narrative to: 'Actually, maybe I won't get disappointed or rejected'.

My memories no longer hold crushing emotions, but feelings that help me grow, learn and shape what I want for the next chapter of my story.

If something doesn't feel right, I can listen to those feelings attached to it and make a change, rather than feeling like I have to suffer and endure.

Thank you for allowing me to share my journey with you. I hope you find inspiration to move toward your own personal growth. Remember, ups and downs are part of getting to this point. Just because it's not a straight road doesn't mean you aren't moving forward. Keep persisting, and things will change for you. It just takes a bit of time to unwind it all – we can keep unwinding together!

Don't underestimate that this has been a many-years-long process for me. I know I've put everything in one place in this book, but the process takes practice and time. Use this book like a blueprint and keep going back to it.

I want to leave you with one more thing before you close this book.

As we've learnt, trauma limits your enjoyment of life. One of the things I had written down on my recovery goals was to allow more fun and experience joy. This is my final challenge to you in your recovery journey.

Find something that you enjoy, that makes you laugh – even if it's just for a few minutes. Trauma survival is a serious business – it has to be because surviving is serious.

Dr Rachel asked me to find something I enjoyed doing that was separate from achievement, something that was playful and about having fun, for fun's sake. This is a hard concept to grasp when your brain is wired to be on high alert as it would mean letting my guard down. I thought about it and said, 'Running!', but that was something I did to cope. Although it is therapeutic and grounds me, running had achievement linked to it and to past harmful behaviours.

So what else could I find? I've always loved music and I could dance all night. Just give me a dance floor and you'll have to drag me off it. So, dancing! Dancing is my fun, for fun's sake.

For a while after I'd realized this, I didn't go dancing, but I did write it on my goals in my Recovery/Growth Goals connection card. And every time I saw the card it said 'Dancing, have fun'.

And, eventually, I did. I went dancing all night. I laughed, I jumped up and down, I threw my arms about, I was carefree, I joined in with the energy of the crowd, and I experienced the euphoric feeling of joy. I felt like I could breathe freely for the first time in, well, I can't quite remember when. While I was busy having fun, my mind for those moments was at peace. I went again a few months later, and the same thing happened. I laughed, jumped around, felt free and had fun. I felt like I was actually living rather than just trying to survive.

In our trauma recovery it's so important to find enjoyment, because it will actually help rewire the brain. Again, it comes back to making the brain feel safe. Being able to have fun and realize that everything is still okay slowly starts to tell your brain and body that you're safe and worthy of finding joy. You don't need to spend your life treading water, you can show up a different way.

Dancing was my fun, for fun's sake. My challenge to you is to find what that moment of fun and feeling of joy is for you. Yes, trauma recovery takes work, but it also takes adding in a little bit of fun. After all, spontaneity and play is one of our basic universal needs to survive through trauma, grow through its challenges and thrive at the other end. Have fun finding the thing or things that bring you joy.

Appendix

ASKING FOR HELP: HOW TO FIND THE WORDS

If you ever find yourself lost for words or not quite sure how to describe the help that you need when seeing a professional and/or seeking external help, I thought some guidance on this may be helpful. I know it can be really hard to find the right words – remember, when I first met Dr Rachel I said I was fine, even though I'd reached out for help and needed it.

Use the simple structure below, and pick some phrases from each section that apply to you. Write them down and use these notes like a script. Have them in front of you when talking to a professional. This will also help take the immediate emotion out of the conversation, like overwhelm or any feelings of shame that can prevent you from getting the help you need.

This is what's happening:

Phrases:
- I can't get out of bed in the morning.
- I don't want to spend time with anyone.
- I have no energy.
- I am having flashbacks.
- All my days blend into one.
- I can't think straight or make decisions.
- I have nightmares.
- I lie awake at night.
- I can't eat.
- I'm irritable.
- I'm on edge.
- I am using alcohol or drugs to cope.
- I'm finding it hard to take care of myself/do basic tasks.

This is what I'm feeling:

Phrases:

- I am feeling numb/low/sad/angry.
- I have a heavy fog in my head.
- Everything looks grey.
- I am having intrusive thoughts.
- I feel emotionally drained.
- I am having suicidal thoughts.

This is what I've been through:

You don't have to disclose what you've been through if you don't want to, but you can tell them without telling them. Also remember that patient confidentiality will be in place when talking with health professionals.

Phrases:

- I have been through some very distressing/horrible things. It is affecting my quality of life and my relationships. I need help.
- I have been through a lot of trauma. I need help from a professional because it is causing me problems in my day-to-day life.
- I'm not sure what to say but I'm really struggling with my mental health.
- I'm struggling with the things that have happened to me and it's making me feel like I'm not safe.

Example:

"I am having flashbacks. I don't want to spend time with anyone. I'm finding it hard to do basic tasks. I am feeling numb to everything. I have been through a lot of trauma. I'm not sure what to say but I'm really struggling."

References

ACADEMIC PAPERS

Elbert, T, Schauer, M, Neuner, F (2022). 'Narrative Exposure Therapy (NET): Reorganizing Memories of Traumatic Stress, Fear, and Violence.' In: Schnyder, U, Cloitre, M (eds) Evidence Based Treatments for Trauma-Related Psychological Disorders. Springer, Cham. https://doi.org/10.1007/978-3-030-97802-0_12

English, A, McKibben, E, Sivaramakrishnan, D, Hart, N, Richards, J, Kelly, P (2022). 'A Rapid Review Exploring the Role of Yoga in Healing Psychological Trauma.' Int J Environ Res Public Health, Dec 3; 19(23):16180. https://www.ncbi.nlm.nih.gov/pmc/articles/PMC9741324/

Gilbert, P (2015). 'Affiliative and prosocial motives and emotions in mental health.' Dialogues Clin Neurosci. Dec; 17(4):381-9. https://www.ncbi.nlm.nih.gov/pmc/articles/PMC4734876/

Gilbert, P (2009). 'Introducing compassion-focused therapy.' Advances in Psychiatric Treatment, 15 (3), 199-208. https://doi.org/10.1192/apt.bp.107.005264

Gilbert, P (2014). 'The origins and nature of compassion focused therapy.' Br J Clin Psychol, 53: 6-41. https://bpspsychub.onlinelibrary.wiley.com/doi/abs/10.1111/bjc.12043

Hayes, SC, et al. (2013). 'Acceptance and commitment therapy and contextual behavioral science: examining the progress of a distinctive model of behavioral and cognitive therapy.' Behav Ther. Jun; 44(2):180-98. https://www.ncbi.nlm.nih.gov/pmc/articles/PMC3635495/

International Society for the Study of Trauma and Dissociation. 'Trauma and Complex Trauma: An Overview.' https://www.isst-d.org/wp-content/uploads/2020/03/Fact-Sheet-I-Trauma-and-Complex-Trauma_-An-Overview-1.pdf

Lee, DA, Scragg, P, Turner, S (2001). 'The role of shame and guilt in traumatic events: a clinical model of shame-based and guilt-based PTSD.' Br J Med Psychol. Dec; 74(Pt 4):451-66. https://pubmed.ncbi.nlm.nih.gov/11780793/

Lewis SJ, et al. (2019). 'The epidemiology of trauma and post-traumatic stress disorder in a representative cohort of young people in England and Wales.' Lancet Psychiatry. 2019 Mar; 6(3):247-256. doi: 10.1016/S2215-0366(19)30031-8

O'Beney, R, Salm, AM, Lavender, T (2019). 'An exploration of members' experiences of group therapy: an interpretive phenomenological analysis.' Group Analysis, 52(1), 82-99. https://doi.org/10.1177/0533316418814054

Schauer, M, Neuner, F, Elbert, T (2011). 'Narrative exposure therapy: A short-term treatment for traumatic stress disorders (2nd rev. and expanded ed.).' Hogrefe Publishing. https://psycnet.apa.org/record/2011-16922-000

Sweeney, A, et al. (2018). 'A paradigm shift: relationships in trauma-informed mental health services.' BJPsych Adv. Sep; 24(5):319-333. https://www.ncbi.nlm.nih.gov/pmc/articles/PMC6088388/#ref34

Thompson, MG, Leavy, SA (1994). 'Working-Through ("Remembering, Repeating, and Working-Through," 1914).' In *The Truth About Freud's Technique: The Encounter with the Real* (pp. 192–204). NYU Press. http://www.jstor.org/stable/j.ctt9qfvqq.29

BOOKS

American Psychiatric Association, *Diagnostic and Statistical Manual of Mental Disorders* (Fifth Edition, 2022)

Beah, I, *A Long Way Gone* (Farrar, Straus & Giroux, 2020)

Farrell, J, Reiss, N, Shaw, I (2014). *The Schema Therapy Clinician's Guide: A Complete Resource for Building and Delivering Individual, Group and Integrated Schema Mode Treatment Programs.* New York: Wiley

Gilbert, P, *The Compassionate Mind* (Constable, 2010)

van der Kolk, B, *The Body Keeps the Score* (Penguin, 2015)

Kübler-Ross, E, *On Death and Dying* (Routledge, 2008)

Tedeschi, RG, Shakespeare-Finch, J, Taku, K, and Calhoun, LG, *Posttraumatic Growth: Theory, Research, and Applications* (Routledge, 2018)

Tierney, J and Baumeister, RF, *The Power of Bad* (Penguin, 2019)

Acknowledgements

Thank you for reading this book. Thank you for trusting me and for being willing to take a step with me on this journey. The reason why I wrote this book was for you. They say write a book like no one is reading – I did the opposite. I wrote with you always in my mind, readers. You were my motivation, to try in some way to support, help and show that you aren't alone on your journey. So the biggest of thank yous to you!

Mindtalk (the mental health group I ran during the pandemic), thank you for trusting me, sharing with me and inspiring me to put it all down into a book.

Thank you to the many people that have followed and supported me. I will never forget the outpour of love and prayers when I was critically ill. You may not see in person how much your comments mean but I promise they do. They have given me hope and determination to keep on fighting many times over.

Mum, I know that some of what I have written in this book is also a part of you. I am so proud of you. Thank you for loving me and fighting for me from the very beginning. You are the reason I am able to write this book. Ben, Joe and Toby, my brothers, you are the most precious things to me. Thank you for giving me the gift of being your sister. You give me strength to speak out and to tell my story – I know some of it is also yours. I love you all so much.

Grandma, thank you for always showing me I could be whatever I wanted to be. 'Never let the buggers get you down.' I know you have your own trauma. I am proud of you for getting help. It's never too late.

Thank you to all my friends who have loved me unconditionally – you are my family. A special mention to Tanya for being my rock and Matty, well, for also being my rock, and to both of you for taking my late-night calls and drinking endless cups of tea with me.

Dr Rachel, working with you helped me see myself for who I really am. You gave me the strength to feel, the courage to be vulnerable and the tools to give myself a chance in life to allow myself to be loved. Thank you for giving your care and knowledge not only to me but to all the readers of this book.

Thank you, Dr Niki – you helped me understand what I had gone through and helped me stop blaming and shaming myself. Thank you for contributing your expertise to this book and helping bring awareness to the mental and emotional trauma that physical illness has on us.

Jo, my literary agent, thank you for believing in what I had to say and for being with me and making me feel safe throughout this process. This book exists because of you. Thank you, Beth, my editor – you gave me confidence in what I had written, you helped me order with clarity the many things I had to say and always with encouragement and guidance. Thank you to all the team involved in publishing this book – Matt, Isabelle, Lucy, Joe, Margarida – I appreciate every one of you and the time you've put into me. My heartfelt thanks to you incredible people that not only took the time to read my book (some while on holiday!) but also gave your name in support of it.

To my former running group – you're all with me and I'm grateful for the family I had in you through such tough times – and to Katie and Georgina who are no longer with us. Our story will live on and I will do everything I can to make sure people do not go through what we did.

Thank you to the people in my therapy group for giving me a safe space to share my deepest self. I am always with you.